Sharon Pollock

THE WEST SERIES

Aritha van Herk, Series Editor

ISSN 1922-6519 (Print) ISSN 1925-507X (Online)

This series focuses on creative non-fiction that explores our sense of place in the West - how we define ourselves as Westerners and what impact we have on the world around us. Essays, biographies, memoirs, and insights into Western Canadian life and experience are highlighted.

Sharon Pollock
First Woman of Canadian Theatre

Edited by
DONNA COATES

UNIVERSITY OF CALGARY
Press

University of Calgary Press
2500 University Drive NW
Calgary, Alberta
Canada T2N 1N4
www.uofcpress.com

LIBRARY AND ARCHIVES CANADA CATALOGUING IN PUBLICATION

Sharon Pollock (2015)
         Sharon Pollock : first woman of Canadian theatre / edited by Donna
Coates.

(The West ; 8)
Includes bibliographical references and index.
Issued in print and electronic formats.
ISBN 978-1-55238-789-4 (paperback).–ISBN 978-1-55238-791-7 (pdf).–
ISBN 978-1-55238-792-4 (epub).–ISBN 978-1-55238-793-1 (mobi)

     1. Pollock, Sharon–Criticism and interpretation. I. Coates, Donna,
1944-, author, editor II. Title. III. Series: West series (Calgary, Alta.) ; 8

PS8581.O34Z95 2015   C812'.54   C2015-904581-9
                                               C2015-904582-7

The University of Calgary Press acknowledges the support of the Government of Alberta through the Alberta Media Fund for our publications. We acknowledge the financial support of the Government of Canada through the Canada Book Fund for our publishing activities. We acknowledge the financial support of the Canada Council for the Arts for our publishing program.

This book has been published with the help of a grant from the Canadian Federation for the Humanities and Social Sciences, through the Awards to Scholarly Publications Program, using funds provided by the Social Sciences and Humanities Research Council of Canada.

Canada Council
for the Arts
Conseil des Arts
du Canada

Printed and bound in Canada by Marquis
♻ This book is printed on FSC® Enviro 100 paper

Cover design, page design, and typesetting by Melina Cusano

Contents

Acknowledgements

I would like to thank the staff at the University of Calgary Press, particularly Peter Enman, Karen Buttner, and Melina Cusano, for their encouragement and patience in seeing the manuscript into print. Thanks also to Jaclyn Carter, doctoral candidate in the English Department at the University of Calgary, whose computer skills, far superior to my own, proved invaluable to the production of the manuscript.

Introduction

Sharon Pollock: First Woman of Canadian Theatre is an appropriate title for this new collection of essays on the life and work of the foremost woman in Canadian theatre. As playwright, actor, director, theatre administrator, critic, teacher, and mentor, Sharon Pollock has played an integral role in the shaping of Canada's national theatre tradition. Not surprisingly, the number of awards and prizes she has won for her enormous and lengthy contribution to Canadian theatre is truly staggering. Pollock was the first recipient of the Governor General's Award for Drama in 1981 for *Blood Relations*, a play about Lizzie Borden, the acquitted American axe-murderer. In 1986, Pollock won that award a second time for *Doc*, a play loosely based on her family background in Fredericton, New Brunswick, where she was born and raised. Three years earlier, *Whiskey Six Cadenza*, another historical murder case set in the Crowsnest Pass, Alberta, had been nominated for another Governor General's Award. Pollock has also received a number of provincial and national awards both for acting and play-writing, beginning in 1966, the year she moved to Calgary, when she won the Dominion Drama Festival Best Actress Award for *The Knack*. In 1971, she received the Alberta Culture Playwriting Competition for *A Compulsory Option* (which she wrote while pregnant with her sixth child), and in 1981, she was granted the Golden Sheaf Award (Television) for *The Person's Case*. *Doc* won the Chalmers Canadian Play Award in 1984, and in 2009, *Kabloona Talk*, a courtroom drama about two Inuit charged with murdering two Oblate priests, commissioned by Stuck in a Snowbank Theatre, earned the Gwen Pharis Ringwood Award for Drama at the Alberta Literary Awards.

Pollock has also received provincial, local, and national awards for her support of theatre. In 1983, she won the Alberta Achievement Award; in 1999, the Harry and Martha Cohen Award for contributions to theatre in Calgary; and in 2008, the Gascon-Thomas Award from the National Theatre School of Canada. She has also achieved considerable international recognition: in 1987, she received the Canada-Australia Literary Prize, and in 1995, the Japan Foundation Award. Her plays continue to be performed in major theatres throughout Canada, in the United States, and Europe; she has conducted playwriting and theatre workshops nationally and internationally, and she continues to collaborate with national and international groups in the development of new scripts. Pollock also holds five honorary doctorates – from the University of New Brunswick (1987), Queen's University (1989), the University of Calgary (2003), the University of Alberta (2005), and Mount Royal University (2010). In 2012, she was made an Officer of the Order of Canada.

Pollock has also held an amazing array of positions in local, provincial, and national theatre scenes. She was a member of the Prairie Players, MAC 14 Theatre Society (Calgary); chairperson of the Advisory Arts Panel for the Canada Council; head of the Playwrights Colony at the Banff Centre of Fine Arts; associate artistic director of the Manitoba Theatre Centre; associate director of the Stratford Festival Theatre; artist-in-residence at the National Arts Centre, Ottawa; playwright-in-residence at the National Arts Centre, Alberta Theatre Projects, Theatre Calgary, and Theatre Junction in Calgary. She was also writer-in-residence at the Regina Public Library; head of the Playwriting Lab at Sage Writing Experience, Saskatchewan; associate director and artistic director of Theatre Calgary and Theatre

New Brunswick, as well as founding member and artistic director of the Performance Kitchen and the Garry Theatre, Calgary. She has also been president of Alberta Playwrights Network (APN) and director of Playwrights Lab (APN).

In 2008, when Sherrill Grace's *Making Theatre: A Life of Sharon Pollock* appeared, Pollock became the first woman in Canadian theatre history to have had a volume produced on her life and work. Pollock is also one of the few Canadian women playwrights to have had several collections of her plays published. Diane Bessai's *Blood Relations and Other Plays* ("Blood Relations," "One Tiger to a Hill," "Generations," "Whiskey Six Cadenza") appeared in 1981, and Cynthia Zimmerman has recently assembled twenty-two of Pollock's works into a three-volume set titled *Sharon Pollock: Collected Works* (2005, 2006, 2008). As Zimmerman writes in her preface to Volume 1, both she and the publisher agreed that "this was a timely and important way to honour both Sharon Pollock's significant contribution to Canadian theatre and the range of her work" (iii). The collections include some of her "best-known works for the stage, but also some of her lesser known ones, several of her radio plays and scripts for young audiences, and a couple of plays that have not yet been published" (iii).

Although most people at Pollock's age – she is now in her late seventies – would be winding down their careers, retirement does not seem to be a word in her vocabulary, as she continues to produce politically provocative plays. In 2008, she travelled to Kosovo to meet with young Kosovar artists; that meeting led to an ongoing project of collaboration and creative exchange with playwright Jeton Neziraj, former artistic director of the Kosovo National Theatre and current executive director of Qendra Multimedia, Pristina. (Neziraj has produced a brief essay for this collection, which pays tribute to Pollock and describes their work in progress.) In 2014, the Turner Valley, Alberta, historical society commissioned Pollock to write a play she titled *Centennial* that would celebrate the one-hundredth anniversary of the discovery of oil in Alberta. Pollock is also currently working on a script about the American journalist, writer, correspondent, and activist Agnes Smedley, best known for her supportive reporting of the Chinese Revolution. Remarkably, Pollock has also added several new positions to her extensive theatrical repertoire. Since 2006, she has served as dramaturge and artistic consultant for the Atlantic Ballet Theatre of Canada based in Moncton, New Brunswick, and from 2006 to 2008, she gathered a large following for her weekly reviews of Calgary theatre productions, titled "Pollock on Plays," for CBC Radio's *The Homestretch*.

Throughout her theatrical career, Pollock has continued to direct, most recently the third monologue ("Instruments of Yearning") in Judith Thompson's *Palace of the End*, for Downstage Theatre in 2009. Other directorial credits include productions at numerous theatres across the country such as the Manitoba Theatre Centre, the National Arts Centre, Neptune Theatre (Halifax), Theatre New Brunswick, Theatre Calgary, Alberta Theatre Projects, Theatre Junction, and Magnus Theatre (Thunder Bay). She has also continued to act. Among her favourite roles are Dr. Livingstone in *Agnes of God*; Nurse Ratchett in *One Flew Over the Cuckoo's Nest*; Sister George in *The Killing of Sister George*; Eleanor in *The Lion in Winter*; Eme in her own play, *Getting It Straight*; Lysistrata *in Lysistrata*, and Miss Lizzie in *Blood Relations*. In 2004, Pollock appeared on stage at the Timms Centre for the Arts at the University of Alberta in 2004, where she performed the role of Nell Shipman in her own *Moving Pictures*, about the career of the Canadian-born silent film star and independent filmmaker, which had premiered at Calgary's Theatre Junction in 1999. In 2008, she played the role of Margaret in Downstage Theatre's production of Judith Thompson's *Habitat*, and in 2011, with Verb Theatre, she played the role of Marg in the one-woman show *Marg Szkaluba: Pissy's Wife*, by Alberta playwright Ron Chambers, which required her to sing several country-and-western songs.

Pollock has frequently acknowledged that it was her acting career that inspired her to write plays, in part because she was frustrated with the dearth of Canadian voices and stories on Canadian stages. According to Grace, none of the works Pollock acted in at that time were from Canada; they were all from "elsewhere (England or the United States, London or New York), and the actors were expected to sound like Brits or Americans or like some odd mid-Atlantic alien" (Grace 26–27). As she wrote in an essay, "'The only voice and accent one never used . . . was the Canadian voice and accent, the Canadian voice as it was heard when it fell from the lips of white Canadians . . . People found nothing odd about its absence in our theatres for virtually no plays were set in Canada'" (Zepetnek and Yui-nam 116.). Although Pollock was not the first playwright to lament the lack of Canadian voices and stories on Canadian stages, she was nonetheless one of the first to take up the challenge to produce Canadian scripts. During an interview with Margot Dunn in 1976, Pollock stressed that she felt obliged to tell "Canadian-oriented" stories about the country she inhabited:

> I couldn't live in the States. I couldn't work for the States either. I really believe that the artist has a job, a responsibility not just to her/himself but to the society s/he comes from. I represent the kinds of questions some Canadians are asking and my responsibility is here. (6)

Typically, many of those "Canadian-oriented" stories, such as *Walsh* (1973), *The Komagata Maru Incident* (1976), and *Whiskey Six Cadenza* (1983), shine a light on the dark side of the nation's history. According to Grace, the writing of *Walsh* began Pollock's abiding concern with "the interrelated problems of racism, oppression, and the treatment of First Nations people in Canadian history and contemporary society" (101). These early plays, which earned Pollock a reputation as a playwright of conscience, continue to be staged and critically assessed. (Two of the essays in this collection examine these three plays either in whole or in part.) But arguably, no matter whether her works are considered "domestic," or "feminist," or "psychological," or "mysteries," most continue to explore the kinds of injustices which arise out of hypocrisy, bigotry, patriarchy, and racism. Her most recent work, *Man*

Out of Joint, produced by Calgary's Downstage Theatre in Calgary in 2007 (also discussed in two essays in this collection), is no exception.

In 2012, Pollock became the first playwright in Canada to have a conference held to celebrate her life and work. Although the event was organized by mainly academics and graduate students from the University of Calgary who wished to honour Pollock as a local, national, and internationally respected artist, uppermost was their desire to acknowledge Pollock's fervent support of her local community: her tireless work with students and teachers at high schools, colleges, and universities has become the stuff of local legend. By all accounts, the conference was a rousing success. Local theatre practitioners and academics came together with their counterparts from across Canada, as well as from Kosovo, Serbia, and India, to present papers on academic and/or theatre-practitioner panels, view archival displays, listen to readings of Pollock's work, and take in several productions of her plays. Although Pollock informed a CBC Radio interviewer that she felt slightly uneasy about the conference ("I should be dead," she quipped), the organizers were grateful she was not, because she took on a great many "roles" herself, including reprising her performance as Marg in *Marg Szkaluba: Pissy's Wife*. (As Grace writes in her essay, included in this collection, Pollock found performing a role of "eighty-to-ninety minutes in length . . . quite a challenge for a seventy-five-year-old memory"). To no one's surprise, her performance was flawless.

Pollock is also one of the few playwrights in Canada to have had several collections of critical examinations produced on her work, upon which this collection builds. Editor Anne F. Nothof's *Sharon Pollock: Essays on Her Works*, appeared in 2000; editors Sherrill Grace and Michelle La Flamme's *Sharon Pollock: Critical Perspectives on Canadian Theatre in English* was published in 2008. In testament to the sustained attention paid to Pollock's work, six of the nine critical essays included in *Sharon Pollock: First Woman of Canadian Theatre*, are by scholars who have never before written on the playwright. But the collection is also enriched by three essays from among the best-known scholars on Pollock's work to date (Sherrill Grace, Jerry Wasserman, and Cynthia

Zimmerman), each of whom welcomed the opportunity to produce new critical assessments.

Jerry Wasserman's "*Walsh* and the (De)Construction of Canadian Myth" provides an excellent opening to this new collection of essays. Wasserman's essay, written in an engaging personal style, explores the relationship between Sioux Chief Sitting Bull and James Walsh of the North West Mounted Police. As "almost a draft-dodger" from the United States during the Vietnam War, Wasserman had considered the movement of political refugees across the border reminiscent of the Sioux's attempt to obtain political asylum in Canada during the period after the Battle of the Little Bighorn (1877–1881). Hence he confesses that when he first taught *Walsh,* he tended to regard the Canadian treatment of the Sioux as "morally superior" to the Americans', but he soon realized that Pollock's vision, which both "shattered and shored up" the national mythology, was the more accurate. Wasserman concludes that Walsh, whom Pollock depicts as a "basically good man" is, like many of her dominant male characters, hampered by a "combination of internal weakness and institutional loyalty or social conformity."

Shelley Scott's "Sharon Pollock and the Scene of the Crime" focuses on a curiously neglected area of Pollock's work. Scott asserts that while numerous critics have paid considerable attention to Pollock's mystery plays, they have generally viewed them as vehicles for the exploration of larger thematic concerns. Scott analyzes *Blood Relations,* which remains the most frequently produced of Pollock's plays; *Constance,* which has received scant critical attention; and the later works *End Dream* and *Saucy Jack,* in order to demonstrate that Pollock adheres much more closely to the conventions of the genre than critics have acknowledged in the past.

Like Scott, whose essay offers a cogent reconsideration of previous critical assessments of Pollock's mystery plays, Jason Wiens challenges traditional readings of one of Pollock's early political prairie plays in his essay. In "Ownership and Stewardship in Sharon Pollock's *Generations,*" Wiens offers a refreshing consideration of this work by drawing attention to the extent to which Pollock has often chronicled the events of her day, but with perhaps unacknowledged foresight. While Wiens's essay underscores that *Generations* operates, as do so many of Pollock's plays, on several levels of conflict – here the domestic, the local, and the national – it stresses that although Pollock tended to displace the third, which consisted of disputes between the local Aboriginals and their reserve's irrigation water and the distribution of energy resources on a national level in favour of the domestic, it was the timeliness of the play, which premiered just prior to the energy-revenue sharing scheme that became known as the National Energy Policy, that concentrated reviewers' and audiences' minds on the current economic climate, as well as on the perennial problem of Western alienation.

In "Different Directions: Sharon Pollock's *Doc*," Cynthia Zimmerman examines another of Pollock's important early works in order to express her frustration with audiences and critics who have often placed their sympathies with either of the parents in the play – that is, with Everett Chalmers, the famous doctor, or with Bob, his neglected alcoholic wife. Zimmerman believes that the story of Catherine, the daughter caught between two warring parents, has been sidelined and hence requires more examination. To that end, she selects two productions – one staged in 1984, the other in 2010 – to demonstrate how directorial choices influenced interpretations of Catherine's role in the play.

In "'The art a seein' the multiple realities': Fragmented Scenography in Sharon Pollock's Plays," Wes D. Pearce identifies another neglected aspect of Pollock's work. He asserts that critics' tendencies to focus on the "political and/or historical underpinnings of her plays and, to an extent, the biographical/autobiographic conventions that haunt some of them," have led them to ignore Pollock's use of scenography (or the visual world of the play), which plays a crucial role in how she "creates, writes, and dramatizes." Like Scott, Pearce examines several texts – *Walsh*, *The Komagata Maru Incident*, *Generations*, *Whiskey Six Cadenza*, and *Doc* – to demonstrate how Pollock's use of scenography has developed over time. He insists that while her techniques may be viewed as commonplace today, they were not when she began experimenting with them more than forty years ago.

The next two essays in the collection return to Pollock's interest in history; both examine *Fair Liberty's Call*, which explores the migration of the United Empire Loyalists to the Maritimes after the American War of Independence, and which critics have also tended to overlook. In "Listening is Telling: Eddie Roberts's Poetics of Repair in Sharon Pollock's *Fair Liberty's Call*," Carmen Derkson once again turns to an examination of Pollock's ongoing concern with the marginalization of Aboriginal people. Derkson argues that Pollock's stage directions make use of a "performative strategy" that emphasizes sound and its relationship to listening practices in order to foreground indigenous presence. Similarly, Kathy K. Y. Chung's "Loss and Mourning in *Fair Liberty's Call*" combines a perceptive reading of stage directions with an abundance of secondary sources on rites of mourning and loss in arguing that while the play highlights the "historic brutality and injustices" that took place during Canada's past, it also emphasizes that the well-being of a community and nation depends on the recognition and support of all its members' losses and suffering, including those of its indigenous peoples.

The final two essays, which offer textual analysis, are the first to comment on *Man Out of Joint* (2007); both reveal that while Pollock has played a major role in informing Canadians about shocking events in Canadian history, she is also keenly attuned to current injustices. In "Questions of Collective Responsibility in Sharon Pollock's *Man Out of Joint*," Tanya Schaap finds that the play, which chronicles the abuse of detainees at Guantanamo Bay as well as the controversies surrounding 9/11 conspiracy theories, functions stylistically and thematically as a "trauma narrative." (To my knowledge, Schaap is the first to apply trauma theory to Pollock's work.) But Schaap's essay also reiterates familiar concerns in Pollock's work, such as "distrust of power" and "accountability" (Nothof, "Introduction," 9), and thus further emphasizes that Pollock does not want audiences to leave the theatre without recognizing their own culpability if they fail to pay attention to those who suffer, or fail to comprehend that it is their social indifference that makes possible the abuse of power. Donna Coates's "Equal-Opportunity Torturers in Judith Thompson's *Palace of the End* and Sharon Pollock's *Man Out of Joint*" concentrates on the representation of "torture chicks" in these two works. It argues that Thompson's focus on the ignorance and moral deficiencies of her character Soldier (loosely based on the "real-life" US Army Specialist Lynndie England) makes it difficult to address the serious ethical and political questions that emerge from women's involvement in systems and structures of dominance, whereas Pollock recognizes that women's exclusion from power has not necessarily made them immune to its seductive qualities, nor has it led them to use power differently from men. Coates's essay concludes by drawing upon the works of a number of feminist critics who insist, as does Pollock, that any admission of women to existing hierarchies in the military must be accompanied by a powerful critique of the institution itself. Both Schaap's and Coates's essays point to Pollock's tendency to use complicated structures which consist of interlocking narratives that track how multiple systems of oppression come into existence and how they are connected.

The remaining entries move the collection in a different direction – that is, to the recognition of Pollock's contribution to theatre production, to the making of theatre – hence providing a worthy balance to the essays on textual semiotics. In "Sharon Pollock and the Garry Theatre (1992–97)," Toronto theatre critic Martin Morrow looks back at the years he spent reviewing theatre productions for the *Calgary Herald*, and specifically those at the Garry Theatre, which Pollock ran with her son Kirk, a.k.a. K. C. Campbell. He concludes it was "remarkable" that the pair managed to keep the company afloat without public funding for five years but honestly confesses that (for sound reasons) his own lack of reviews during the last year of the company's venture may have contributed to its demise. The next essay, "Sharon Pollock in Kosovo," is one that I, as editor, invited Kosovar playwright and executive director of Qendra Multimedia, Pristina, Jeton Neziraj to write. In particular, I asked him to describe how his collaboration with Pollock came about. He writes that it was Pollock's generous response to those struggling to keep theatre alive in war-torn Kosovo that began their relationship. In his essay, Neziraj also explains why he and his theatre company decided to produce *Blood Relations* in Pristina in 2010 (a production Pollock attended) and outlines the subject matter of their work-in-progress, a play tentatively titled "The Hotel."

In "Biography and *the* Archive," Sherrill Grace explores some of the challenges biographers face, including their attempts to achieve the impossible task of getting their subject's story "right." Grace also considers the role biography plays in the life-story of a nation such as Canada and firmly rejects the notion that only the lives of "politicians, generals and military heroes, hockey players and business tycoons" matter, or that only "nation building through railways or Vimy Ridge" should be considered identity-forming events. Rather, she insists that biographies of creative people such as Pollock and the writer/dramatist Timothy Findley, the subject of her current research, are essential because they demonstrate "what and who was left out, misrepresented or silenced." The good news, she writes, is that biographies of artists are finally beginning to appear in our local bookstores. Grace concludes her essay by filling in the details of Pollock's life since 2008, affirming that not a moment is dull or wasted in her subject's life.

Grace's essay is followed by "Sharon's Tongue," a new play that again substantiates the kind of impact Pollock has had on the local theatre community. Immediately after receiving the invitation to the Pollock conference, playwright and actor Lindsay Burns, actors Laura Parken and Grant Linneberg, and former artistic director of Lunchbox Theatre Pamela Halstead, began reading *everything* Pollock has written, and then met once a week over a period of many months (the kind of commitment equivalent to a two-term university graduate course) to discuss the thematic concerns they identified in the playwright's work. Then, drawing almost exclusively on Pollock's own words, they produced a play which, with its insight into the wide range and diversity of ideas and concerns that have captured the playwright's imagination, will undoubtedly prove to be an invaluable resource for future teachers and students of Pollock's work. The collection concludes with a sampling of Pollock's CBC radio reviews, which indicate that she approached this new aspect of her theatrical career with the same professional style those who know her have come to expect. The radio format consisted of a conversation between Pollock and the CBC host based on the review Pollock produced and handed over just prior to the interview, but the audience never got the chance to exactly hear what she had written; many of the reviews were posted online, however, as were some of the interviews. The weekly reviews were always skilfully researched, fair, and delivered with frankness and humour.

That so many of the essays in this collection refer to previously disregarded areas, even on works that have been critically examined many times in the past, speaks to the complexity of Pollock's plays and suggests that, even with the addition of this new collection to the existing body of criticism on her opus, there remains much work to be done. The inclusion of Pollock's reviews should serve to inspire future research on her contribution to the making of theatre as critic.

Works Cited

Dunn, Margo. "Sharon Pollock: In the Centre Ring." *Makara* 1.5 (August–September 1976): 2–6. Print.

Grace, Sherrill. *Making Theatre: A Life of Sharon Pollock*. Vancouver: Talonbooks, 2008. Print.

—— and Michelle La Flamme, eds. *Sharon Pollock: Critical Perspectives on Canadian Theatre in English*. Vol. 10. General ed. Ric Knowles. Toronto: Playwrights Canada P, 2008. Print.

Nothof, Anne F., ed. "Introduction: Illuminating the Facets." *Sharon Pollock: Essays on Her Works*. Writers Series 1. Series eds. Antonio D'Aalfonso and Joseph Pivato. Toronto: Guernica, 2000. 7–11. Print.

Pollock, Sharon. "The Evolution of an Authentic Voice in Canadian Theatre." *Canadian Culture and Literature: A Taiwan Perspective*. Ed. Steven Tötösy de Zepetnek and Leung Yui-nam. Edmonton Research Institute for Comparative Literature, University of Alberta, 1998. 114–24. Print.

Zimmerman, Cynthia, ed. Preface. *Sharon Pollock: Collected Works*. Vol. 1. Toronto: Playwrights Canada P, 2005. iii–iv. Print.

Walsh and the (De-)Construction of Canadian Myth

Jerry Wasserman

The Sharon Pollock celebration at University of Calgary in 2012, which marked, among other things, Pollock's seventy-fifth birthday, had special meaning for me as well. The year 2012 was the fortieth anniversary of my arrival in Canada from the United States. Pollock and her work have been an important part of my Canadian theatre experience since the late 1970s, when I started reading Canadian plays in preparation for teaching my first Canadian drama course at the University of British Columbia. *Walsh* was the Pollock play on my first syllabus. It chronicled a moment in Canadian history that I knew nothing about. (I knew nothing about Canadian history at all, but what American did?) The play packed a powerful punch. It was, and remains, dramatically stunning, a great character study with epic quality. But it had additional particular resonances for me. Although ostensibly about the relationship between North West Mounted Police Superintendent James Walsh and Hunkpapa Sioux Chief Sitting Bull during the years 1877–1881 that the Sioux spent in Canada after the Battle of the Little Bighorn, it seemed obvious to me back then that it was also about the present, the time in which it was written and first performed: the early 1970s, the Vietnam War era.

I was almost a draft dodger. Classified 1A and draftable in 1968, when virtually every young American who was drafted was sent to Vietnam, I had decided I would not go into the army, and – after great anguish – determined to go to Canada instead. At that time there was no notion of any future amnesty; it seemed an irrevocable decision. I applied and was accepted for graduate school at McGill and literally had my bags packed for Montreal when I received, on appeal, what I came to call my middle-class-white-boy medical deferment. I didn't have to leave the United States. But my decision to accept a teaching job in Vancouver a few years later was certainly influenced by my fond feelings for the country that would have been willing to take me in when my own country wanted to send me off to fight an unjust war and possibly kill me.

My reading of *Walsh* was filtered through that lens.[1] And I was not the only one who saw a connection between the history Pollock chronicled in her play and the relationship of Canada to the United States and its political dissidents in the 1970s. Alan Haig-Brown's book *Hell No, We Won't Go: Vietnam Draft Resisters in Canada* begins with the testimony of a Vietnam War resister living in Canada who said he "understood the differences between the two nations when he learned about Sitting Bull coming to Canada after General Custer's defeat at Little Big Horn" (Haig-Brown 18). For American war resisters fleeing to Canada in the 1960s and 1970s, the lesson could not have been clearer. The story of Sitting Bull in Canada seemed a template for Canada–U.S. difference, an early historical illustration of what Daniel Francis calls the Canadian myth of the Mild West versus America's Wild West (*Dreams* 229–35): the kinder, gentler, more liberal, more open-minded, more open-hearted nation that we all wished – and that many of us believed – Canada was, compared to the racist, warmongering United States. This was a common Canadian feeling in the intensely nationalistic 1970s. "I don't need your war machines / I don't

JERRY WASSERMAN

need your ghetto scenes," sang the Guess Who. "American Woman, stay away from me."

I would subsequently learn that comparative Canadian–American policies toward the opening of the West and the management and policing of Native people had long comprised a presumptive site of Canadian good sense and moral superiority to the United States. In 1873, journalist Nicholas Flood Davin stated, "in the way we have dealt with Indians on this continent, I think we have displayed more humanity than the authorities and officers of the Washington government" ("British" 41). (Ironically, Davin's 1879 The Davin Report, is thought to have given rise to the Canadian residential school system.)

The year 1873 also saw the establishment of the North West Mounted Police and the beginnings of the iconic mythology of the Mounties' non-violent, humane peacekeeping successes in contrast to the blood-soaked history of the American frontier and its Indian wars. A key narrative attributing the moral high ground to the Mounties as a peacekeeping force was the story of Sitting Bull and the Sioux finding asylum in the Cypress Hills. A cartoon appearing on the cover of *Canadian Illustrated News* in September 1877, titled "Sitting Bull on Dominion Territory," shows an Aboriginal man sitting against a post marked Boundary Line. Above him stand an American soldier and a North West Mounted policeman. The caption reads,

> U.S. Soldier – Send him over to our side of the line and we'll take care of him.

> N.W. Mounted Police Officer – So long as he behaves himself, the British right of asylum is as sacred for this poor Indian as for any royal refugee. (McGrady 72, illus. 10)

Whereas the Americans had tried and failed to suppress the Sioux by means of military force, leading to the infamous destruction of General Custer and his men, a tiny North West Mounted Police contingent under the command of Major Walsh maintained peaceable relations with the Sioux, without resort to force, for the entire four years they remained in Canada. This story, reifying into myth, says Francis, "had a powerful influence on the way Canadians felt themselves to be distinct from, and superior to, the United States" (*Imaginary* 69).

Early in *Walsh*, Pollock stages what Francis calls "the familiar confrontation stereotype" scene at the heart of the Mountie legend (*Imaginary* 70): "On one side stands the solitary, unarmed Mounted Policeman; on the other side, a much larger number of desperadoes, armed to the teeth and ready to make trouble" (*Dreams* 33). In the play Major Walsh, along with only three of his men, rides out to meet thousands of Sioux who have just crossed the border into the land of the Great White Mother (Queen Victoria), led by fierce warrior chiefs Gall and Sitting Bull. The Sioux ask for sanctuary based on a promise made by George III to their people who had fought alongside the British against the Americans a century before during the Revolutionary War. Before responding to the request, Walsh confronts the Assiniboine warrior White Dog over some stolen horses. According to Pollock's stage directions, *"belligerent"* White Dog carries a rifle and *"there is a swell of sound from the surrounding Sioux"* (46), but Walsh faces him down, *"oblivious of his rifle"* (47), without ever drawing his own weapon. Walsh's bravery, his fairness and firmness, his integrity and strength of character, all symbolized by the red coat of the Mounties, subsequently convince Sitting Bull to shake his hand and reach an agreement without violence or compulsion, based on mutual respect and trust.

Pollock's theatrical version of this scene corresponds very closely to most of the authoritative historical versions. Pollock takes a little licence, backing Walsh up with only two other Mounties, Sergeant McCutcheon and Clarence, plus the Métis scout Louis, whereas most historical accounts have Walsh accompanied by McCutcheon, three other troopers and two scouts (Manzione 45; Anderson 106). But the gist of the scene is the same, and most of the rest of the play is remarkably faithful to the details of the scholarly histories. As Hayden White has taught us, however, a historical narrative is "necessarily a mixture of adequately and inadequately explained events, a congeries of established and inferred facts, at once a representation that is an interpretation and an interpretation that passes for an explanation of the whole process mirrored in the narrative" (281). And as Sitting Bull's biographer, Robert M. Utley, points out, "For the first meeting with Sitting Bull ... Walsh's [own] reminiscence is the major source" (Utley 370n1). This reminiscence, according to Utley, "is a long, rambling, frequently illegible or incoherent account of police service penned by Walsh for his daughter [Cora]. Despite its flaws, including exaggeration and even fabrication, it contains much valuable information" (370n1).

All sources agree that Major Walsh became Sitting Bull's most trusted white ally and a champion of the Sioux. In the play, as he gets to know them, Walsh becomes their increasingly passionate advocate, increasingly appalled by the injustices done to them. "Yes, they're starving and destitute, yet they endure," he writes to his wife, Mary:

> They share what little they have, and they observe the law – god damn it, they'd be a credit to any community. . . One thing I know, across the line there's been gross and continual mismanagement of the Sioux. An able and brilliant people have been crushed, held down, moved from place to place, cheated and lied to – And now they hold on here in Canada, the remnants of a proud race, and they ask for some sort of justice – which is what I thought I swore an oath to serve! (87–88)

He becomes known as White Forehead or White Sioux, a man on whom Sitting Bull and his people can depend. In contrast, the sole American representative in the play, General Alfred Terry, is a racist, sexist, unapologetic advocate of Manifest Destiny and the "imperative. . . elimination of the savage" (69).

If this were all there were to the play, it would merely re-inscribe the cultural truisms developed by the mythmaking machinery of nineteenth-century Canadian nationalist historiography that endured well into the twentieth century – and beyond. In his 1975 book *Hollywood's Canada: The Americanization of Our National Image*, Pierre Berton mocks the distortions of Hollywood movie treatments of Canadian historical scenarios. He cites as particularly blatant the absurdities of the 1954 movie *Saskatchewan*, featuring Mounties and Indians riding up and down the Canadian Rockies, predatory Sioux attacking Shelley Winters's wagon train, and Alan Ladd "avert[ing] a bloodbath and sav[ing] the Canadian west" from the savages (107). Berton scoffs at what he calls "the geographical mumbo-jumbo" as well as the distorted history, asserting that "the peaceful movement of the Sioux across the border after the battle with Custer is one of the remarkable chapters in the history of the Canadian frontier" (108). He dramatically re-stages their first meeting on the Canadian side, describing how the Mounted Police treated the Sioux "with dignity and pomp, including a fanfare of trumpets. The police were drawn up in their dress uniforms and the Sioux were given presents. In return, the Sioux danced and sang for their hosts" (108). For several years before they returned to the United States, he concludes – without explaining *why* they returned to the United States – Sitting Bull and his people "were model refugees" (108).

As an object lesson defining perceived differences between Canada and the United States, the Sitting Bull/Walsh story resurfaced during the free trade negotiations of the 1980s. In a 1989 special issue of *Maclean's* magazine, aiming to explain what made the countries and their cultures distinct, Peter C. Newman used as his primary illustration of cultural difference "the curious fate of . . . the great Sioux warrior [who] had valiantly" resisted and then defeated Custer's cavalry (24). Newman, too, felt it necessary to stage the primal scene. Crossing the border with his people, Sitting Bull was met by Major Walsh, "wearing his resplendent scarlet jacket" (24). Walsh "sternly explained that the Indians could stay only if they obeyed Canadian laws" (24). And that alone seems to have done the trick. "Sitting Bull remained on the Canadian side of the border for a peaceful half-decade,

[Newman slightly exaggerates], returning to North Dakota in 1881, where he again placed himself in jeopardy and was gunned down by government agents a few years later" (24).

James Laxer, in his 2003 book *The Border*, cites the Sioux quest for asylum in Canada and Walsh's friendship with Sitting Bull in the context of, and as an implicit parallel to, a post–9/11 Homeland Security crackdown on illegal Pakistani immigrants in the United States, which sent them fleeing across the border en masse into Canada (121–26). And for speculative spin it would be hard to beat the conclusion of Grahame Woods' article on Walsh and Sitting Bull in the *Cobourg* (Ontario) *Daily Star*, also from 2003. "It could be said Walsh saved the west for Canada; that if his enormous gamble of riding into Sitting Bull's camp for the first time had failed and he and the rest of the NWMP had met the same fate as Custer, the American army would have flooded across the border – and perhaps stayed, swallowing up the rest of western Canada in the process. The Saskatchewan Rough Riders might be in the NFL today" (4).

There also exists, however, a counter-mythological reading of the story different from either Hollywood's or the Canadian nationalist version. Dee Brown's revisionist *Bury My Heart at Wounded Knee: An Indian History of the American West* is as scathing in its account of Canada's role in the fate of the Sioux as it is in its challenge to official American versions of frontier history. If the Canadian government had been more co-operative, Brown argues, the Sioux "probably would have lived out their lives on the plains of Saskatchewan. From the beginning, however, the Queen's government viewed Sitting Bull as a potential troublemaker, as well as an expensive guest. . ." (Brown 393-94). Although contradicted by every other historical account I have read, and by Pollock's play, Brown claims that "no aid of any kind was offered" to the Sioux by the Canadian government, "not even food or clothing. . ." (394). But he does find compelling proof of the government's repellent attitudes in the archive of Canadian House of Commons debates for 1878. He cites this mocking exchange between

Prime Minister Alexander Mackenzie and the then leader of the opposition, Sir John A. Macdonald:

> MR. MCDONALD [*sic*]: I do not see how a Sitting Bull can cross the frontier.
>
> MR. MCKENZIE [*sic*]: Not unless he rises.
>
> SIR JOHN: Then he is not a Sitting Bull. (394)

"This," Brown drily concludes, "was the usual level of discussion reached in the Canadian Parliament whenever the problem of the exiled Sioux arose" (393–94). Macdonald and his Conservatives would return to power by the end of that year, but the change in government would do nothing to improve the lot of the Sioux in Canada.

Richard Gwyn's award-winning biography of Macdonald mentions Sitting Bull and the Sioux only in passing, but Gwyn devotes a full chapter – full of uncomfortable contradiction and equivocation – to Macdonald's Indian policy previous to the Riel rebellion. He argues that "Macdonald knew more about Indian policy and the Indians themselves than any of his predecessors, or any of his successors until Jean Chrétien and Paul Martin a century later" (419), and that, for his time, Macdonald had a particularly enlightened attitude toward Aboriginal people. Gwyn also repeats the contention that "Canadian Indian policy was far superior, in effectiveness and sensitivity, to American Indian policy" (426). It was Macdonald's bad luck, Gwyn insists, to have governed during the period when the disappearance of the buffalo essentially destroyed Plains Indian civilization. Not just the Sioux were suffering on the Canadian side of the Medicine Line. Gwyn cites reports of Blackfoot having to eat the flesh of poisoned wolves and Cree starving and destitute between 1879 and 1882. One band survived a winter only because the Mounted Police at Fort Walsh shared their rations with them. Yet, Gwyn acknowledges, "Macdonald shared fully the prevailing fear of creating a permanent dependent underclass. So he vacillated, temporized and clung to the hope that things would somehow sort themselves out" (424). In fact "the unofficial operating slogan" of the new Department of Indian Affairs, of which Macdonald appointed himself minister, was "'work or starve'" (425). Historian J.R. Miller confirms that "the government used denial of food aid to the starving bands [of Cree] as a weapon to drive them out of the Cypress Hills" in 1882 (Miller 228). If that was his strategy toward Canadian Aboriginal people, it would be no surprise to learn that Macdonald might have been anxious to have the Sioux problem in the Cypress Hills, with all its American complications, taken off his hands.

Sharon Pollock follows both Dee Brown and her Canadian sources more flattering to Canada in excavating the story for its revelations of political immorality and personal failure on both sides of the border. In doing so, she simultaneously helps shore up the myth and deconstruct it. As bad as the Americans may have been, Pollock suggests that Canadians were no better in their insidious complicity with American Indian policy and their desire to rid themselves of the troublesome Sioux. As she writes in her oft-quoted "Playwright's Note" to the published script of *The Komagata Maru Incident*, "As a Canadian, I feel that much of our history has been misrepresented and even hidden from us. Until we recognize our past, we cannot change our future" (Pollock 1978, n.p.). In *Walsh*, Pollock asks us to see the significant differences between Canadian and American behaviour toward the Sioux, and at the same time to see through the self-flattering cultural myths Canadians have built up around the story, in order that we not commit similar sins in the present or future. As Sherrill Grace has argued, "Through the writing and revising of *Walsh*, Pollock learned how history can be changed by theatre. . ." (137).

At first Walsh's frustration with Canadian government policy focuses on its hopeless attempt to turn the nomadic Plains Indian hunters into farmers, as he keeps getting sent shipments of seed and agricultural implements rather than the guns and ammunition the Indians need for the buffalo hunt that sustains their culture. Early in the play, he half-heartedly tries to convince Blackfoot Chief Crow

Eagle that "When the white man comes, the buffalo goes . . . And with the buffalo goes the life you have known," so he should take the Great White Mother's gift of agricultural equipment. But when Crow Eagle wittily replies, "I do not wish to be servant to a cow," Walsh easily concedes and grants him ammunition (37).

As the play progresses, Walsh comes under increasing pressure first to persuade and then to starve the Sioux into returning to the United States. Washington has been putting pressure on London, which in turn has pressured Ottawa, whose emissary to Walsh is his commanding officer, Commissioner of the North West Mounted Police, Colonel James Macleod. "Persuade [Sitting Bull] to return across the line," he urges Walsh. "Goddamn it, he's a thorn in our flesh. We can't discuss a bloody thing with the Americans without they bring it up!" [sic] (93). When Walsh resists, Macleod voices his government's strategy, ordering Walsh to cut off supplies to the Sioux: "The Prime Minister feels that, whereas common sense has not prevailed upon the Sioux, hunger will" (98).[2] Reluctantly, Walsh agrees, and his capitulation is complete when he abjectly accedes to Macleod's order that he apologize to the American government. As Heidi J. Holder points out, "The disgrace in *Walsh* is not simply in what one does, but in what one is bullied into doing" (109).

Earlier, in an attempt to persuade Sitting Bull to return with his people to the United States, Walsh had clearly defined his bifurcated loyalties and divided self: "I tell you this because I am a soldier, and I must follow orders, but I am friend also. White Forehead (*indicating himself*) does not say this; Major Walsh says this" (54). In the end his loyalty to the Force and his own military identity trumps his sense of morality and responsibility to Sitting Bull and the Sioux, just as he had deferred to his role ("my red coat") and "duty" in his excruciating decision to deny Canadian sanctuary to the bloodied, frozen Nez Perce women and children on the last leg of their flight from the murderous American cavalry (59). Pollock makes clear that this strategy is tragic for both the Aboriginal people and (pointedly in the Prologue)

JERRY WASSERMAN

for Walsh himself – a man of genuine conscience – as it ultimately destroys him.

Pollock's portrait of Walsh, a title character rent by internal conflict, is necessarily dramatically complex. Like Pollock's, all the historical accounts paint Walsh as a compassionate man, genuinely committed to trying to find a just resolution to the dilemma of the Sioux refugees. They all agree with Pollock's portrayal of him as a man caught in an elaborate political squeeze play involving the American, British, and Canadian governments, all trying to foist off responsibility for the Sioux onto one another. The most detailed scholarly account, Joseph Manzione's *"I Am Looking to the North for My Life": Sitting Bull, 1876–1881*, provides a particularly scathing description of the machinations of David Mills, the Canadian minister of the interior, who, Manzione says, "played a mercenary game":

> He voiced concern to the President of the United States about the plight of a group of destitute, homeless human beings, and pointed accusingly at the government and the American people for breaking treaties . . . Mills tried eloquently to persuade American officials that they could best serve the interests of the United States by offering to return the Sioux to their reservations, where their needs could be met . . . Then he ordered subordinates to collect information about the atrocities committed against the Indians to use against the United States in negotiations. He characterized the same Indians whose plight he had described so graphically as murderous savages . . . The minister intended to get rid of the Sioux by whatever means was possible. (69)

All sources agree that after Macdonald regained the post of prime minister from Mackenzie in 1878, he began working to neutralize Walsh's influence with the Sioux and institute what Manzione calls "the rather barbaric policy of starving the Sioux in order to force their return across the border to prison" (5) – although there are alternative explanations of why, ultimately, the Sioux returned to the United States and surrendered to the American Army, including opposition from other Aboriginal people in Canada (McGrady 86; Pennanen 135).

Pollock refuses to whitewash Walsh's character, although she does not build into her portrayal the specific criticisms rendered by certain historians: that Walsh suffered from "vanity and ambition . . . conceit and romanticism" (Utley 214–15), or that Walsh's memoirs were "self-congratulatory," making himself the hero of his own tale (LaDow 2). What we do see, I think, in Pollock's Major Walsh is a certain weakness of character and a propensity to feel sorry for himself. His decision to give in to the prime minister's ultimatum that he help starve the Sioux into submission and to Macleod's that he write a letter of apology to the Americans or resign seems to me a rationalization couched in bad faith: "They say one's strongest instinct is self-preservation . . . and I've made the force my life," he tells Macleod. "To whom do I send this letter?" (99). This is not a matter of *instinct* at all; nor is the choice for Walsh life or death, as it will be for the Sioux.

Shortly after this, in the play's most powerful scene, an angry, frustrated Walsh "*does up the top button on his tunic*" (110), as if locking himself into his official bureaucratic policeman's role, then attacks Sitting Bull when the latter comes in, ragged and hungry, to beg for food for his people: "And I can give you nothing!" Walsh explodes. "God knows, I've done my damndest and nothing's changed. Do you hear that? Nothing's changed! Cross the line if you're so hungry, but don't, for Christ's sake, come begging food from me! . . . I don't give a goddamn who you are! Get the hell out!" (111). As Sitting Bull goes for his knife, Walsh throws him to the floor and plants his foot on his back as the young recruit Clarence, the conscience of the play, screams, in an echo of the Prologue, "Noooooooo!" (112–13). That, of course, is Pollock's cry as well. James Walsh would prove the model for a whole series of basically good males in later Pollock plays – *One Tiger to a Hill*, *The Komagata Maru Incident*, *Blood Relations*, *Doc* – who are fatally compromised, to Pollock's great regret, by a combination of internal weakness and institutional loyalty or social conformity. This incident, by the way, the fight in which Walsh humiliates Sitting Bull, is cited in many of the historical accounts, although Manzione points out that it originates in a 1955 history whose author "does not cite sources for this story" (118n26).

However much may be truth, however much invention, the story of Walsh and the Sioux retains great staying power as Canadian cultural myth, not just for historians and journalists but for a range of writers in a variety of literary genres. The last few years alone have produced an excellent suite of poems by Colin Morton called *The Hundred Cuts: Sitting Bull and the Major*; Guy Vanderhaeghe's novel *A Good Man*, which covers the same time frame and many of the same events as Pollock's play and in which Walsh is a major character, Sitting Bull a lesser one; and a Ken Mitchell play about Walsh and Sitting Bull called *Spirits of the Trail*, performed outdoors with the actors on horseback (Riess B1). But for me, none of these could have the power, the resonance, or the relevance of Pollock's *Walsh*, written in the midst of a new flood of political refugees coming across the border from the United States a century after the flight of the Sioux, marking and erasing at the same time apparent differences between Canadian and American *modi operandi*, and providing a sobering reminder of the *realpolitik* of Canadian–American border diplomacy.

NOTES

1   My reading of Walsh has also been filtered through the lenses of the many excellent scholarly articles written about the play. See Grace, Holder, Nothof, Nunn, Page, and Salter. See also reviews by Adele Freedman, Jamie Portman, and Herbert Whittaker in Conolly, especially Whittaker's opening night review of the Stratford Festival production in 1974, which begins with these eloquent lines: "The color of the red coats in Walsh . . . is not the color of Rose Marie, or of the Union Jack, for that matter. It is a faded, dusty, unspectacular red, and it is the true color of one of the saddest episodes in the history of the Canadian West" (Conolly 138).

2   This line was one of the generative sources of the play for Pollock, according to Malcolm Page. He quotes her as saying at a lecture in 1976, "I began with an interest in Walsh as a character, as a rebel. Then I discovered John A. Macdonald had written, 'If words will not prevail with the Sioux, hunger will.' I was angry at my own ignorance, and that the historians hadn't told me" (13).

Works Cited

Anderson, Ian. *Sitting Bull's Boss: Above the Medicine Line with James Morrow Walsh*. Surrey, BC: Heritage House, 2000. Print.

Berton, Pierre. *Hollywood's Canada: The Americanization of Our National Image*. Toronto: McClelland & Stewart, 1975. Print.

Brown, Dee. *Bury My Heart at Wounded Knee: An Indian History of the American West*. New York: Bantam, 1970. Print.

Conolly, L.W. *Canadian Drama and the Critics*. Rev. ed. Vancouver: Talonbooks, 1995. 135–44. Print.

Davin, Nicholas Flood. *British versus American Civilization: A Lecture*. National Papers 2. Toronto: Adam, Stevenson, 1873. Print.

———. "Report on Industrial Schools for Indians and Half-Breeds." 14 Mar. 1879. Canada. Annual Report, 1880, Department of the Interior.

Francis, Daniel. *The Imaginary Indian: The Image of the Indian in Canadian Culture*. Vancouver: Arsenal Pulp, 1992. Print.

———. *National Dreams: Myth, Memory, and Canadian History*. Vancouver: Arsenal Pulp, 1997. Print.

Grace, Sherrill. "Imagining Canada: Sharon Pollock's *Walsh* and *Fair Liberty's Call*." *Sharon Pollock*. Ed. Grace and La Flamme. Toronto: Playwrights Canada P, 2008. 133–50. Print.

——— and Michelle La Flamme, eds. *Sharon Pollock*. Toronto: Playwrights Canada P, 2008. Print.

Guess Who, The. "American Woman." Written by Randy Bachman, Burton Cummings, Garry Peterson, Jim Kale. RCA, 1970. LP.

Gwyn, Richard. *Nation Maker: Sir John A. Macdonald: His Life, Our Times. Volume Two, 1867–1891*. Toronto: Random House Canada, 2011. Print.

Haig-Brown, Alan. *Hell No, We Won't Go: Vietnam Draft Resisters in Canada*. Vancouver: Raincoast, 1996. Print.

Holder, Heidi J. "Broken Toys: The Destruction of the National Hero in the Early History Plays of Sharon Pollock." *Sharon Pollock: Essays on Her Works*. Ed. Anne F. Nothof. Toronto: Guernica, 2000. 100–127. Print.

LaDow, Beth. "Sanctuary: Native Border Crossings and the North American West." *American Review of Canadian Studies* 31 (Spring/Summer 2001): 25–42. Print.

Laxer, James. *The Border: Canada, the U.S. and Dispatches from the 49th Parallel.* Toronto: Doubleday Canada, 2003. Print.

MacEwen, Grant. *Sitting Bull: The Years in Canada.* Edmonton: Hurtig, 1973. Print.

McGrady, David G. *Living with Strangers: The Nineteenth-Century Sioux and the Canadian–American Borderlands.* Toronto: U of Toronto P, 2010. Print.

Manzione, Joseph. *"I Am Looking to the North for My Life": Sitting Bull, 1876–1881.* Salt Lake City: U of Utah P, 1991. Print.

Miller, J.R. *Skyscrapers Hide the Heavens: A History of Indian–White Relations in Canada.* 3rd ed. Toronto: U of Toronto P, 2000. Print.

Morton, Colin. *The Hundred Cuts: Sitting Bull and the Major.* Ottawa: Buschek, 2009. Print.

Newman, Peter C. "Bold and Cautious." *Portrait of Two Nations.* Special Issue of *Maclean's* 102 (3 July 1989): 24–25. Print.

Nothof, Anne F., ed. *Sharon Pollock: Essays on Her Works.* Toronto: Guernica, 2000. Print.

———. "Crossing Borders: Sharon Pollock's Revisitation of Canadian Frontiers." *Sharon Pollock.* Ed. Nothof. Toronto: Guernica, 2000. 81–99. Print.

Nunn, Robert C. "Sharon Pollock's Plays: A Review Article." In *Sharon Pollock.* Ed. Nothof. Toronto: Guernica, 2000. 26–43.

Page, Malcolm. "Sharon Pollock: Committed Playwright." In *Sharon Pollock.* Ed. Nothof. Toronto: Guernica, 2000. 13–25. Print.

Pennanen, Gary. "Sitting Bull: Indian without a Country." *Canadian Historical Review* 51 (June 1970): 123–40. Print.

Pollock, Sharon. *The Komagata Maru Incident.* Toronto: Playwrights Co-op, 1978.

———. *Walsh.* Rev. ed. Vancouver: Talonbooks, 1983. Print.

Riess, Kelly-Anne. "Travelling Show Brings History to Life." *Leader Post* (Regina) 12 Aug. 2010: B1. Print.

Salter, Denis. "(Im)possible Worlds: The Plays of Sharon Pollock." *Sharon Pollock.* Eds. Grace and La Flamme. Toronto: Playwrights Canada P, 2008. 13–32. Print.

Utley, Robert M. *The Lance and the Shield: The Life and Times of Sitting Bull*. New York: Henry Holt, 1993. Print.

Vanderhaeghe, Guy. *A Good Man*. Toronto: McClelland & Stewart, 2011. Print.

White, Hayden. "Interpretation in History." *New Literary History* 4 (Winter 1973): 281–314. Print.

Woods, Grahame. "A Great Historical Figure Who's Largely Forgotten." *Cobourg Daily Star* 6 May 2003: 4. Print.

Sharon Pollock and the Scene of the Crime

Shelley Scott

This essay originates with two comments Sherrill Grace makes in *Making Theatre: A Life of Sharon Pollock*. First, in reference to Pollock's play *End Dream*, Grace writes, "Both in its historical basis and in her dramatic treatment of the subject, this play belongs with *Blood Relations, Saucy Jack,* and *Constance*" (333). Each of these four plays, which span the period 1980–2000, deals with an unsolved real-life murder. A few lines later, Grace makes the further comment that "Sharon . . . adores murder mysteries" (333). Pollock's interest in the murder-mystery genre comes as no surprise, since scholars frequently make passing reference to the mystery component in many of her plays and point out the sources of the real-life cases. However, scholars usually insist that Pollock's intentions extend far beyond a simple "whodunnit" plotline to explore larger thematic concerns. For example, in her introductory essay to Pollock's *Collected Works*, Cynthia Zimmerman notes, "A number of these historical works include an explicit mystery component" ("Anatomising" 5), but quotes Pollock herself as saying she is only interested in manipulating historical mysteries for a bigger purpose. Most often, Pollock's plays have been admired for their multitude of angles, the contrasting perspectives of various characters, and the fragmentation of time and narrative, devices that do indeed lend themselves to multiple interpretations and thematic richness. Zimmerman, for example, has pointed out that "in a Pollock play the multiplicity of vantage points is not only critical to the story, it is also married to the play's structure" ("Anatomising" 8). But Pollock's technique of telling a story from competing points of view, her complex layering of versions of the truth, and her preoccupation with relations of power, also lend themselves particularly well to murder mysteries.

In this essay, rather than brushing aside the murder-mystery designation, I will look closely at the selection of plays Grace identifies in order to examine how they work when considered squarely within the conventions of the genre. Instead of dismissing that association as somehow a lessening or cheapening of the dramatic form, I will argue that genre conventions of the murder mystery play a significant part in making these plays effective. According to Grace, in 1992 Pollock made a proposal to CBC Radio to write "a series called 'A.J. Jones' . . . that featured a young, female, would-be detective and her talking cat" (*Making Theatre* 320). The proposal was rejected (apparently because of the cat), but as I will demonstrate, Pollock's interest in working within the detective genre has manifested in other ways in her more serious plays. *Blood Relations*, Pollock's most famous play and winner of the Governor-General's Award for Drama in 1981, treats the acquitted American axe-murderer Lizzie Borden as its subject. *Constance* (1992), a radio play, deals with the notorious killing of a child in England in 1860. *Saucy Jack* (1993) is set in 1888 and springs from the crimes committed by the most infamous of English serial killers, Jack the Ripper. With *End Dream* (2000), the story of the murder of a young nanny in Vancouver in 1924,[1] Pollock turns to Canada for source material.

Each of these plays can be understood to demonstrate features of the mystery genre. According to Lucy Sussex, crime writing is "marked by the subject matter of crime and its solution; structured around the gradual revelation of criminous information (the mystery) of which detective fiction is a refinement; [and] focussed on the detective as ratiocinator of the narrative" (6). Sussex further identifies the "generic crime narrative form: the discovery of a murder, followed by investigation into whodunnit, the discovery of the culprit and the motive" (11). She points out, however, that the historical evolution of policing and prosecuting brought adjustments to fictional depictions too: "When lawyers came to dominate court proceedings, legal combat ensued, and also a theatre of narrative, the different accounts of how a crime had occurred" (11). Mystery novels have been popular since their earliest appearance in the nineteenth century and were being dramatized for the English stage as early as the 1840s (57).[2] Certainly, the four plays under consideration here fit the definition of the crime narrative, concerned as they are with the gradual revelation of a mystery. They also display some flavour of the courtroom, as competing theories are argued and characters take on the language of prosecution and defence. The question of the "detective" complicates matters, since there is no representative of the law in these plays per se; rather, the role of investigator or sleuth is embodied by an interesting range of characters that are never entirely successful in their efforts. In *Blood Relations* and *Saucy Jack*, the investigator is an actress and therefore someone already operating outside the norms of social convention, a woman unusually free to take on the typically male role of the detective. In *Constance*, the investigator is an unnamed male and the antagonist in the play, a representative of patriarchal oppression who tries to force a confession from the accused murderer. Most intriguingly, in *End Dream* the victim and the investigator are one and the same, a woman on the threshold of death who mentally replays the events leading up to her own murder. These wide variations should not necessarily be seen as exceeding the generic possibilities of the murder mystery because, for example, according to film critic Philippa Gates, "A genre is a body of films that have narratives, structures, settings, conventions and/or characters in common and that are readily recognizable to audiences and promotable by producers" (6). But she also points out that, while audiences like to see the same *kind* of film, they do not want them to be *exactly* the same: change and innovation are also important.

One thing all four plays do have in common is a private, indoor, domestic setting. *Blood Relations* unfolds in 1902 in the same family home where the murders were committed ten years earlier. *Constance* is set in 1944 in Miss Kaye's room at a nursing home and recalls the murder that took place at her childhood home eighty-four years earlier. While Jack the Ripper murdered his victims in a public place, *Saucy Jack* plays out in a private home on the Thames, "*the week-end getaway of Henry Wilson, a senior bureaucrat at the Home Office*" (11). The murder that is committed within the time frame of the play, the poisoning of Montague, happens in this domestic location. *End Dream* occurs in the summer of 1924 in Vancouver, at "*The home of Doris and Robert Clarke-Evans*" (100). *Blood Relations* and *Constance* have narrative frames that take the audience back to the time of the murders, while *Saucy Jack* and *End Dream* deal with crimes much more immediate, but all take place in one confined and confining setting, the one place where all the clues and evidence of the mystery must come out. The circumstances of each murder are inextricably linked to the conventional gender roles, making the traditionally female domestic realm an appropriate location for every play.

Blood Relations illustrates one way Pollock deals with unsolved murder: she introduces an outsider, someone who was not present at the scene of the crime, an investigator who tries to uncover the truth. In a traditional murder mystery, this would be the character of the detective, a figure of authority who eventually puts the clues together. In *Blood Relations*, Lizzie Borden's friend, the Actress, takes on the role of investigator and stages a detailed re-enactment of the events leading up to the murders that Lizzie was accused of committing. She pieces together the events and arrives at a motive much as a traditional detective would. The audience journeys through the re-enactment of the crime along with the Actress until the very end, when Pollock undermines her "detective" and exposes the limits of her ability to know what happened. As Anne Nothof writes, in many of Pollock's plays,

"The compulsion to 'know the truth' is sabotaged by a demonstration of the impossibility of knowing the truth: the ambiguity is fascinating" ("Painting" vii). The Actress does not learn what Lizzie did; rather, she learns what she would have done in Lizzie's place and we, as audience members, are left wondering what we might have done in the same circumstances. We have been led, not to the solution of the crime, but to a profound understanding of Lizzie's sense of entrapment in a patriarchal household and an oppressively conventional society. As Pollock has confirmed in an interview with Robert Wallace in regard to *Blood Relations*: "I'm saying that all of us are capable of murder given the right situation" (123). In an interview with Nothof, Pollock conceded that her play appeals to "the people who are just looking for a suspenseful murder-mystery" ("Essays" 167). While the play does work within those generic parameters, this appeal does not preclude those same spectators from simultaneously appreciating the sophisticated meta-structure and the feminist social commentary that *Blood Relations* also provides – whether they expected to or not.

In her preface to the second volume of Pollock's collected works, Zimmerman also observes the parallels between the plays under discussion in this essay: "Like *Blood Relations*, *Saucy Jack* and *End Dream*, which also re-vision historical crimes, *Constance* is structured as an investigation and moral inquiry" (iii). Zimmerman says of the 1992 radio play, "in *Constance*, Pollock produces a sophisticated and complicated 'why done it'" (iv). As in *Blood Relations*, Pollock introduces an outsider who plays detective although, unlike the Actress, this investigator is cast in the role of an unsympathetic persecutor. Identified in the script only as "*Male, about 40*" (272), the character remains unnamed in the dialogue. At her advanced age (she is over one hundred years old), Miss Kaye at first mistakes her visitor for Death (275) and later dismisses him as "a seedy newsman" (291). He has come to visit Constance Kent, who now goes by the name Ruth Emilie Kaye, in her room at a nursing home, in order to force her to confess to the murder of her half-brother Francis eighty-four years ago. Explicitly constructing himself as a detective, the Male boasts, "I'm one who's penetrated your disguise, that's who I am ... Cracked the façade. Seen through you" (291). The strange thing is that, as a young woman, Constance/Miss Kaye had already confessed to the murder and served a prison sentence. Upon her release, she joined her brother William in Australia and lived a full and useful life, including setting up the very nursing home where she now lives. The motivation of the Male interrogator seems not so much to confirm the confession as to provoke Miss Kaye into displaying guilt and remorse. In that sense, he continues the patriarchal role begun by her abusive father and continued by her bullying bishop, another in a series of men intent on condemning her as: "Obstinate! Proud! Sullen! Envious! Thoughtless! Thoughtful! Insubordinate! Rude Independent Assertive Fanciful, Contrary" (308). Miss Kaye does not confess again. Instead, she actively embraces the litany of criticisms levelled against her and tells her Male visitor to "go to hell." The stage directions indicate that her last words of the play are spoken in a *"strong and clear"* voice: "Not! Guilty!" (309).

Constance supplies an interesting example of how Pollock uses her source material for her own creative and political ends. Zimmerman has argued that Pollock loves the historical mystery for the larger use she can make of it: "The issue under investigation is not so much if the incident happened, but rather why it might have happened, how it might have happened" ("Anatomising" 5). Zimmerman notes that it is injustice for the victims and potentially for the accused that moves Pollock: "From a deep, personal core comes Sharon Pollock's sustained preoccupation with justice, authority, betrayal, self-sacrifice, the marginalised, the silenced, and the high price of both surrender and resistance" ("Anatomising" 3). These preoccupations lead Pollock to imagine the circumstances of the crime. In the case of *Constance*, Pollock takes the known fact that Constance's father was cheating on his wife with their children's nanny and that, upon his wife's death, he married the nanny and had another child with her, a son named Francis. From this evidence, Pollock imagines that the father in fact murdered his wife by poisoning her food and drink. On her deathbed, Mother struggles to tell her daughter Constance of her suspicions, repeating the words:

SHELLEY SCOTT

"Your father . . . brings . . . drink food . . ." (285). The elderly Miss Kaye takes on the voice of legal prosecution when she tells her Male visitor: "I state – that Constance Kent's mother, in general good health except for depression, died suddenly in great agony of an ailment diagnosed by the attending physician as an 'obstruction of the bowels.' I state – that Constance Kent's father married the nursemaid Mary after the death of his wife. I state – an intimate relationship existed between the nursemaid and father prior to the death of the mother. Does this set of circumstances – suggest – anything to you?" (288–89). The Male refuses to take Constance's accusations seriously, as did the Doctor at the deathbed who dismissed Constance and called her "girlie" (287). Pollock is clearly portraying a culture where the Father can behave with impunity. He abuses his wife and children, he carries on an affair with the nursemaid Mary and later, after he has married her, he begins an affair with the next nursemaid, Jeannie. And, Pollock suggests, he may well have gotten away with two murders: that of his first wife and that of his child, Francis.

Here we return to the murder Constance is accused of committing, the killing of three-and-a-half-year-old Francis. The child is found stuffed down the privy with his throat slashed, but the surprising lack of blood at this location suggests he may have been killed elsewhere and his body moved, and that he may already have been dead when his throat was cut. From these known details, Pollock again concludes that the father was the murderer. Miss Kaye suggests: "A hand perhaps, clasped tightly over a small child's face . . . To prevent him crying out perhaps . . . As Father and Jeannie silence him for fear of discovery" (303). Pollock uses the devices of the murder-mystery genre in *Constance* to create intrigue and tension, which includes the graphic description of the victim's wounded body and the introduction of possible motives among more than one suspect: did the father kill the child accidentally while quieting him and then stage his death as a murder to avert suspicion? Did Constance kill the adored child in an act of revenge against her father and stepmother, a retribution for their murder of her mother and their cruelty to her and her full-blooded siblings? Pollock draws deliberate attention to the conventions of murder mysteries when the Male visitor brings up the fact that one of Constance's nightgowns was found to be missing at the time, and Miss Kaye responds with exasperation that could almost be humorous: "Why why why is there always a missing nightgown? Covered with blood no doubt to explain the absence of same. Were waistcoats counted, I wonder"? (303).

But *Constance* deviates from a more traditional murder mystery by remaining unsolved. The Male visitor and the radio listener waiting for an explanation for why Constance confessed are left unsatisfied. For Pollock it is enough, as it was in *Blood Relations*, to create an unjust, patriarchal world where we might imagine a young woman driven to domestic murder. As Grace puts it, "True to form, Sharon explored the story of Constance Kent from a fascinating angle because she was not interested in whether or not Constance had murdered her little half-brother. Instead, she wanted to explore the broader context of what might have led a teenager to commit such a crime and to examine the contradictory circumstances surrounding the case" (*Making Theatre* 318). Pollock's choices become even clearer when her version of the Constance Kent story is compared to another of the many considerations it has received. For example, in her 2008 non-fiction book, *The Suspicions of Mr. Whicher*, subtitled "A Murder and the Undoing of a Great Victorian Detective," Kate Summerscale concludes that Constance did in fact commit the murder, along with her brother William, and confessed in order to protect him, to allow him to receive his inheritance and move to Australia to become a scientist. Summerscale credits the promotion of the theory that the Father was the murderer to none other than Charles Dickens (207). And most contrary of all, Summerscale uses the case to detail the rise of the professional detective and the simultaneous popularization of detective fiction. When considered against this other treatment, we see an excellent example of how Pollock has used the murder mystery for her own, quite different creative ends.

SHELLEY SCOTT

Saucy Jack provides another historical example for Pollock's creative treatment and, as in *Blood Relations*, Pollock uses another actress character to re-enact the circumstances of the crime. While the Actress in *Blood Relations* acts out of curiosity as a sympathetic friend to Lizzie (who may be a killer), in *Saucy Jack*, the music hall entertainer, Kate, has been hired to portray Jack the Ripper's victims for the perverse entertainment of two wealthy gentlemen (one or both of whom may be a killer).[3] Pollock has explained that "the end or objective or motivation for the re-enactment of the women's deaths in the play is not to achieve the death of the women, but to achieve some other end or objective that relates to the relationship between the men" (5).[4] The murders and their re-enactments are acts of purported loyalty and friendship that bind the male characters together as a sort of extension of their extreme social privilege. As Nothof writes, "*Saucy Jack* (1993) replays the murders of Jack the Ripper from a woman's perspective, to show the ways in which social systems and habits are implicated in gender crimes" ("Painting" v–vi). Just as the Fathers in both *Blood Relations* and *Constance* get away with whatever they wish by virtue of their patriarchal status in a sexist society, here the two privileged gentlemen, Eddy and Jem, live in a world where, as Pollock writes, "women are killed because they can be killed with relative or complete impunity" (5). It is a chilling vision of a world of absolute power familiar to fans of the crime genre, except that Pollock allows her women – Lizzie, Constance, and Kate – to escape alive.

The dynamic between Prince Albert Victor (known as Eddy) and his brain-damaged tutor and friend, Jem, drives the play, and as far as they are concerned, Kate is a mere object of exchange between them. Perhaps more than in any of the other plays under consideration here, *Saucy Jack* operates within the parameters of a conventional murder mystery. As in the other plays, there are graphic descriptions of the murder victims' wounds, but in *Saucy Jack* the murder weapons (two knives in a blood-stained case) are constantly and threateningly present onstage. Furthermore, the audience is fed a steady stream of clues about the identity of Jack the Ripper. From Eddy's first appearance, it is established that he is good at "slipping away" unnoticed from his life in royal society (21). He boasts that he is also good at killing things, such as quail, "And other things, larger things, more dangerous" (23). Eddy himself produces physical evidence by removing two rings from his pocket, rings that Kate has already revealed as belonging to one of the victims (29). Eddy is the suspect and Jem attempts to inhabit the role and position of the detective. He tries to interrogate Eddy, asking him about his whereabouts on a certain evening, reporting suspicions he has heard, and warning that a witness has come forward (32). Even in his defiance of Jem's line of pursuit, Eddy's choice of words implicates him: "You mustn't try to catch me up. You may be smart, but I'm cunning" (31). The problem is that Jem has recently suffered a serious head injury, his recollections are scattered and confused, and he may also be implicating himself as Eddy's accomplice.

As the play begins, Jem is already convinced that Eddy is Jack the Ripper and, in order to protect his friend and former student, he has concocted a plan to pin the blame on another mutual friend, Montague. Montague has just been dismissed from his position as a schoolteacher due to allegations of impropriety with a male student. The insinuations could look bad for a known friend of the prince, but if he succumbs to guilt and depression and dies at his own hand, he can be set up as the deviant serial killer Jack the Ripper and take all suspicion away from Eddy. Jem tries to convince Eddy to go along with his plan; he insists, "You lie and you know I know it" (37) and stresses that, "We're all in this together" (39). But Eddy is evasive: "I've not acknowledged that" (39). Montague generates further suspicion that in fact both Eddy and Jem are involved when, already feeling the effects of the poison they have given him, he says to Eddy, "What do you think would follow if suspicion as to the identity of the Whitechapel murderer fell on one so close to you, Eddy? And . . . there is . . . certainly a suggestion that – a second individual may be involved" (57).

Despite Jem's pretensions and efforts to play the detective, he is far too implicated in class privilege and insider status to function in this capacity. By virtue of her sex and her class, Kate is the outsider in this play, and Pollock positions her against the triumvirate of highly privileged men. They see the role they have hired her to fill, which is enacting the murdered women, but she is playing another role of her own choosing all along. Kate serves as the real detective here, almost an undercover agent, who listens carefully as Jem and Eddy reveal their plan, pieces together the clues, and attempts to warn their victim Montague. At the end of the play, she explicitly assumes the traditional prerogative of the detective at the end of a murder mystery and reveals the fate of all three men in her final summation. Kate foretells the future deaths of the three men, and then walks out of the room alive. While the identity of Jack the Ripper has not been definitively revealed, in this play at least, his authority has been negated by the woman who outsmarts him.

Pollock's most recent murder mystery, *End Dream*, is based on the shocking death in 1924 of Janet Smith, a young Scottish nanny, whose body was discovered at the home of her wealthy employers in Vancouver. As Grace writes of the real-life case, "the Chinese houseboy quickly became a suspect. The newspapers went wild. Rumours of drug dealing, drunken parties, rape, and torture filled the headlines" ("Art" 4). This was an era of overt anti-Asian racism in Vancouver, a time when, among many other measures, "Caucasian women and Asian men were forbidden to work in the same public places" ("Art" 4).[5] The Chinese servant, Wong Foon Sing, was abducted and tortured by law enforcement officers; tried and acquitted; and sent back to China, with the mysterious death of Janet Smith still unsolved. As Nothof suggests, "*End Dream* (2000), like *Blood Relations*, uses a murder mystery to interrogate notions of responsibility, truth, and lies" ("Painting" vi).

Grace notes that the unsolved case of Janet Smith has inspired other literary treatments, but praises Pollock's approach, which is to create a threatening dreamscape, to conjure up Janet Smith as a sort of ghost figure and let her piece together the story through her own vague memories. Grace points out that "in *End Dream* Janet Smith, the one person whose voice was never recorded – who was indeed a non-entity until she died – gets to speak" ("Art" 2). As in *Constance*, Pollock uses the source material of the case to make her own points and to tell the story in her own way. *End Dream* is told in a highly imagistic and fragmented manner. Grace interprets it as "a psychodrama with many expressionistic qualities, presented from Janet Smith's unbalanced perspective in a series of flashbacks just before she dies," (*Making* 334). Nothof agrees that "in *End Dream*, events are collapsed into the final seconds of a woman's life, evoked through light and sounds as lived nightmare" ("Staging" 140). Pollock evokes a sinister environment of crime and corruption through inventive staging techniques such as sound effects, lighting, and spatial dynamics ("Art" 5). The characters in *End Dream* never leave the stage; when not involved in the action, they remain on the periphery, watching, contributing to a claustrophobic atmosphere of secrets and suspicion.

As a murder mystery, *End Dream* works through a series of revelations, as Janet Smith labours under false first impressions and deliberate obfuscation, and then gradually uncovers one shocking truth after another. Young Janet has been seduced by wealthy Robert Clarke-Evans to come to Canada to care for his daughter; their meeting in London was conducted in a hotel room, but Robert failed to mention that his wife Doris would also be in the picture. When she first arrives, Janet continues to flirt with Robert and looks down her nose at Doris, whom she despises as an alcoholic liar. Besides the surprise of her existence, Doris is also the first to hint that things in the household are not what they seem. She tells Janet that they call their houseboy, Wong Foon Sing, Willie, as a private nickname. Doris says: "A very silly private joke and you must promise not to breathe a word of it. Never never never! Not to a living soul. See? You're a member of the family already. Privy to private jokes and sworn to secrecy" (104). Doris goes on at great length about all the things Janet will need to find out about the household; she emphasizes secrecy and loyalty in a peculiarly insistent way.

In addition to misleading Janet, Robert turns out to be a threatening figure. Like Eddy in *Saucy Jack*, Robert makes it a point of pride that he is potentially dangerous; he tells Janet that she is looking "at a man who's killed men" (133) in the war. As the play progresses, Janet comes to understand that Robert and Doris run a lucrative business smuggling drugs hidden in pieces of furniture and in suitcases, and that they socialize with the most influential strata of society, including the son of the Lieutenant Governor (127). As Janet begins to understand more of what goes on in the house, she moves from innocent to investigator, looking for evidence of wrongdoing and finding a handgun (130). The discovery of the gun, which changes hands several times and is used in a threatening manner, heightens the atmosphere of danger. According to Gates, there are different kinds of "investigative protagonists, the detective/criminalist who solves the case by intelligence after the crime has been committed, and the more active undercover agent, who infiltrates the criminal community and dismantles it from inside" (*Detecting* 7–8). Like Kate in *Saucy Jack*, Janet Smith could be described as this second type of undercover agent, as she finds herself working for criminals and trapped in their home and centre of operations. The scandal of Janet's death brings her employers unwanted publicity and public scrutiny. The Clarke-Evans's insider status is also why the case attracts so much attention, as the men who abduct and interrogate Foon Sing are eager to make an accusation against Robert. But Foon Sing sticks to the story that Janet committed suicide, and even when he himself is arrested and tried for murder, nothing is ever proven. As Grace points out, we still do not know if Janet Smith killed herself or was murdered; although her corpse was disinterred, a proper autopsy could not be performed because it had been embalmed: "despite investigations and a trial, a host of conflicting details, a number of possible suspects, and a potential motive, the clues were destroyed or covered up" ("Art" 4). Grace argues that there are a number of possibilities surrounding Janet's death: perhaps "psychological and emotional pressure" pushed Janet to commit suicide; she might have been murdered by the drunken, jealous wife; "or has some drunken party guest – the son of the lieutenant-governor of the province maybe? – tried to rape Janet and killed her in the process?" (*Making Theatre* 335). Within the context of the play, the most logical conclusion is that Robert discovered that she knew more than she should about his illegal drug smuggling operation and silenced her, either by his own hand, or by forcing her to shoot herself, or – most likely of all – by coercing Wong Foon Sing to kill her.

Another murder mystery feature of the play is the character Wong Sien, an older Chinese man who at first seems to be peripheral to the action, but in fact is central to its unfolding. He acts as a business contact for Robert; he serves as translator during the brutal interrogation of Wong Foon Sing; and then he acts as interpreter at Wong Foon Sing's trial. In this privileged capacity, it is Wong Sien that tells the audience the grisly details of Janet's fatal wound, conveys Wong Foon Sing's testimony that Janet killed herself, and contradicts that verdict by showing us forensic evidence: Janet's stockings, the feet covered in blood. Wong Sien asks: "These are bloody stockings worn by person who shoots themself. At time of death person is wearing shoes, and stockings. How does this blood come to be on feet of stockings, if shoes are on feet, at time of death?!" (158). Pollock writes Wong Sien as a classic mystery character who produces evidence that appears to contradict the official verdict and who turns out to be far more involved in the crime than he first appears.

Pollock invents an ironic twist to the story; in another revelation, Janet goes from disliking Wong Foon Sing to begging him to run away with her. Janet implores him to get the gun and escape with her. She insists, "We've got to help ourselves Willie because nobody else will help us. You were right, it is bad business and powerful friends and what can we do? I know what they're doing, and I know what they've done, everything that they've done, and it's not your fault Willie you're caught, and the two of us here, in this house, caught in this house" (158). Janet seduces him in an attempt to win his assistance. In a powerful moment of simultaneous time periods, Wong Sien describes the exit wound on Janet's corpse, even as Janet and Foon Sing share an erotic embrace. But in a final betrayal, it is Foon Sing who does Robert's dirty work by killing Janet at his request. The play ends poignantly, with Foon Sing kneeling beside Janet's dead body; he says,

"I did not want this. I do care for you. Did you have feelings for me?" (163). In this interpretation, as in *Saucy Jack*, the woman's murder is an act of loyalty between two men. In that play, it was based on their shared class privilege, while here, Foon Sing's allegiance is an act of survival, a dependence on the protection of his powerful employer in a country where his race makes him horribly vulnerable.

Many worthy scholars have written about Pollock's work and have explored a wide range of topics, from her use of historical material, to her complex framing devices, to the autobiographical elements, and much more. But in this essay, I have suggested that, for the spectator, listener, or reader, a large part of the reason that at least some of Pollock's plays work so well is their adherence to the conventions of one of the most successful of all genres. Zimmerman has observed of all Pollock's work that "inquiry provides the play's structure, as well as its moral imperative. This is most obviously the case when the play is structured as a murder mystery" ("Anatomising" 12).

Ann Saddlemyer further argues that theatre is the ideal place for "the process of judgment, assigning responsibility for action, distinguishing truth from fiction, sifting the pertinent from the irrelevant," the discriminating audience serving much like a jury (215). In his review of an early Canadian thriller, Carol Bolt's 1977 play *One Night Stand*, Alexander Leggatt agrees that a murder mystery can allow a playwright to investigate bigger ideas. He writes: "the thriller format carries, easily and naturally, a commentary on the characters and their world" (367). Jack Batten further observes that mysteries demand "intricacy in the plotting, surprise twists and rational explanations – the eventual certainty, as John Leonard of the *New York Times* has pointed out, of 'someone to blame and perhaps to forgive'" (qtd. in Batten 4). Most explicitly, Canadian novelist Ross Macdonald insists that mystery novels are really about the search for the meaning of life, a quest for a saving grace (qtd. in Batten 4).

As feminist film critic Jeanne Allen has written, part of the pleasure for the spectator is the "tightness and symmetry" of the murder mystery form: "it is pleasure produced by a highly controlled 'imagined world' representing the chaos of psychic and physical violence and disorder" (34). Furthermore, Gates points out that, "The detective film . . . presents a fantasy of resolution for social anxieties concerning crime – and, more interestingly, gender" (16). While none of Pollock's plays under consideration here provide the certainty or the tidy conclusions that these theorists suggest is integral to the murder mystery, they do leave the audience with a very clear sense of blame and judgement, and a strong sense that a kind of justice has been done. Lizzie and Constance, as accused murderers, have had a version of their story told that takes into account their experiences and clearly indicts the patriarchal oppression under which they lived. Whether we believe them to be guilty or not, we have at least been witness to their circumstances. Kate and Janet give voices to the victims: Kate brings to life the victims of Jack the Ripper, women who otherwise would have remained nameless and unknown, and Janet Smith gets a chance to remember and recount her story in a way the real-life victim did not. Thus while the murder remains unsolved in each play, there is definitely a sense that some theatrical justice has been done and some injustice exposed. In this sense, *Blood Relations*, *Constance*, *Saucy Jack* and *End Dream* are all successful murder mysteries.

NOTES

1   "One Tiger to a Hill" also features the murder of a woman and is based on a real-life hostage-taking incident in a BC prison. "The Making of Warriors" includes the murder of American Indian Movement activist Anna Mae Pictou Aquash. In both cases, however, Pollock's focus is on indicting institutionalized violence and the plays do not easily lend themselves to a murder-mystery discussion. (Sharon Pollock, "One Tiger to a Hill," *Blood Relations and Other Plays*, ed. Anne Nothof [Edmonton: NeWest Press, 2002, 77–151]; "The Making of Warriors," *Airborne: Radio Plays by Women*, ed. Anne Jansen. [Winnipeg: Blizzard, 1991], 99–132).

2   Today there are also murder mysteries written for the stage, although many continue to be adaptations. According to its website, Calgary's "Vertigo Mystery Theatre is the only professional theatre company in Canada that produces a full season of plays based in the mystery genre. Since our very first production in 1978 – Agatha Christie's *The Mousetrap* – we have continued to expand our boundaries. Our seasons include everything from the classic *Blithe Spirit* to the highly contemporary and critically acclaimed *Sweeney Todd: The Demon Barber of Fleet Street*. Our loyal audience is also growing. We currently welcome over 5,200 subscribers who are

SHELLEY SCOTT

joined each season by 25,000 single and group ticket buyers" (www.vertigotheatre.com). Vertigo produced *Blood Relations* as part of its 2009–10 season.

3   Craig Walker shows that while the Actress in *Blood Relations* enters into Miss Lizzie's telling of the events, Kate in *Saucy Jack* is more autonomous because she is not coached by the men as the Actress is coached by Lizzie. Walker suggests Kate's role is to compete in preserving memories of the victims: "Kate is engaged in a sort of mortal competition with the men for the control of the past" (148–49).

4   Grace reminds us that Pollock's comments about the women as objects of social exchange between men are similar to the ideas of Eve Kosofsky Sedgwick and other theorists that work with the idea of the homosocial ("Portraits" 129).

5   Grace points out that, for example, Asians born in Canada were not citizens and not allowed to vote, and that the infamous "head" tax made immigration difficult ("Art" 4).

Works Cited

Allen, Jeanne. "Looking Through Rear Window: Hitchcock's Traps and Lures of Heterosexual Romance." *Female Spectators: Looking at Film and Television*. Ed. E. Deidre Pribram. London: Verso, 1988, 31–44. Print.

Batten, Jack. "The Maltese Beaver." *Books in Canada* 10.2 (Feb. 1981): 3–5. Print.

Gates, Philippa. *Detecting Women: Gender and the Hollywood Detective Film*. Albany, NY: SUNY P, 2011. Print.

Grace, Sherrill. "The Art of Sharon Pollock." *Sharon Pollock: Three Plays*. Toronto: Playwrights Canada P, 2003. 1–11. Print.

———. *Making Theatre: A Life of Sharon Pollock*. Vancouver: Talonbooks, 2008. Print.

———. "Sharon Pollock's Portraits of the Artist." *Theatre Research in Canada* 22.2 (Fall 2003): 124–38. Print.

Leggatt, Alexander. "Drama." *University of Toronto Quarterly*. 47.4 (Summer 1978): 367–78. Print.

Nothof, Anne. "Introduction: Painting the Background." *Blood Relations and Other Plays*. Sharon Pollock. Ed. Anne Nothof. Edmonton: NeWest, 2002. v–xi. Print.

———. "Interview with Sharon Pollock (May 1999)." *Sharon Pollock: Essays on Her Works*. Ed. Anne F. Nothof. Toronto: Guernica, 2000. 167–79. Print.

———. "Staging the Intersections of Time in Sharon Pollock's *Doc, Moving Pictures* and *End Dream*." *Theatre Research in Canada* 22.2 (Fall 2003): 139–50. Print.

Pollock, Sharon. "Blood Relations." *Blood Relations and Other Plays*. Ed. Anne Nothof. Edmonton: NeWest, 2002. 2–73. Print.

———. "Constance." *Sharon Pollock: Collected Works*. Vol. 2. Ed. Cynthia Zimmerman. Toronto: Playwrights Canada P, 2006. 272–309. Print.

———. "End Dream." *Sharon Pollock: Three Plays*. Toronto: Playwrights Canada P, 2003. 98–139. Print.

———. *Saucy Jack*. Winnipeg: Blizzard, 1994. Print.

Saddlemyer, Ann. "Crime in Literature: Canadian Drama." *Rough Justice: Essays on Crime in Literature*. Ed. Martin L. Friedland. Toronto: U of Toronto P, 1991. 214–30. Print.

Summerscale, Kate. *The Suspicions of Mr. Whicher: A Murder and the Undoing of a Great Victorian Detective*. Vancouver: Raincoast, 2008. Print.

Sussex, Lucy. *Women Writers and Detectives in Nineteenth-Century Crime Fiction: The Mothers of the Mystery Genre*. New York: Palgrave Macmillan, 2010. Print.

Walker, Craig. "Women and Madness: Sharon Pollock's Plays of the Early 1990s." *Sharon Pollock: Essays on Her Works*. Ed. Anne. F. Nothof. Toronto: Guernica, 2000. 128–50. Print.

Wallace, Robert. "Sharon Pollock Interview." *The Work: Conversations with English-Canadian Playwrights*. Ed. Robert Wallace and Cynthia Zimmerman. Toronto: Coach House, 1982. 114–26. Print.

Zimmerman, Cynthia. Preface. *Sharon Pollock: Collected Works*. Vol. 2. Ed. Cynthia Zimmerman. Toronto: Playwrights Canada P, 2006. iii–iv. Print.

———. "Introduction: Sharon Pollock Anatomising the Question." *Sharon Pollock: Collected Works*. Vol. 2. Ed. Cynthia Zimmerman. Toronto: Playwrights Canada P, 2006. 1–15. Print.

Ownership and Stewardship in Sharon Pollock's *Generations*

Jason Wiens

Concerns around the ownership and stewardship of land and resources are central to Sharon Pollock's 1980 play *Generations*.[1] The conflicts of the play extend into three frames. At the primary, domestic level, the play represents a conflict within the Nurlin family, who have farmed in the Medicine Hat area for several generations. The main conflict is over patrilineal privilege and obligations, with the eldest of two sons, Young Eddy, having rejected the farming life for a law career in the city, and the youngest, David, having decided to continue the farming life to the overt approval of his grandfather, Old Eddy, and the more equivocal support of his father, Alfred. The action of the play concerns Young Eddy's return to the farm in the hopes his father, grandfather, and brother will release the equity capital of his birthright by selling a section of the land, thereby providing him with the liquid capital to fund his own law practice. Further complicating the domestic conflict is David's girlfriend, Bonnie, a schoolteacher and Young Eddy's tacit ally, who encourages the Nurlins to abandon the farming life.

47

At the level of the wider rural community near Medicine Hat, Pollock presents a conflict between white farmers and the local Indian reserve, some of whose members have blockaded the "irrigation water from the reserve river" (165). Pollock stages that conflict primarily through conversations between Old Eddy Nurlin and Charlie Running Dog, an elderly member of the reserve, and the only Aboriginal character in the play. Characters also refer to off-stage actions and characters relating to this conflict, including community meetings and Sneider, a "hothead" local farmer and friend of David Nurlin.

That conflict in turn invokes a third frame of conflict, that between the local community and the federal government, which has negotiated the arrangement over the irrigation water with the Indian reserve, an arrangement the reserve is reneging on because, according to Charlie, the band council has decided the government is not paying them enough for the water, and "Council says the government don't hear us yellin', maybe they hear yuh" (165). The disagreement between the reserve and the federal government leads to frustration with and hostility toward the latter on the part of the white farmers. The play subordinates the second conflict involving access to water and Aboriginal title to the other two conflicts.

I read *Generations* through the intersection of two regionalisms: a literary prairie regionalism that the play deliberately both extends and modifies, and a political regionalism that was informing the increasingly hostile debate over federal versus provincial control of natural resources in the 1980s, though of course the resources of concern then were not the resources at issue in the play. The more topical question over control of energy resources becomes displaced in the play, I argue, onto the context of a struggling family farm, a context more suitable to naturalist treatment and, I suspect, more evocative of audience sympathies.

I wish to historicize both the political conflict during which the play was staged (and which shaped audience response to the play) and the literary regionalism that the play appears to embrace. One might read *Generations* as performing the ideological work of naturalizing patriarchal property rights at the domestic level of the family farm and colonial relations at the normative political level of Canada's fraught federal arrangements and treaty agreements with First Nations. In this reading, the construction of the land as a mythical space, which compels an inescapable organic relationship with those who farm it, is part of this ideological work. However, I suggest that despite Pollock's ostensible attempts to cast the land as an "omniscient presence" having "mythic proportion" (Pollock 156), as well as the play's subordination of what Carole Corbeil observed was an "underdeveloped plot concerned with the Indians' ownership of property rights" (cited in Conolly 272) to the dominant, normative political conflict of federal-provincial rights, *Generations* actually works to make visible the material reality of invented property relations at both the domestic and wider political level.

The strongest anti-government, and more specifically anti-Ottawa, voice in *Generations*, is David Nurlin, the youngest man in the play. Indeed, the play makes clear that it is the younger generation, among both the farmers and the Natives, who are more willing to voice their frustration with government and take drastic steps to have their message heard. In the first exchange between Old Eddy and Charlie, Charlie explains why the Natives are holding the local farmers' water hostage in order to get the attention of the federal government:

> CHARLIE: Council says the government don't hear us yellin', maybe they hear yuh.
>
> OLD EDDY: That's not yuh talkin'.
>
> CHARLIE: No?
>
> OLD EDDY: No, it's them others, the young ones.
>
> CHARLIE: Yuh got 'em too. (165)

For David, the structural problems facing the farm go far beyond the immediate concerns with irrigation; at one point he tells his father Alfred, "We're not talkin' water, what the hell, water! So the crop dies in the field, we lose money – shit, we can harvest and sell it and lose money! That's the problem and gettin' reserve water is not gonna solve it!" (171). David's solution is the "alternative action" of holding back "the product of our labour" (172), and the play ends with David joining his neighbours in their mass cull of livestock by setting fire to one of his own fields to send the government a message. At various times in the play, David rails against the lot of the farmer in general: "Fair? You wanna talk fair! What's fair about Eddy and the whole fuckin' city sittin' drinkin' scotch and feedin' their faces while we bust our ass to put food on their tables! Two-thirds of the goddamn world dies of starvation and the farmer's low man on the totem pole!" (206). At other times he directs his anger at eastern Canada: "Look we been carryin' the East on our back for so goddamn long they think we're the horse and they're the rider" (204). And in one exchange with Young Eddy and Bonnie he targets the Liberal party specifically:

> DAVID: Hey listen Eddy, it's gonna be a humdinger tonight – first of all we got media types, and Stocker from Edmonton, and a dingbat from Native Affairs – that's for the dam business – and then to top her all off, a coupla Liberal interpreters for national agriculture – Jesus, wanna bet when they travel west they're wearin' bullet-proof vests – and earplugs?
>
> BONNIE: Maybe you should try voting Liberal.
>
> DAVID: Maybe they should try listening.
>
> BONNIE: Maybe you should run for office, Dave.
>
> DAVID: Maybe you should mark papers, Bonnie.
> (181)

In addition to this overt invective by David, the jokes in the play tend overwhelmingly to have political overtones, which either express cynicism toward normative politics in general or hostility to Central Canada and the federal government in particular. For example, in the opening scene of the play, when a hungover David Nurlin talks with his grandfather in the morning, the two exchange jokes:

> DAVID: You wanna hear a joke, Grampa?
>
> OLD EDDY: Fire away.
>
> DAVID: How is a politician like a church bell?
>
> OLD EDDY: Yuh tell me.
>
> DAVID: One peals from the steeple – the other steals from the people!
>
> *They laugh.*
>
> OLD EDDY: Here's one for yuh – do yuh know how Canada is like a cow?
>
> DAVID: How is Canada like a cow, Grampa?
>
> OLD EDDY: Well sir – she feeds off the West – she's milked dry by Ontario – and she shits on the Maritimes! (161)

Other jokes reference particular politicians, including Pierre Elliott Trudeau. At one point David asks Old Eddy if he heard "they found out who was mutilatin' all the cattle . . . About someone cuttin' off their sex organs," and when Old Eddy asks "Who was it?" the punchline delivers "Trudeau – he needs more pricks for his cabinet" (177). Joe Clark, the federal opposition leader – and briefly prime minister – of the time, does not get off the hook, either. David tells Young Eddy this joke: "Trudeau is walkin' along the street and he sees Clark carryin' this here duck and he hollers, 'Where are you goin' with that turkey?' and Clark, he says, 'Look stupid, this is not a turkey!' and Trudeau says, 'I am talkin' to the duck!'" (184).

If *Generations* draws upon and speaks to what came to be called Western alienation, the producers could hardly have asked for a more fortuitous time to stage its premiere. The play opened during a week marked by conflict between Alberta and Ottawa over changes to the energy revenue sharing scheme that would eventually become known as the National Energy Policy. Its premiere, at the Canmore Opera House on October 28, 1980, took place the same evening the Liberal government in Ottawa passed a federal budget which promised that the domestic oil and gas industry would be 50 percent Canadian-owned by 1990; proposed that Petro-Canada, then a Crown corporation, take over one of the foreign-owned oil companies; introduced a new tax on natural gas and gas liquids sold in Canada or exported; imposed an 8 percent production tax on oil and gas companies; and promised that the Canadian price of oil and gas would never exceed 85 percent of world energy prices. The proposed changes would see Ottawa's share of revenues from oil and gas rise to 24 percent from 10 percent, see the industry's take decline from 45 percent to 33 percent and the provinces' share fall from 45 percent to 43 percent (Simpson 1). Two days later, then-Alberta premier Peter Lougheed delivered a televised address in which he stated Alberta had decided to cut its oil production by 15 percent in retaliation for what it saw as a federal threat to its resource ownership. In his speech, Lougheed described the federal government's moves as akin to someone stripping off a farmer's topsoil, or "walking into our homes and occupying our living room" (Sallot and Williamson 2). His were interesting choices of metaphors that sought to compare the oil and gas industry to a family farm and shift the debate to the domestic level. This is precisely the metaphorical displacement, I argue, that is at work in *Generations*.

A number of contemporary reviewers of the play did not hesitate to situate the performance within the wider political context of the day, or at least allude to that context, even by remarking on its absence from the play. In his *Theatre in Review* response to the Alberta Theatre Projects production, Allan Sheppard remarked that "*Generations* is nothing less than an attempt to confront the question of why Albertans are as they are, and act as they do. And it does so without once mentioning oil and gas, the constitution or multi-national corporations (though Trudeau and Clark jokes do pop up from time to time)" (Sheppard C26). Brian Brennan observed in his *Calgary Herald* review that while he had not found Pollock's work to that point to be particularly funny, this play was an exception, and "the anti-Trudeau jokes seem so timely, one would have sworn Pollock sat down to write the play after watching Lougheed on television the other night" (cited in Conolly 270). Carole Corbeil begins her *Globe and Mail* review by quoting David Nurlin's statement "I feel a power out there," and then remarking that he "is talking about the prairie land, not oil" (cited in Conolly 271). And Martin Stone somewhat bizarrely concludes his review of Toronto's Tarragon Theatre's production by observing that "The play focuses on a part of Alberta where life for the working farmer is far removed from the luxury of TV's Dallas. Or Calgary's oil scene" (Stone n.p.)

But the contemporary response to the play that most elaborated on its relationship to the political context was Philip McCoy's review of the play for CBC's Arts West and Arts National on October 31, 1980, the day after Lougheed's speech. McCoy begins by quoting Kenneth Tynan's observation that a play review "is a letter addressed to the future; to people thirty years hence who may wonder what it felt like to be in a certain playhouse on a certain distant night" (n.p.). McCoy suggests that "Pollock's play is about the burdens and responsibilities of ownership, a subject preoccupying the minds of Albertans these days with a worrying and fearful persistence. *Generations* is about the ownership of land and not about the ownership of oil and gas production rights, but that only makes it all the more thought-provoking since land has about it a mystique which petroleum does not" (n.p.). McCoy then reminds his listeners that "on the way to the theatre on Thursday evening nearly all of us in the audience had listened to Peter

Lougheed's calm suggestion that if Ontario owned the oil, we'd all be paying world prices for it. So it was with the shock of recognition that we listened to Sharon Pollock's farmers accusing Ottawa and the East of ruthlessly riding the backs of the wheat producing provinces of the West. Their metaphors were earthier and their language was coarser than Lougheed's but the message was the same" (McCoy n.p.). *Generations*, it should be noted, actually aired in an earlier incarnation as a radio play in 1978,[2] but the degree to which it anticipated and spoke to the normative political context of late 1980 was remarkable, even if, as I suggest, the conflict is displaced from the resources deep within the earth to its produce at the surface.

According to Alison Calder and Robert Wardhaugh, recent arguments about the prairie "region" and the literature produced there have begun to question the way in which "the particulars of prairie history are subsumed into a generalized timelessness" (7). Calder and Wardhaugh further observe that "up to the late 1990s, critics of Canadian prairie literature [. . .] seem to have constructed a category of 'Canadian prairie writing' in which landscape dominates culture and geography effaces history" (8). One might be tempted to read *Generations* as fitting neatly into this construction, given the insistence on the geography's "mythic proportion" in Pollock's stage directions (Pollock 156), or some of the dialogue in the play, such as when David and Alfred look at the horizon, and David asks his father what he sees, to which his father replies, "Nothin'" (202), which seems to imply a timeless landscape. On the other hand, I read the play as continually emphasizing the cultural construction of the landscape and the historical and economic contingencies upon geography, given the play's emphasis on property relations as an invented, historical system.

Diane Bessai has observed that the "standard notion of doctrinaire 'prairie naturalism' primarily has its roots in the earlier modern fiction of the region" (189), including the work of fiction writers such as Sinclair Ross, Frederick Philip Grove, and Martha Ostenso. She further argues that this tradition evokes a view of the pioneer and early post-pioneer stages in the social development of rural prairie society. Characters are caught in a perennial struggle with a hostile wind-swept landscape that continually defies human effort to bring it under human control. They endure poverty, social isolation, personal alienation and domestic entrapment. (189)

In the context of a broader discussion of Barbara Sapergia's play *Roundup*, Bessai, as an aside, aligns *Generations* with the work of regional dramatists in the 1980s who write out of a consciousness of this rural tradition in fiction, "not in slavish conformity to it, but in order to re-examine it, enrich it and in some measure to subvert it through dramatic form" (189). In *Generations*, she argues, "the stereotypical conflict between allegiance to the land and the need to escape its tyranny takes on a positive note with the re-alignment of expectations and the recognition of individual power of choice" (190). I would further argue that *Generations*, despite Pollock's emphasis on the "omniscient presence and mythic proportion of **The Land**" (Pollock 156), demystifies the ties of the Nurlins to the land not only by emphasizing the materiality of those ties but also, in raising the competing claims to ownership and stewardship repeatedly in the play, by questioning the legitimacy of invented patrilineal property rights themselves. That is, while *Generations* seems intended to mystify the relationship between the land and its inhabitants, both Aboriginal and non-Aboriginal, in a fashion consistent with how prairie naturalism had been understood to that point, the underdeveloped elements of the play ultimately reveal the political contingencies and historicity of those relations.

Pollock has commented in an interview that the eventual dramatic naturalism of the play's set design was at odds with her initial vision. As she tells Robert Wallace and Cynthia Zimmerman,

> I had a lot of problems with *Generations*. We went through that whole thing where you paint rooms, you build the set, you take it down. If I had had my druthers, if I could

have found a way to do it, the play would not have happened in the house. There would be no kitchen because once you're in the kitchen, you've got all the stinking things you've got to do in the kitchen, like cook the food. If I could have placed the characters into space, into that field with the prairie going on forever, I think I could have created a more interesting piece. (Wallace and Zimmerman 120)

We need to distinguish between the prairie naturalism which Bessai describes above and which is particular to critical discourses shaping what had come, by the 1980s, to be known as "prairie literature," and the broader tradition of dramatic naturalism which has its roots in the nineteenth century, while recognizing the overlapping concerns of these different naturalisms. To me, the play's insistence on assigning the land mythic significance, while consistent with prairie naturalism, runs counter to what I understand as the hyperrealist conventions of dramatic naturalism. The naturalistic set design of the play sets up a contrast between the new place, realistically rendered as a kitchen, and the old place, evocative of a past passing into myth and associated with the "eternal Aboriginal," but most of the action of the play takes place in the domestic space of the former. Readers of the play will note immediately the importance Pollock places on the land, not only in her comments describing the setting, in which she writes, "There should be some sense of the omniscient presence and mythic proportion of **The Land** in the design," but in her designation of the land itself as "a character revealed by the light and shadow it throws on the Nurlin's [sic] lives" (Pollock 156). It also seems significant that in her notes on the characters, she aligns the two oldest characters, Old Eddy and Charlie Running Dog, explicitly with the land. She writes, "[the land] has many faces, but Old Eddy sees it most clearly when he stands in the heat of summer or the dead of winter in his Southern Alberta back section watching the sunrise, and looking right across the expanse of Saskatchewan all the way to Winnipeg" (156). Despite the impossibility of seeing Winnipeg from southern Alberta, this detail should alert us that, in this play, Pollock imagines the prairie region as a cohesive unit, thereby further aligning it with the concurrently burgeoning regionalism in prairie literature. She also suggests that a presumed geographical uniformity defines the prairie provinces as this cohesive unit. Of Charlie Running Dog she writes, "Time and the elements have so conditioned and eroded his skin that he looks less like a Native Canadian, and more like some outcropping of arid land" (156). This identification, however brief, of the Native character with the land might be read as problematic, though significant, given the struggle in the play over control of the land's resources. But here Pollock is not differentiating between Old Eddy and Charlie by suggesting the latter enjoys a more authentic, because autochthonic, relationship to the land, but rather equating them as men who have forged an organic relationship to the land after working it for decades. Denis Salter concurs and refers to a "phallocentric desire to make the land submit to their will" (xxvii) in the play, and one exchange between Old Eddy and Charlie, which Young Eddy recalls, nicely supports Salter's observation, "Old Eddy, Grampa, was sayin' the land was like some kind of monster a man had to wrestle and fight, and it was always throwing drought and frost and I don't know what at you – and you fought away like some kind of Greek hero I guess – and Charlie was sayin' no, no, it's like a woman, you gotta woo her and win her" (Pollock 183–84).

Images of aridity and thirst proliferate in *Generations*, and not just in explicit reference to the drought conditions or the conflict over irrigation. The play opens in the morning in the Nurlin house, the stage directions tell us. Old Eddy enters the kitchen and proceeds to make strong coffee, filling "*liberally the filter basket of an automatic coffee appliance with coffee*" (158). We then see David enter the kitchen, and "*take[. . .] out a large jar which once contained mayonnaise but now contains water. David drinks from the jar, leans on the fridge, rests his forehead on the cold interior*" (158). Seeing David, Old Eddy recognizes his grandson is hungover, and the following exchange occurs:

OLD EDDY: Hard night?

DAVID: Uh-huh.

OLD EDDY: You stick to a good rye like I tell yuh, yuh wouldn't be so dry in the mornin's.

DAVID: Yeah. *He takes another swig from the jar.* (158)

This exchange sets up a discussion of alcoholic beverages, which leads to a further discussion of the differing class significations between such beverages, but what interests me is the emphasis on David's self-inflicted dryness at the beginning of play, as well as the fact that he drinks the water from an old mayonnaise jar. The parsimony of the farm household in which no container goes to waste immediately equates with the necessity of hydration. The exchange between Old Eddy and David ends with Eddy announcing that he is heading out to "speak to Charlie 'bout them blockin' the irrigation water" (161), an exchange which makes explicit the overt conflict between the Natives and non-Natives.

In fact, the opening sequence establishes drinking as a motif that extends throughout the play, which is replete with references to and scenes of characters drinking various beverages, including beer, coffee, rye, scotch, tea, iced tea, and water. This is an element of the play's naturalism — there is a drought and the dialogue mentions the heat of the day numerous times — but it also comes to emphasize thirst as an ongoing concern in the play. Other domestic exchanges subtly remind the audience of the lack of water. In the initial exchange between Alfred and Margaret, Alfred asks her about the water pressure as she prepares to rinse dishes. When she tells him it's low, he responds, "It's the well, coupla more days and that'll be it" (168). In Act Two, after an exchange between Old and Young Eddy in which Young Eddy is about to ask his grandfather about selling a piece of land but decides against it, we see Alfred enter the yard and try to draw water from the water pump, but with no results: "Come on you beggar, don't go dry on us now," he says, before greeting his oldest son (194). Young Eddy takes a turn at the pump and manages to draw water before they enter the house. He then offers his grandfather a glass of water before the grandfather changes the topic to whether or not Young Eddy drinks scotch. I note these domestic exchanges over water is to point out that while characters can and do reference the wider concern in the community over access to water – they mention the crops withering for lack of water as well as the native blockade – the dramatic naturalism of the play iterates the water issue at the domestic level.

The primary, domestic conflict of the play turns on Young Eddy's rejection of patrilineal privilege and its obligations, as well as his encouragement of his brother to do the same, albeit in his own interests in raising capital to fund the launch of his own law firm. This conflict also turns on the question of what ties these men to the land. Salter argues that the play suggests "the land will ultimately possess those who try to tame it" (Salter xxvii), and, in fact, at the end of the play, David appears to resolve his own conflict over his rights and obligations to his family's property through a mystification of the land. In his final exchange with Bonnie, he tells her,

> *Out there* . . . is . . . something – I know it. Out there . . . is a feelin' . . . you don't get other places. Other places its hidden in all the dinky scenery, but on the *prairies* it's just there. A *power*. Can you understand that? [. . .] I don't care if you understand it or not, I understand it! Sure I could do some stupid job somewhere else, but when I'm standin' out there . . . well . . . there's just somethin' 'bout a person standin' there on the prairies, everything else stripped away. It makes things simple. (Pollock 223)

David's references here to a "power" and his inability to articulate what holds him to this land suggests a transcendent, mystical force that exceeds human material concerns. David makes this speech immediately after the climactic scene in which he has fired his own fields and physically fought with his grandfather as rain falls, quenching the earth's thirst and extinguishing the flames in the fields and with it the men's conflict, itself a scene with mythic implications that departs from the play's naturalism. The fact that he makes this speech in the closing minutes of the play suggests we accept it as the play's resolution of the domestic conflict by appealing to the men's enduring, mythic, and phallocentric relationship to the land.

Generations, then, might be read as exemplary of a dominant dramaturgical structure that Ric Knowles identifies in post-centennial Canadian drama:

> Variations on patriarchal, socially affirmative dramatic and narrative structures (and their mutually affirmative social formations and structures of consciousness), while they have dominated the Western world since Aristotle first articulated them in *The Poetics*, were (for various social and cultural reasons) particularly influential in Canada in the years following the centennial celebrations of 1967. (*Theatre*, 31)

Generations illustrates Knowles's argument, as its explicitly patriarchal thematic concerns and implicitly phallocentric structure – complete with the violent quasi-Oedipal struggle between grandfather and grandson at the play's climax – demonstrates that "this Aristotelian / oedipal / biblical narrative, then, has become the standard structural unconscious of dramatic naturalism in Canada as elsewhere, and the meanings and ideologies that it inscribes, fundamentally conservative and patriarchal (imitating as it does the rising action, climax, and return-to-status quo falling action of the male orgasm and focusing as it does on the male experience), constitute the primary and affirmative social impacts of the plays that use it, whatever their (conscious) themes or subject matters" (31). Yet this reading of the play would accept that the marginalization of its voices of alterity – specifically of the women and of the First Nations – effectively silences them. It would also ignore the fact that the play hardly ends with a satisfactory resolution of all conflicts. Finally, it would not recognize that the play offers an alternative, materialist presentation of patriarchal and colonial property relations, as opposed to a mythic, naturalized presentation.

Other scenes in *Generations*, after all, suggest that the men's connection to the land is material rather than mythic. Old Eddy tells David early in the play, "She's all yours . . . and your father's . . . and Young Eddy's, it's a legacy" (176), but this legacy entraps rather than empowers the men. Alfred's complaint at one point in the play, that "I sometimes wonder who owns who" (174), is less a personification of the land as hostile and resistant to human domination but persistently drawing the men to it, than it is a recognition of the economic entrapment and frustration he feels. Bonnie is hardly a sympathetic character in the play, but she voices a critique, which the action of the play seems to support, of Old Eddy's obsession with patriarchal legacy. When David says of his grandfather, "He paid for [the land] with his own flesh and blood" she responds, "And now you're gonna pay, why can't you see that? You're gonna serve in Old Eddy's place when he dies – in Young Eddy's place – and our kids would be expected to do the same! I don't want that – this country uses people up and wears them out and throws them away!" (191). When Old Eddy tells Bonnie near the end of the play, "when I go, what I'm leavin' is land, not money" (219), he imagines the land as eternal and money as ephemeral. But the play as much suggests that the land – as equity capital – imprisons, and money – as liquid capital – empowers.

Knowles has argued that "Pollock's earliest plays to deal with issues of race do so primarily by pointing out injustices historically performed and historiographically erased by Canada's current dominant cultures. As such, they tend to focus on the white men who perpetrate the injustices rather than on the 'Indians'" (*Theatre*, 138). He is writing here of *Walsh* and *The Komagatu Maru Incident*, but the same might be said about *Generations*: the play certainly foregrounds the "white" perspective in the conflict over irrigation water. Yet *Generations* invites us to read significance in Charlie's silences and laconic responses.

The play ends with Old Eddy and Charlie together at the Old Place, and with Eddy telling Charlie in the play's final line, "We're still here, Charlie. Hell, we'll always be here" (Pollock 224). This ending, with the two oldest characters in the eternal space of the Old Place, might suggest a very different reading of the play from what I am advancing here. Cynthia Zimmerman, for instance, writes that "Pollock grants this pair of ancestors a mythic, archetypal dimension. Representing endurance and proud continuity, they voice the play's optimistic conclusion" (80). But in a brief exchange in Act I, Young Eddy asks David if Charlie is still alive, to which David responds, "Oh yeah, still hangs around the Old Place, Grampa says just down from the rise is where Charlie's mother's people used to camp . . . so . . . I guess he feels like he owns it in some kinda way" (183). The "some kinda way" Charlie feels he owns it might cast an ironic light on Old Eddy's final words, the Nurlins' struggle throughout the play over who should own the land, and the broader constitutional conflict of the time, in which I have suggested the play might be read. *Generations'* acknowledgment, however brief, of an alternate claim to the land, and in fact an alternate understanding of ownership and stewardship, at the very least historicizes the colonial, patriarchal property relations which the play might be seen to otherwise naturalize, and from which all its conflicts derive.

NOTES

1   *Generations* was first performed by Alberta Theatre Projects, Calgary, at the Canmore Opera House, 28 October 1980. It was later performed by Tarragon Theatre in Toronto in 1981. In 1994, the Centre for Canadian Studies at M.S. University Baroda in India staged a single performance of the play as part of a workshop conducted by visiting professor Robert Fothergill. I am not aware of any recent Canadian production. I have not seen a performance of *Generations*; as such I find myself more or less limited to the textual, literary analysis of the play, which Knowles has asked us to eschew in favour of an emphasis on the contingencies of performance ("Voices", 110).

2   I would have liked to compare the script of the radio play with that of the 1980 stage production, but the Sharon Pollock Papers at the University of Calgary do not include a typescript, nor does Pollock have a copy in her personal papers.

Works Cited

Bessai, Diane. "Centres on the Margin: Contemporary Prairie Drama." *Contemporary Issues in Canadian Drama*. Ed. Per Brask. Winnipeg: Blizzard, 1995. 184–207. Print.

Calder, Alison, and Robert Wardhaugh, eds. *History, Literature, and the Writing of the Canadian Prairies*. Winnipeg: U of Manitoba P, 2005. Print.

Conolly, L.W. *Canadian Drama and the Critics*. Vancouver: Talonbooks, 1987. Print.

Knowles, Richard Paul. *The Theatre of Form and the Production of Meaning: Contemporary Canadian Dramaturgies*. Toronto: ECW, 1999. Print.

———. "Voices (off): Deconstructing the Modern English-Canadian Dramatic Canon." *Canadian Canons: Essays in Literary Value*. Ed. Robert Lecker. Toronto: U of Toronto P, 1991. 91–111. Print.

McCoy, Philip. Rev. of *Generations*, by Sharon Pollock. Arts West and Arts National. Canadian Broadcasting Corporation, 31 Oct. 1980. Sharon Pollock Papers, University of Calgary Special Collections. 54.7.6.3a.

Pollock, Sharon. *Blood Relations and Other Plays*. Edmonton: NeWest, 2002. Print.

Sallot, Jeff, and Robert Williamson. "Canada Won't Freeze, Lougheed Promises." *Globe and Mail* 31 Oct. 1980: 1–2. Print.

Salter, Denis W. "Biocritical Essay. (Im)possible Worlds: The Plays of Sharon Pollock." *Sharon Pollock Papers: First Accession*. Ed. Apollonia Steele and Jean Tener. Calgary: U of Calgary P, 1989. ix–xxxv. Print.

Sheppard, Allan. "One Rose among the Thorns." Rev. of *Betrayal*, by Harold Pinter, *Generations*, by Sharon Pollock, and *Sherlock Holmes and the C.P.R. Murders*, by Martin Keeley. Sharon Pollock Papers, University of Calgary Special Collections. 54.7.6.1a.

Simpson, Jeffrey. "Ottawa Taking Bigger Energy Share." *Globe and Mail* 29 Oct. 1980: 1–2. Print.

Stone, Martin. "Farming, a Way of Life." Rev. of *Generations*, by Sharon Pollock. *CanadianTribune* April 13, 1981. N.p. Sharon Pollock Papers, University of Calgary Special Collections. 54.7.6.5.

Wallace, Robert, and Cynthia Zimmerman, eds. *The Work: Conversations with English-Canadian Playwrights*. Toronto: Coach House, 1982. Print.

Zimmerman, Cynthia. "Sharon Pollock: The Making of Warriors." *Playwriting Women: Female Voices in English Canada*. Toronto: Simon & Pierre, 1994. 60–98. Print.

Different Directions:
Sharon Pollock's *Doc*

Cynthia Zimmerman

I have long been intrigued by Sharon Pollock's most autobiographical play to date, *Doc*. Commissioned by Rick McNair of Theatre
Calgary, it was first produced at that theatre in 1984, directed by
Guy Sprung. Substantially rewritten, it was remounted in September
1984 at Toronto Free Theatre, again directed by Guy Sprung. *Doc*
won the Chalmers Canadian Play Award, the Alberta Writers' Guild
Award and then, after publication, went on to win the 1986 Governor
General's Award for Drama. It has been restaged innumerable times
since, including at Theatre New Brunswick, where Pollock herself
directed it in March 1986; for that production only it was re-titled
Family Trappings.

　　Doc is a play I find as compelling, intense, and honest as Eugene
O'Neill's autobiographical play, *Long Day's Journey into Night*. Both
plays are semi-autobiographical, fictionalized reconstructions which
revisit a traumatic time in the playwright's past. O'Neill did not permit *Long Day's Journey into Night* to be published or produced until
after his death. Sharon Pollock was more of a risk taker. "Here's how

crazy I am," she said in an interview with Richard Ouzounian. "All the characters [except Katie/Catherine] bear their real-life names." She explained that she had not intended to write an autobiographical play. It was originally conceived as a "study of how family medicine has changed over the years." Her father, Everett Chalmers, who died in 1993, had been a renowned New Brunswick physician who had a hospital named in his honour in 1977. "Sometimes you don't know what you are writing," she said. "If I knew I was going to delve so deeply into my past life, I never would have done it."[1] As journalist Russell Smith remarked, it is important to remind ourselves that "the fact that it has autobiographical elements is not what makes it a good play."[2] Real life does not make satisfying fiction: a play needs crafting into something significant for others; it needs artful structure, focus on interesting parts and characters; it must be both emotionally moving and intellectually insightful.[3] *Doc* is.

Any good work will encourage multiple readings and lend itself to multiple interpretations. What particularly intrigued me in the case of Sharon Pollock's *Doc* was the empathy generated by audiences and critics for the character Bob, the neglected wife of the famous doctor in the play, Everett Chalmers. While he was the ostensible central character and was even given the title to the play, hearts went out to his alcoholic wife who would eventually commit suicide. According to Sherrill Grace, "The reviewers . . . showed little interest in any of the characters except Ev and Bob" (Grace 243). But my concern was always for the young girl caught between these two powerful combatants, her parents. It seemed to me that it was her story that had been overlooked and needed to be better appreciated. Given that the character Catherine is a recreated version of Pollock, and given that the memories reconstructed and revisited to make this play are mainly Catherine's, why weren't people talking about her? Taking the daughter's overlooked perspective as my main concern, I have selected two productions staged in 1984 and 2010 respectively to illustrate how directorial choices can influence interpretation. Directorial decisions are able to guide reception to a different focus and to a much-altered understanding of what has just been seen. *Doc* is about a dysfunctional family, but the directorial choices influence where "true" meaning lies and where, if characters are to be put on trial for past actions, blame is to be placed.

To make my point, it is necessary to recall the specifics of the complicated plot. At the opening of the play, middle-aged Catherine re-enters the family home after an absence of many years. She is here to see her father Ev because she was told he had had a heart attack; she does not know that this is the evening before his biggest public triumph: he is about to have a new hospital named in his honour. As she comes into the house, voices and ghosts from her past come to life. Between the moment when she greets her father and the moments they share at the play's close, time shifts back and forth. Onstage are enactments from memory (some shared, some only Catherine's or only Ev's) and these take up almost all of the playing time. However, the play begins and ends in the present.

Catherine's parents, Bob and Ev, had both been the gifted and "chosen" ones in their respective families: all of his mother's hopes were "pinned on [him]" (156), Ev says. Bob tells Katie (who later changes her name to Catherine) a similar story:

> And I picked and sold berries, and my mama cleaned house for everyone all around, and my sisters and my one brother Bill, everything for *one thing*. For *me*. For Eloise Roberts. For Bob. (162)

These two fall madly in love, and Ev gives up his dream to train as a specialist. At that time they are both rising to the peak of their careers: he as a doctor, she as a nurse. If he regrets or resents that decision, there is no mention of it in the script. He is charismatic, resourceful, and driven to succeed, and his star continues to rise. However, for Eloise Roberts, becoming Ev's wife and the bored mother of their two children, Katie and Robbie, is hard because she has been ambitious and successful herself. In her case, marriage ends her career.

BOB: . . . I think of my mama who cleaned all around so I could go into nursing . . . and you want to know what's worse? My mama's so happy I married a doctor. I'm successful you see. I made something of myself. (*moves away smiling; lifting her glass in a toast*) I married a doctor. (167)

She falls in love with "the shining light" (156), and then dwindles into his wife. Her sense of entrapment and depression become acute. She is a haunting figure onstage in a housecoat and slip, her confinement thus a visual reality. Alcohol becomes Bob's way of leaving a situation she finds intolerable: "I feel as if I've wasted something" (161), she says, but "There's nothing I can do" (181). Her creativity turns into frustration and anger. She becomes seriously depressed, seriously alcoholic. While Ev cannot be blamed for the whole oppressive system, there is an incident that might have altered the course of events. It occurs when Bob says she wants to go back to work, back to nursing, and Ev refuses, saying, "I don't know any surgeon who wants his wife on staff" (158). He denies her autonomy, declaring,

Look, you're not just an R.N. anymore . . . you're not Eloise Roberts, you're not Bob any more . . . [You're] my wife. (159)

Ev exhibits the same traditional perspective when he says to Catherine, "A woman your age should be raisin' a family" (142). His is conservative small-town prejudice, the conventional male-centred viewpoint of the 1940s and 1950s. In his view, a smart woman is supposed to devote herself to her husband and children. She has to learn the art of substitution: that is, learn to want the lot that fate has dealt her, but Bob cannot. She cannot be the content domesticated wife that Ev, like every other professional man, selfishly wants. The crux of the matter is that he does not want her working for one of his colleagues or taking orders from someone else.

CYNTHIA ZIMMERMAN

Bob cannot see herself becoming a philanthropist; she cannot adapt to Ev's demands and she cannot leave the marriage. Thus Ev sends her to a series of expensive treatment centres where she learns various hobbies like painting and making gloves (161), but his plan does not work out. After several unsuccessful attempts, she will finally succeed in committing suicide. Throughout this time, Ev continues to be a workaholic; he is hardly ever at home and the children are left alone with their despondent mother. Pollock asks us to consider whether his neglect of his family or his absence from them were the cause of Bob's suicide. His friend Oscar tells him:

> It shouldn't have happened.
>
> She asked for so goddamn little and you couldn't even give her that. (194)

Ev defends himself at various points in the play. He says to Oscar, "I was an insensitive son-of-a bitch when she met me, I haven't changed" (175); and later, "Her problem's got nothing to do with time nor work nor any other goddamn thing" (186); and still later, "You got no more idea of what she wanted than I have" (194). However, Ev can also be charged with neglecting his children, a charge his wife would have to share since both of them, for different reasons, have been completely self-absorbed. The consequence for Katie is that she believes it is her fault: because of her they had to marry, because of her and her brother they won't divorce. In a moment of anger, Bob puts this to Katie directly: "Why would he marry me, eh? Why would a brilliant young man, whole life ahead of him, why would he marry me? Eh? Do you know why? Do you know!" (183). Although Katie tells her mother she does not know, she admits to Catherine that "Inside I do know. Because of me – and that's what went wrong" (183).

In the present situation, the prevailing concern for the adult Catherine and her father is the revisiting of this family crisis: trying to understand what happened, ascribing appropriate blame, and coming to recognize the inevitability of guilt. Even now Catherine continues to feel partly to blame because she had been so angry and empathetic with her mother (146). She cannot forget some of the horrible things she had said to her mother, such as "someday you'll be dead and I'll be happy!" (193). Ev is challenged directly by Bob for his mother's suicide, by Catherine, by Oscar. Feeling on trial, he asks, "Was it worth it?" Finally, in his last scene with Oscar, Ev says,

> Supposin' it were, her death my fault, put a figure on it, eh? Her death my fault on one side —and the other any old figure, thousand lives the figure – was that worth it? (OSCAR *exits*). Was it? I'm askin' you a question! Was that worth it! (195)

And this IS the question: worth it to whom? Who sets the standard? Who pays for it? The unanswerable question is asked repeatedly throughout the play – a troubling, rhetorical leitmotif.[4]

More needs to be said of Oscar's place in this story. Essentially he is a mediator and foil. Ev's best friend since childhood, he, too, is a doctor, but one without drive, without ambition. Temperamentally the opposite of Ev, he admires Ev and pines for Bob. Ev says Oscar has no "gumption," that he's been "a pseudo-doctor . . .,a pseudo-husband . . ., and a pseudo-father to my kids!"(195). In contrast to Ev, Oscar's desire to help lies more in the domestic realm. A number of times we watch him fixing things: repairing a hockey stick (129), bandaging Katie's wrist (160), and repairing Katie's shoe (151). However, he cannot fix Ev and Bob's marriage, although he tries to. He keeps Bob company when Ev is away; he even takes her on a trip that Ev has arranged:

> How often do I ask for a favour? Take her to one of those islands you go to, eat at the clubs, lie in the sun, and – Christ, Oscar, I got to go, so gimme an answer, yes or no? (*pause*) You make the arrangements, I'll pick up the tab. (176)

Ev is not nervous in the slightest; "she wouldn't have you," (195) he says. Oscar spends a lot of time with Katie as well, but Katie suspects he mainly wants access to Bob (159). A gentle and sympathetic man in a white suit, Oscar is often there, but always on the periphery. In the midst of these intense characters, he hardly exists.[5] Interestingly, Oscar tells Ev that his mother "had the good sense to get out. Leaving me with [my dad]. How could she do that?" (147). When Catherine says to Bob, "why couldn't you leave" (179), it would seem that the question is arising out of her own contemporary context. But the in-clusion of Oscar's story reminds us that an alternative existed which Bob, because of her own conflicts and character, could not take. Thus Catherine is making a statement and not asking a question. Confined, Bob succumbs; her resourceful daughter will be the one that gets out.

The issue for me is this: Pollock said in an interview with me that she intended the play to be about Catherine, about her journey. As she put it:

> Central to the play is Catherine's journey, the discovery which allows her to accept the responsibility that belongs to her and to lay the rest aside without guilt . . . But because Bob is more present . . . I don't think the audience sufficient-ly realizes what has happened to Catherine. Catherine is the figure that has learned from the tragedy. (Zimmerman 90)

However, it was not only the audience that did not appreciate Catherine's story; the critics and reviewers did not either. Sherrill Grace writes that "Doc is very much Bob's play" (Grace 235); reviewer Marianne Ackerman says, "Doc is less a drama about the struggle between the generations than about the inner mind of a workaholic professional";[6] and Ray Conlogue, in his review, argues that "the remembering writer feels [Katie's] impotence so strongly that Katie – adolescent or adult – never really develops as a character beyond the statement of rage."[7] Most responses focus on the moral and ethical quandaries surround-ing the adults in the gut-wrenching tragedy.[8] Who or what is to blame:

the constricting repressive times; the egotistical workaholic doctor; the self-pitying, self-destructive mother? This happened: how could it? Why? These seem like obvious questions. Nonetheless, Katie's situation remains completely overlooked by the press, just as it is by her parents.

It is common knowledge to suggest that dysfunctional families repeat. Consequently, it is interesting to note that this theme of the neglected, abused, or misunderstood, unconventional daughter also appears in Pollock plays that precede *Doc*. In *Blood Relations* (1980) and *Whiskey Six Cadenza* (1983), the young women protagonists identify with their charismatic fathers, their birth mothers have died, and they are betrayed by the stepmother who fails to protect them. While Katie's mother has not died, Bob is not a good mother to Katie. In fact, the emotional and developmental needs of the young Katie are not met by either of her narcissistic, self-centered parents. Ev is never home and Bob escapes into an alcoholic haze. When Catherine bears witness to Katie's lonely struggle, she calls out repeatedly to her father –"Daddy!!"(169), "Do something" (170), "Help me" (171).

Analyst philosopher Elisabeth Young-Bruehl writes about traumatized and neglected children in *Childism: Confronting Prejudice against Children*. She describes parents who are abusive because they place their own needs above their children's developmental needs:

> At its basis, childism is a legitimation of an adult's or a society's failure to prioritize or make paramount the needs of children over those of adults, the needs of the future adults over the needs of the present adults. It is role reversal at the level of a principle. (280)

This mistreatment, where adults do not "prioritize or make paramount the needs of their children" (279), can have significant consequences. The child comes to feel unloved, a manipulated pawn denied the right to be who she is. In the text, it is clear that Katie's struggle is enormous. "People lie to me" (188), she tells Oscar, and people are always pretending: "I'll pretend too," she says, "pretend that I don't know, I'll pretend that everything's all right":

You all say she's sick, she isn't sick.

She's a drunk and that's what we should say! (193)

She says she hates her brother, that she hates her mother. Later, she deliberately changes her name to Catherine so that it is no longer the same as her grandmother's. She does not want to be like them. When Oscar urges her to look out for her younger brother, she is furious and says, "I am trying to teach Robbie to look out for *himself!*" (162). Later, when Oscar tells her that mother is not well and that she should "think about that," about "How she feels inside," she retaliates with a childish outburst, saying, "I wonder – what my father sees in you . . . You're not a very good doctor. What does he see in you? . . . I hate you! (168). In her eyes, these people are weaklings. She insists, "I can do things for myself" (174). She wants to be like her father who "works hard! [He] works really hard!" (160), and who is totally self-reliant because, as he tells Catherine, "there [is] fuckin' little else to rely on" (173). She hates weakness and she refuses to cry (190). In refusing to succumb to tears, Katie is proving her strength, proving her difference from those who collapse, but it is very difficult. At this point Catherine and Katie share lines as Catherine's memory and Katie's experience merge:

CATHERINE: I'm holding my breath and my teeth are together and my tongue, I can feel my tongue, it pressed hard on the back of my teeth and the roof of my mouth . . .

KATIE: . . . and I hang on really tight. Really tight, and then . . . I don't cry.

CATHERINE: I never cried . . . (*to BOB*) but I couldn't listen like that.

> BOB *releases* CATHERINE's *hands, and moves away from her.* CATHERINE *runs after her as she speaks. It's one of the things you can't do like that!*
>
> KATIE: It's better not to cry than to listen.
>
> CATHERINE: Is it?
>
> KATIE: It's how you keep on. It's one of the ways. I'm surprised you don't know that. (191)

This is Katie's way to "escape" an unbearable situation. Unable to get the nurturing and understanding she seeks, Katie refuses the same to her mother. Katie's need for attention may also be the reason for another form of negative behaviour. "I'm accident-prone," she says to Oscar, "Some people are you know. Accident-prone. I do dangerous things. I like doing dangerous things" (160).[9]

But of course rage and tears are two sides of the same coin. Both arise from feelings of deep hurt. Katie believes that they didn't want to have her (155) and that they had to get married because of her (183). Like Young-Bruehl's patients, she feels a crucial need to understand the abusers' motivations. Thus she keeps notes to help her remember:

> Everything's down in here. I write it all down. And when I grow up, I'll have it all here . . . . I used to pray to God, but I don't anymore. I write it all down in here. I was just little then and now– (174).

The maelstrom of feelings – anger, emotional alienation, isolation, and a sense of abandonment – and the attempt to take control of them is the consequence for young Katie. Catherine remembers it well: "For a long time I prayed to God. I asked him to make her stop. I prayed and prayed. I thought, I'm just a little girl. Why would God want to do this to a little girl? I thought it was a mistake. I thought maybe he didn't know" (132). Her vulnerability goes either unnoticed or

CYNTHIA ZIMMERMAN

disregarded by the adults around her. But Katie keeps track of all the chaotic scenes, and when the adult Catherine returns home, part of her healing will be to love and accept the cruel, angry and confused little girl she had separated herself from. The merger of the split self is clearly articulated in the play:

> CATHERINE: You can cry Katie . . . it's all right to cry . . .
>
> KATIE: Would you want to have me?
>
> CATHERINE: Yes, yes I would. (194)

In the production I saw, this was the point of embrace. Catherine, in her thirties, takes into her arms her younger, unguarded self.

The goal of Catherine's journey is the healing that must take place. First, she must accept and encompass her childhood self; she must close that divide. Second, she has to come to a deeper understanding and compassion for her father's story. At the play's closure, father and daughter together burn the unread letter his mother wrote him just before her suicide which, they both assume, is an accusing one. In agreement now, placed close to each other onstage, they speak gently. But there is also a strong sense that they have come to a new understanding about the limits of responsibility and the limits placed on choice. Perhaps now they have forgiven themselves and each other; perhaps now they can bury the past. Speaking of the 2010 production in which he played Ev, R. H. Thomson said, "everyone felt it was a cleansing thing, a cauterizing of the still bleeding wound."[10] The lights go down on the dying flames from the letter.

In summary, this play is about resurrecting the ghosts of the past to review the story once more. Has time distorted the memories? Has the past been reshaped according to the psychological needs of the present? This is Catherine's reconstruction: what happens to the bright, unconventional, sensitive child? As I have suggested, her story has been neglected and must be reclaimed. Her needs and her experience have been sidelined by the parents (who steal the show); the script (because she mainly bears witness); maybe by the casting decisions; and by critics and audiences alike. Her story must be reclaimed because this IS what happens – in *Doc*, in domestic disputes, especially where children are pressured to take sides, in divorce courts, and by audiences and everyone else. It happens in art, just as it does in life. Is it "childism," as Young-Bruehl believes: the presence of those comforting myths that children are resilient, they won't remember, they won't suffer? Although reviewers have written about how this play not only brilliantly explores family conflict but also looks to "the wider context of social forces and mores which must also assume some responsibility for family events,"[11] there remains a dimension to this drama that deserves more careful attention – that is, how Katie's experiences and her perspective become Catherine's story.

Finally, because I firmly believe in the marriage of text with performance, the recognition of production's interpretative role, this paper includes performance images that illustrate my point. The 2010 production by Soulpepper in Toronto, directed by Diana Leblanc, marries the *mise-en-scène* and the *mise-en-page*. The Leblanc production makes a clear attempt to address the oversight I have been discussing by drawing attention to the importance of Kate/Catherine's role.

This is a "staged photograph," especially arranged for publicity purposes. The production was mounted at the Toronto Free Theatre, September 1984, directed by Guy Sprung and designed by Terry Gunvordahl. Props, costume, and furniture all point to a period piece. There are many props from the time: the coat rack, the vanity mirror, the side table, as well as the ashtrays, glasses, and requisite alcohol. Ev (played by Michael Hogan) is placed in the centre, facing the audience; the other characters all look at him. Catherine (Clare Coulter) and Ev are in the present moment, which the house program states is 1978. They sit at the front of the stage in dark clothing. The ghosts from the past are behind them, dressed in white. We note how young Katie (Henriette Ivanans) looks in her pinafore and saddle shoes. Bob (Kate Trotter), in high heels, appears sophisticated and elegant. A blonde

Photograph by Nir Baraket / Toronto Free Theatre, September 1984

beauty, her satin dressing gown, when she closes it, looks like a stylish dinner gown, a clear marker of her social status. Oscar (Michael Kirby) is placed a bit further back, his doctor's white jacket hanging from the coat rack. The stage has a number of levels, for playing purposes, and although this is a black and white photograph, the stage itself appears to have a black and white emphasis. Ray Conlogue called this "the ultimate memory play set":

> All black with white perspective lines of floor-boards fleeing toward a vanishing point and ghostly doors and millwork hanging in emptiness. . . . It floats the characters in a timeless suspension and lends credibility to the writer's daring jests with time and space. (M7)

The Soulpepper production of 2010 was directed by Diana Leblanc and designed by Astrid Janson. These photographs were taken during performance. In this scene, Doc (played by R. H. Thomson) is speaking to Catherine (Carmen Grant). Her father seems defensive, with his hand placed on his chest as he leans toward her. They are placed

4 | Different Directions: Sharon Pollock's *Doc*   77

Photography by Cylla Von Tiedemann / Soulpepper Production, August–September, 2010 / Young Centre for the Performing Arts, Toronto

far apart, the physical separation marking the emotional gulf. Between them, with her back to us, is young Katie (Hannah Gross). Literally, she seems like a branch from Catherine. The designer, Astrid Janson, known for using texture, fabrics, and careful colour schemes, dresses Catherine completely in red which make her stand out, clearly differentiated from the muted colours—beige, tan, brown—of her surroundings. In contrast, Katie wears the family colours: an off-white blouse and a tan plaid skirt in the same tones as her mother's dress and the couch. Of note too is the dream/nightmare background (the set includes what is called a "ghost chair"), and the stage is essentially bare; there is no attic space, no bedroom area, no foyer. Furniture and props – the couch, a chair, a side table – are minimal. The large, open space facilitates the quick time shifts the play calls for.

The evocation of a dreamscape continues as Ev and Catherine bear witness to a scene – Bob's enraged attack on Katie – from the past.

CYNTHIA ZIMMERMAN

Soulpepper, 2010

This is the point in the text where Catherine says, "Let her go" (190). Ev and Catherine peer out from the plexiglass structure the designer created, each standing in an Ev-sized opening. This Bob (Jane Spidell) is a markedly different casting choice than in the 1984 version. Spidell is a fierce virago, a whirlwind, a volatile force.

Finally, here is an older-appearing Katie, with her hair neither loose nor braided, but tied back. She holds in her hands the notebook referred to in the script. It is red and, strikingly, she is now wearing a red sweater. This Katie is becoming Catherine.

What has happened? The period piece by Guy Sprung in 1984 has been reinterpreted by Diana Leblanc in 2010, twenty-six years later. Not one word of the script has been altered, but the interpretative focus has dramatically changed. The original production enacted the times: it placed the inset play in the restricting, constricting, and conservative small-town setting of Fredericton, New Brunswick, in the

Soulpepper, 2010

1950s. The attitudes and social expectations, like the furniture and costuming, were of that period. In the Leblanc production, the focus has entered into the realm of dream and nightmare, into the revisiting of the past, so much a part of psychodrama where participants recall and enact the physical and psychological material of trauma.

In the Leblanc production, Catherine is vibrant in red. She is the only character who wears highly coloured clothing, and this, I want to argue, makes her constant presence onstage more visible, more palpably *there*. Even when she is placed behind Astrid Janson's plexiglass wall, she stands out. Alert and engaged, even when she is only listening, she has moved, as Sherrill Grace puts it, from "a passive observer of the tragedy" to "an active, remembering participant" (243). She has been taken from the marginalized place of essentially silent witness and given a greater onstage prominence. This is where, I believe, Catherine belongs. In the house program for the Theatre Calgary premiere, Sharon Pollock says the play is "[her] personal journey of discovery." She called the play *Doc*, but it is Catherine's story.

NOTES

1. Richard Ouzounian, "Sharon Pollock: *Doc* – a Taste of Playwright's Own Medicine." *Toronto Star* 18 August 2010, www.thestar.com/print article/849365.

2. Russell Smith, "Want to Write That Book? Read On." *Globe and Mail* 29 Dec. 2011, n.p.

3. For an excellent discussion of the Chalmers family biography, including important facts which have been altered or omitted from the autobiographical play, see "Part II: More Family Trappings – *Doc*," in Sherrill Grace, *Making Theatre: A Life of Sharon Pollock*, 234–49.

4. In an interview, Pollock tells Martin Knelman that she is a workaholic and that she is "baffled by the response of people who see the play as a condemnation of her father" (74).

5. Early in the play, shortly after Catherine arrives, she asks her father about Uncle Oscar. Ev tells her that Oscar "was fly-fishin'. He slipped and fell in the Miramichi with his waders on" (144) and drowned. Perhaps Oscar was another suicide?

6. Marianne Ackerman, "*Doc* Prescribes another Tonic for Calgary's Booming Theatre," *Montreal Gazette* 14 April 1984: E1.

7. Ray Conlogue, "A Highly Personal Drama," *Globe and Mail* 10 Apr. 1984: M7.

8. See, for example, Brian Brennan, "Pollock Offers Best Work Yet," *Calgary Herald*, 8 Apr. 1984 F4; Stephen Godfrey, "*Doc* a Superb Family Drama," *Globe and Mail* 4 October 1984: E5; Martin Knelman, "Daddy Dearest," *Saturday Night* 99 (Oct. 1984): 73–74.

9. According to Young-Bruehl, "delinquency is symptomatic of a child's unmet need; it is not a manifestation of the inborn aggression or wildness or insubordination that childists . . . presume exists in children and youths" (284).

10. Amanda Robinson, unpublished telephone interview with R. H. Thomson, January 2012.

11. Ann Saddlemyer, "Two Canadian Women Playwrights." *Cross-Cultural Studies: American, Canadian and European Literatures: 1945–1985*, ed. Mirko Jurak Ljubljana, Yugoslavia: Edward Kardilj University, 1988. 253.

Works Cited

Ackerman, Marianne. "*Doc* Prescribes another Tonic for Calgary's Booming Theatre." *Montreal Gazette* 14 April 1984: E1. Print.

Conlogue, Ray. "A Highly Personal Drama." *Globe and Mail* 10 April 1984: M7. Print.

Grace, Sherrill. "Part II: More Family Trappings – *Doc.*" *Making Theatre: A Life of Sharon Pollock.* Vancouver: Talonbooks, 2008. 234–49. Print.

Knelman, Martin. "Daddy Dearest." *Saturday Night* Oct. 1984: 73–74. Print.

Ouzounian, Richard. "Sharon Pollock: *Doc* a Taste of Playwright's Own Medicine." *Toronto Star* 18 Aug. 2010. www.thestar.com/printarticle/049365. Web.

Pollock, Sharon. *Doc. Sharon Pollock: Collected Works.* Vol. 2. Ed. Cynthia Zimmerman. Toronto: Playwrights Canada P, 2006. 125–97. Print.

Smith, Russell. "Want to Write That Book? Read On." *Globe and Mail* 29 December 2011. N.p. Print.

Young-Bruehl, Elisabeth. *Childism: Confronting Prejudice against Children.* New Haven, Conn.: Yale UP, 2012. Print.

Zimmerman, Cynthia. "Sharon Pollock: The Making of Warriors." *Playwriting Women: Female Voices in English Canada.* Toronto: Simon & Pierre, 1994. 60–98. Print.

"The art a seein' the multiple realities": Fragmented Scenography in Sharon Pollock's Plays

Wes D. Pearce

> *Typically an early draft of a play is shared with a designer before the director or dramaturge.*
>
> —POLLOCK, "DESIGNERS"

> *I must have a clear sense of the scenic design on which the play takes place, and that design must be a metaphor both for the content and the structure of the work.*
>
> —POLLOCK, "AFTERWORD," 123

To date, much of the critical discourse surrounding Sharon Pollock's oeuvre has traced the development of dramaturgical structures and literary devices within her plays. Somewhat surprisingly, given the extremely theatrical and visually driven nature of her plays, scholars have tended to focus on the political, feminist, and/or historical underpinnings of her plays and, to an extent, the biographical/autobiographic connections that haunt some of them. As the above epigraphs make clear, however, scenography (or the visual world of the play) plays a crucial role in how Pollock creates, writes, and dramatizes. As evidenced in an interview with Cynthia Zimmerman, Pollock, the playwright, is well aware of the role and power that scenography has within her plays:

> Words are . . . only one of the tools you have. Meaning is conveyed . . . by the intersection of all those other elements: the lighting (like where the focus is and how the focus shifts), the placement of people and things, what critical space is there, the design, the colour of everything . . . all of those elements of production . . . ("Anatomising" 9)

Unfortunately, how scenography functions within each play, its essential role in both the formulation/creation process and the production of Pollock's work, has generally been overlooked. This essay argues that as well as employing new dramaturgical strategies, Pollock was simultaneously developing a fragmented or radical scenography. This evolution of the visual world, paralleling similar developments in the written texts, moves her plays from straightforward documentary drama to, as Diane Bessai argues, a complex and satisfying "integration of investigational and psychological realities" ("Pollock's Women" 47). As mentioned, this fragmented scenography is very much tied to complex dramaturgical devices: flashbacks (or in the case of *Walsh* a flash-forward), the conflating of past, present, and future, simultaneous events being presented on stage, and non-linear storytelling, all became hallmarks of Pollock's work.

When *Walsh* premiered in 1973,[1] Canadian scenography (and to a large extent Canadian theatre) was dominated by two opposing visual styles. The most popular was domestic realism, the aesthetic first associated with the plays of Henrik Ibsen and represented by the hyperrealism in the work of Canadian playwrights such as David French's *Leaving Home* and David Freeman's *Creeps*. It is the aesthetic that would become the representative production style for a number of regional theatres and still dominates contemporary theatre. In stark contrast to this "traditional" aesthetic was the imaginative, bare-bones, and highly theatrical style employed by a number of emerging "alternative" theatre companies, including Toronto's Theatre Passe Muraille[2] and Saskatoon's 25th Street Theatre. This visually gripping style, often the result of having to make "something out of nothing," gained national attention with the Canadian tour of James Reany's *The Donnellys*[3] and, like domestic realism, continues to influence Canadian scenography (and theatre) to the present.[4]

Throughout her career, Pollock has developed an aesthetic that refutes both of these scenographic traditions. In an interview with Anne F. Nothof, Pollock suggested that "theatre is at its most powerful when it is least literal" ("Interview" 179), and this statement has often been interpreted as recognition that Pollock favoured a minimalist approach to theatre. Yet in an interview with Robert Wallace, she described the troubles she encountered when trying to stage the naturalistic *Generations* and cautioned, "I don't want to mime it all because then we get into the NDWT[5] style which I don't like, or the Passe Muraille technique: now you're the tractor; I don't want that . . . (120). I would suggest that Pollock's response to this quandary is her development and use of fragmented scenography, a visual bridge between these two existing scenographic styles.

Fragmented scenography allows for naturalistic action to be placed into visual worlds that are expressionistic, surreal, or otherwise completely theatrical. Pollock is drawn to plays filled with "theatrically shuffling past, present, future, external locations, internal landscapes, inner thoughts and uttered words" ("Reflections" 16). Not only does this fragmented scenography emphasize the dramatic elements that she so prizes, but it also supports the feminist dramaturgies at work in her plays. Pollock suggests that feminist dramaturgies and feminist scenographies reject "naturalistic plays that take place in box sets with a unified time span" ("Afterword" 123) and embrace "theatrical environments that . . . [disrupt] linearity of form and of time and space" (Nothof, "Staging" 139).

This essay extends the literary readings of Bessai, Grace, and Nothof by arguing that Pollock's use of fragmented scenography has developed and matured following a parallel trajectory. *Walsh, The Komagata Maru Incident, Generations, Whiskey Six Cadenza,* and *Doc* represent significant markers in the development of this radical theatrical vision, each play challenging the perceived notion of *how theatre does.* I will discuss each of the five plays in terms of how fragmented scenography functions within the text, typically as understood through stage directions, and occasionally through specific text in the script. Pollock is explicit that the structure of a play must be the one that helps her best tell that particular story. Not surprisingly, her use of visuals and the visual world that she creates for the play is subject to similar scrutiny.

Walsh is Pollock's factually inspired play that examines the relationship between Major James Walsh (Superintendent of the North West Mounted Police) and Chief Sitting Bull. At the heart of *Walsh* is a theme to which Pollock will return frequently. In an interview with Rita Much, Pollock states: "I write the same play over and over again. It's about an individual who is directed or compelled to follow a course of action of which he or she begins to examine the morality. Circumstances force a decision . . . and it usually doesn't end very well" (210). Walsh is just the first of many Pollock protagonists who, according to Nothof, "[struggle] with [their] own sense of justice . . . [but in the end opt] for 'self-preservation'" ("Borders" 86).

Ric Knowles argues that the Brechtian prologue, "through which Pollock forestalls empathy and identification with the potentially charismatic Walsh by showing him in his later years as a broken and bitter man" (138), not only provides a theatrical *frame* for the rest of the play, but also clearly situates the theatrical eye of the play:

WES D. PEARCE

The scene is from WALSH's point of view, and the freezes are momentary arrests in the action and are broken by the character's speech or action following. The impression given is similar to that experience when one is drunk or under great mental stress. CLARENCE stands outside of the prologue scene, never taking his eyes off of WALSH. He has on his red tunic and he exists only in WALSH's mind. He is not part of the prologue scene and his scream is heard only by WALSH.

There is no break in staging between the prologue and Act One.

The sound of wind is heard – a mournful sound. In a very dim light, the characters suddenly appear on the periphery of the playing area. WALSH is not among them. They freeze there for a moment, and then, quickly and silently, like ghosts, take their positions onstage . . . (33).

By setting the prologue simultaneously inside the mind of Walsh and in a saloon in Whitehorse, Pollock introduces a new way of seeing and experiencing the action that is about to unfold. *Walsh* is one of the first "mainstream" Canadian plays to explicitly visualize what Delores Ringer calls "the feminist stage . . . [a space] contain[ing] internal and external experience and internal and external images in one space" (301). The prologue expands Ringer's definition of the feminist stage while offering up a glimpse of Pollock's fragmented scenography. This use of "shifting perspectives" is a common visual device in almost all of her plays and one she uses to great effect throughout this play:

WALSH looks at SITTING BULL, then off at the muffled sounds of people approaching. The light begins to flicker, as if people were passing in front of it. WALSH turns slowly, looking outside of the light. The sound of people moaning is heard. A blue light picks out CLARENCE as he makes his way toward WALSH. (60)

As the aforementioned examples demonstrate, Pollock's fragmented scenography re-positions, provokes, and challenges the stage picture and its relationship with the audience.

In a gesture that erases the foundations of theatrical realism, Pollock not only presents select aspects of the stage action/picture (instead of the entire picture) but simultaneously presents the stage action/picture from different points of view. In creating a world that is represented through fractured scenography and multiple points of view, Pollock establishes a visual link between *Walsh* and the expressionistic visions and scenography found in George Ryga's *The Ecstasy of Rita Joe*.⁶ These scenographic explorations and experiments come to more satisfying fruition in later works such as *Whiskey Six Cadenza* and *Doc*, but the use of imaginative and theatricalised scenic moments to propel the narrative forward is something not found in Pollock's earlier plays such as *A Compulsory Option* or *And Out Goes You?*

Pollock, taking what she has learned from her experience with *Walsh*, re-imagines, re-visions, and re-presents what theatre can do in the 1976 premiere of *The Komagata Maru Incident*. Pollock's "landmark play" is the compelling retelling of the ignoble 1914 incident in which the Japanese ship *Komagata Maru*, with 376 East Indian immigrants/British citizens aboard, was refused the right to land in Vancouver. After two months of legal wrangling, the ship, with almost all of the passengers still on board, was forced to return to India. Set in a brothel, the play, as Grace comments, "stages history as a carnival or circus" ("Imagining" 134) and all the action is controlled, with necessary exposition provided by T.S., "a greasy barker and magician, with gloves, hat and cane" (20). Like the prologue for *Walsh*, the play seems to be set both in the real world and also inside the mind of someone (perhaps Hopkinson), but the possibilities of this fragmented presentation are used for greater effect. Unlike *Walsh*, the play deconstructs both the narrative and the scenography, splitting the visuals of the play into distinct but connected fragmented images:

WES D. PEARCE

It is important that the scenes flow together without black-outs and without regard to time and setting. The brothel is the main playing area. Surrounding it is an arc or runway used by T.S. and HOPKINSON for most of their scenes. Although T.S. cannot intrude upon the WOMAN'S space, he is free to move anywhere else on the set to observe or speak. As the play progresses, T.S.'s scenes move from the arc into the brothel area.

The characters never leave the stage . . . The WOMAN is on a level above and behind the area used by the other characters. An open grill-like frame in front of her gives both the impression of a cage, and of the superstructure of a ship. (100)

Pollock suggested this theatricality in *Walsh*, but in *The Komagata Maru Incident*, both the theatricality and the fragmented scenography are more obvious and more effective than in the previous play.

The opening stage directions reinforce not only the *impressionism* of the writing, but also the *theatricality* of the play. This theatricality is witnessed in a number of innovative ways: the meta-theatrical nature of T.S., the way in which time and space operate within this world, and a heightened visual dramaturgy. This fragmenting of text and space allows the story to be told in a radical manner. Instead of setting each scene in a particular location and moving the narrative forward from scene to scene, as was the case in *Walsh*, Pollock tells the story by using multiple locations and multiple narratives simultaneously:

WOMAN: Go to sleep. Go to sleep. Shut your eyes, go to sleep.

It is very hot and WOMAN turns from the child, wipes her forehead and looks out with a sigh, then turns back to the child.

Still not asleep?

HOPKINSON: (*pinning broach on*) There. Everything's forgotten. Alright?

EVY: Alright.

By meshing Brechtian staging techniques with cinematic practice, Pollock exploits the stage picture, and by creating two stage pictures, allows each to comment on the other. In fragmenting the traditional stage picture and in creating a new theatrical vision – "a theatrical impression of an historical event seen through the *optic* of the stage and the mind of the playwright ("Introduction" 98) – Pollock liberated herself from the dramaturgical tyranny of "the well-made play."

After writing *The Komagata Maru Incident*, Pollock commented, "I started to explore structure, and it was exhilarating, and I decided that I never wanted to write a naturalistic play again" (Council of Education Ministers 139). Denis Salter suggests that *The Komagata Maru Incident* highlights Pollock's "commitment to experiment with different techniques of dramatic engagement" (13), insofar as the play both challenges and plays with accepted notions and shapes of dramatic form. Pollock's biographer Grace argues that with this play, Pollock rejects the very form that naturalism demands while insisting that the "theatrical envelope" must be appropriate for the play:

> As a dramatist, [the] challenge was shifting from finding the facts out of which to make a story to creating the appropriate way (the structure or "theatrical envelope") to present these facts in the process of being perceived, interpreted, remembered and recombined into a story. (150)

While Salter and Grace are specifically writing about dramatic structure and literary devices, I would argue that Pollock is also manipulating and exploiting the visual world of the play and its scenography in order to support *and* serve the play's subject. Pollock recognizes that a unique visual world must respond to and reflect the play's structure and, as Zimmerman argues, "she gives great care to realising [the] visual component" ("Anatomising" 10).

According to Salter, *Generations*[7] is a play full of detailed components and visual minutia: "every aspect of the naturalistic style contributed effortlessly to the pervasive lifelike impression. . . . Even something as ordinary as making the morning coffee manage[s] to convey something small but important about the characters" (23). Set on a homestead in contemporary southern Alberta, *Generations* involves the interactions of three generations of the Nurlin family. With this play, Pollock turns from the historic to the domestic and while the play's "major political-social concern: the survival of the family farm" (Zimmerman, "Warriors," 78) provides the back story, the chief conflict of the play centres around Young Eddy's return to the farm. In contrast to almost all of her other plays *Generations*, in both look and style, is quite naturalistic and, as such, it might seem odd to include it in an essay focused on radical scenography. The description of the setting that Pollock provides rivals that of any champion of realism or television drama:

> *DSL is the kitchen of the Nurlin's "New Place" which is what they call the house built in the fifties when Alfred and Margaret were married. It has all the usual accoutrements of a kitchen. The back door of the kitchen . . . opens on a back veranda or porch which runs the width of the house. There is a pump in the yard . . . Off SL lies Nurlin's back section which is lying fallow. Extreme SR, in reality, some distance from the "New Place," a portion of the "Old Place" can be seen. This is the original homestead; it is extremely weathered, grey tumbled, but still standing* (280).

Yet in contrast to this seemingly naturalistic (and functioning) contemporary farmhouse, Pollock fragments the notion of naturalism when she insists that "there should be some sense of the omniscient presence and mythic proportion of THE LAND in the design . . . The prairie extends as far as the eye can see" (280). Zimmerman's contention that the land becomes "a powerful character that the Nurlins respond to differently" ("Warriors" 78) is more fully explored by Corinna Chong, who suggests the "invoked landscape subsumes the characters trapped within it, so that the land effectively becomes a character in its own right" and in doing so, the "rules" of naturalism are upset. Pollock seems uneasy with the results, and in an interview with Robert Wallace, she discusses the frustration with writing the play and the dissatisfaction when the play was staged:

> I had a lot of problems with *Generations*. We went through that whole thing where you paint rooms, you build the set, you take it down. If I had had my druthers, if I could have found a way to do it, the play would not have happened in the house. There would be no kitchen because once you're in the kitchen, you've got to do all the stinking things you've got to do in the kitchen, like cook the food. . . . You can't put the Prairies on the stage so you have to find another way of doing the outside scenes . . . Someday there'll be a director who'll come up with an idea of how to do it in that kitchen and not feel bound by Naturalism. (120)

The inevitable outcome of staging these two oppositional visions seems to be aesthetic conflict. Nothof and Salter, however, have both suggested that the play is not nearly as naturalistic as it seems. In the newest edition of *Blood Relations and Other Plays*, Nothof challenges Bessai's traditional reading of the play as a "conventionally naturalistic work" (Bessai, "Introduction," 9), and Nothof does so by examining the plays "expressionistic elements." Nothof argues that in *Generations*, Pollock's use of place and space is unexpectedly complex, "suggesting variant perspectives or psychological dimensions . . . Lives are conditioned by spaces. Place is not only 'regional,' even though specific. It is multi-dimensional" (vi). Salter also disrupts the familiar reading of the play, noting that "the stage directions [call] for a setting with a double perspective (24). The visual world of the play, as indicated in the stage directions, is not simply a kitchen within a traditional box set; rather, it should be read as a fragmented collage of naturalistic, symbolic and mythic elements set against each other. Not surprisingly, given the nature of the play, the fragmented scenography is subtler and gentler than in any of Pollock's other works, but it has not been abandoned. Salter even suggests that Pollock layers time and space into the setting insofar as the Old Place is "an enduring connection between the old and new worlds, [and] has a kind of mythic dimension, summarizing the family's history in a single vivid image which is more poetic than real" (24).

Craig Walker argues that like *Doc*, *Whiskey Six Cadenza*[8] is "a memory play" (168) in which ghosts of the past seemingly paralyze those in the present. *Whiskey Six Cadenza* recounts the story of Johnny Farley, who returns to his hometown of Blairmore, Alberta, after an unsuccessful attempt to find work in "Tronna." In an interview with Nothof, Pollock has stated that *Whiskey Six Cadenza* is probably her favourite play, but despite garnering some of the best reviews of her career, has never had a professional production after the premiere ("Interview" 168). While situating the play in the Crowsnest Pass during 1919–20, *Whiskey Six Cadenza* avoids the "history play" label because Pollock re-employs a number of scenographic techniques that she has worked with before in order to intertwine seamlessly the (more or less) naturalistic action(s) of the stage world with a visual world that is illusionary, fragmented and cinematic. Perhaps more so than any of her other plays, the scenography and the structure of *Whiskey Six Cadenza* supports Nothof's claim that Pollock's dramaturgies "suggest the illusion of reality and the reality of dreams" ("Introduction" vi):

> *The front of the stage is filled by a gossamer depiction of the Crowsnest Pass . . . All is seen as if through a soft rain . . . Light builds behind the image, exposing it as no more than a grey, dusty, cobwebby affair, much as a spider might spin in the entrance of an abandoned mine-shaft . . . Images and figures*

often appear fractured, refracted, fragmented . . . The landscape
extends into the infinite, giving an impression of viewing eterni-
ty through a glass, a telescope, a microscope, a kaleidoscope. (39)

Pollock's use of fragmented scenography in *Whiskey Six Cadenza*
reflects elements from many of her earlier plays by presenting multiple locations and multiple story lines simultaneously, scenic elements
offering multi-perspectival, highly theatrical visuals that subvert naturalism, and the use of seemingly unrelated visual elements to comment on the story's action. The play reveals a significant maturity in
Pollock's understanding and use of visual dramaturgy insofar as the
fragmented images are inescapable – the play simply cannot function
without fully embracing the visual world she has created. It is, however, a visual world that is not always easy to achieve, and while *Whiskey
Six Cadenza* seems built on the visual, the scenographic elements are
more seamlessly integrated in *Doc*.

Walker maintains in *Whiskey Six Cadenza* that Pollock structures
the narrative and locates the play "within the expressionistic frame of
Johnny's memory" (176); this is not just a memory play but rather a
play placed inside memory. Like *Walsh*, the play opens with a dream-
like prologue, a musical sequence placed outside the constraints of
time, space or narrative logic, and like the circular structure of *Walsh*,
an image to which the play will (eventually) return:

> *The figures, now complete, now fractured, refracted images*
> *of Mr. BIG and LEAH, WILL and DOLLY, CEC and MRS.*
> *FARLEY, GOMPERS and MAMA GEORGE dance; OLD*
> *SUMP dances alone. Occasionally they change partners. BILL*
> *THE BRIT watches, dancing with no one. JOHNNY is ab-*
> *sent. (39)*

The collage of figures, "now complete, now fractured, refracted . . .", is a
device that Pollock uses frequently within the written text. At times, as
with the brass band, the use of abstracted visuals, "*fragmented images of*

trumpets, trombones, light glancing off brass instruments" (49), represent an aspect of the authentic story insofar as the stage directions indicate the band is real and not a figment of the narrator's imagination (this seems to be true, even if the band is only seen in shadow). Similarly, the images can be used to help stage the unstageable, as *"refracted image of glint on motorcycle and gun fades in and out"* (113). At other times, Pollock employs the images to extend moments of the narrative, as is the case at the end of the first act:

> MRS. FARLEY: (*yells after him*) And what will you do with his whore?!
>
> *JOHNNY runs across the stage out of sight. We are left with fractured images of his fleeing. They glint as light fades.* (87)

Pollock's use of the ruptured images/scenography is most effective when the images are inscribed with multiple readings, simultaneously foregrounding memory while commenting upon the onstage action:

> *WILL and DOLLY exit from the Alberta Hotel. Will is whistling. They stop. WILL kisses DOLLY. They make their way off, WILL whistling.*
>
> *JOHNNY sits watching MAMA GEORGE and LEAH restore a bit of order. MAMA GEORGE tidies. LEAH looks as if she might leave.*
>
> *The reflected and softly blurred image of DOLLY and WILL kissing. WILL'S whistling heard faintly from offstage. The image fades. Whistling continues, growing fainter for slightly longer.*
>
> JOHNNY: Do you gotta go right now?
>
> LEAH: Why?

JOHNNY: I thought maybe we, you and me, we could … sit and talk.

LEAH: What do you want to talk about?

JOHNNY *shrugs* … (76)

At the moment when Will and Dolly leave the hotel, having finally resolved the conflicts of their relationship, they are genuinely content, possibly even in love. The image reinforces this perfect second in time, while simultaneously gently critiquing the budding (and possibly dangerous) relationship between Johnny and Leah and foreshadowing the tragedy that soon follows.

Pollock's use of fragmented scenography and her use of reflected and fractured images are essential elements of how she tells stories. In *Whiskey Six Cadenza*, they are foregrounded and made explicit and, Salter suggests, the fleeting images become inextricably connected to structure:

> So-called normal reality is but a pretense here; characters move easily in and out of focus as though they, like Blairmore itself, feel compelled to resist permanent definition; and with all the fluency of film, multiple perspectives are superimposed, fade from view and then magically re-appear in strange new forms. (28)

In *Whiskey Six Cadenza*, Pollock's scenography makes manifest Mr. Big's claim of mastering "the art a seein' the multiple realities a the universe" (89), but this scenography also visualizes and makes manifest the multiplicity of "vantage points" which has always been critical to the way that Pollock tells the story (Zimmerman, "Anatomising," 8).

Telling the story is central to *Doc*.[9] Katie reminds her older self, "Everything's down in here. I write it all down. And when I grow up, I'll have it all here" (174). Yet neither the story nor the structure of the play is linear or expected. Like Johnny in *Whiskey Six Cadenza*,

WES D. PEARCE

Catherine makes the difficult journey "home" for a visit with Ev (her father), but unlike Johnny's singular and linear memory, which frames that play, the "truth [emerges] from the fragmented recollections of two equally haunted minds" (Walker 177). As Pollock suggests in her introduction, the kaleidoscopic views of *Whiskey Six Cadenza* return in new forms:

> Much of the play consists of the sometimes shared, sometimes singular memories of the past, as relived by Ev and Catherine, interacting with figures from the past. Structurally, shifts in time do not occur in a linear, chronological fashion, but in the unconscious and intuitive patterning of the past by Ev and Catherine. (126)

With the ghosts of the past awakened, Katie (Catherine as a child), her dead mother (Bob), and "Uncle" Oscar (Ev's best friend and surrogate husband and father to Bob and Katie), Catherine and Ev re-enact the family history.

The Playwright's Notes for the play indicate how complex and "radical" Pollock's use of scenography has become:

> The "now" of the play takes place in the house in which Catherine grew up and in which Ev now lives alone. The play is most effective when the set design is not a literal one, and when props and furniture are kept to a minimum. I think of the setting as one which has the potential to explode time and space. (126)

For the purposes of this study, however, *Doc* is best understood as the play that fuses the individual scenographic elements that have been discussed into one, enabling multiple points of view, multiple truths, multiple times, and multiple memories to exist simultaneously, ensuring that multiplicities of stories are remembered.

If Malcolm Page's comment is to be believed and Pollock did want the Sioux warriors to ride horses in *Walsh* (19), then *Doc*, "realistic only in its observed detail and lifelike conversations" (Salter 30), demonstrates a remarkable evolution in her use of scenography. *Doc* emerges as another seminal work because it merges everything Pollock has learned about working in the theatre, everything that she has learned about seeing her plays in production, and everything that she has learned about being a playwright. In *Doc*, the montage that Robert Nunn refers to as "not quite working" in her earlier plays, is seamless, as past and present mesh to become one, and the action of the play becomes a unified collage of time and spaces. Pollock creates a world in which Catherine exists simultaneously in the present and the past, a technique that she will develop even further in *Moving Pictures* and which echoes earlier fragmentations in *The Komagata Maru Incident* and *Generations*. Bessai suggests that Pollock's re-presentation of memory has also matured: "The memory images that alternately fade and resurge throughout the play are more often heated accusatory moments than the fully articulated dramatized recollections of earlier plays" ("Pollock's Women," 63). The fractured images that are so prominent in *Whiskey Six Cadenza* are less literal and more ethereal in *Doc*; not only do characters "speak across time," but images and props, such as the music box and the letter, travel across time. Further developing the framing device in *Generations*, the "naturalistic demands of the play" are enclosed within a larger metaphoric world and according to Salter, the "house itself becomes a symbol" (31). Nothof seems to suggest that *Doc* marks the beginning of a recognizable Pollock style because many of her subsequent plays employ a similar structure and exploit scenographic devices in a similar manner ("Staging").

The innovative manner in which Pollock manipulated and exploited scenographic potentials had a profound impact on Canadian theatre, creating an individual scenography that responds to, and visualizes, the stories she is telling. Yet it is this necessary flexibility and deconstruction of form, structure and theatrical visions that have, at times, crossed and upset critics and audiences. Looking back on this collection of plays, it is easy and perhaps clichéd to argue that many of the literary and visual dramaturgical devices employed by Pollock

John Wood's *production of* Walsh. *Photo by Robert Ragsdale, courtesy of the Stratford Festival Archives.*

were ahead of their time: the use of flashbacks (or flash forwards), the conflating of past, present, and future, events being presented simultaneously on stage, and non-linear storytelling, are all dramatic devices that today's budding playwrights take for granted, but that forty years ago critics refused to accept. Eventually, Canadian theatre, Canadian aesthetics, and Canadian audiences caught up to the visual worlds that Pollock so provocatively created throughout her career, so much so that the visual worlds and scenographies of her earliest plays still seem contemporary today.

The intimate venue of Stratford's Patterson Theatre encouraged John Wood to re-imagine the scenographic space of Pollock's *Walsh* in a way that transformed the play from an epic pageant to an intimate experience. Shown here is Donna Farron as Mary Walsh and Michael Ball as Walsh.

Larry Lillo's premiere production of The Komagata Maru Incident. *Photographer unknown. Image provided courtesy of University of Calgary Special Collections [Msc 54.13.21.4]*

Photographer unknown. Image provided courtesy of University of Calgary Special Collections [Msc 54.13.21.5]

In Larry Lillo's premiere production of *The Komagata Maru Incident*, Hopkinson (Richard Fowler), Evy (Heather Beslin), Georg (Leroy Schultz), and Sophie (Nicola Cavendish) inhabit a world that is both realistic and theatrical. Jack Simon's environment is fluid, which allows for the dreamlike play to unfold before the audience. Woman (Diana Belshaw) is both trapped in space and yet is placed in a visual place of power.

Rick McNair's production of *Blood Relations* (1981) featured Sharon Pollock as Miss Lizzie and a realistic world of the Borden's Victorian house that nonetheless allowed for the dreamlike, imaginative and complex world of Pollock's script to unfold in a seemingly flawless manner.

NOTES

1   *Walsh* opened on 7 November 1973 in Calgary's Arts Centre Theatre (later Theatre Calgary).

2   Under the leadership of Paul Thompson and using the collective creation methodology, Theatre Passe Muraille had two revolutionary productions: *Doukhobors* (1971) and the hit production *The Farm Show* (1972).

3   The trilogy is comprised of *Sticks and Stones* (1973), *The St. Nicholas Hotel* (1974), and *Handcuffs* (1975). All three premiered at the Tarragon Theatre, were directed by Keith Turnball, and had sets designed by Rosalyn Mina. NDWT toured the three plays in 1975.

4   One such example is Theatre Newfoundland & Labrador's ongoing tour of Robert Chafe's *Tempting Providence* (2002), a tour de force production featuring four actors, four chairs, a table, and two sheets.

5   Founded in 1975 by Keith Turnbull and James Rainey, NDWT was known for its minimalist aesthetic and actor-driven theatre. The company folded in 1982.

6   Ryga's seminal work opened at the Vancouver Playhouse on 23 November 1967, and the production opened the studio theatre of the National Arts Centre in 1969. The NAC production was subsequently broadcast by the CBC (also 1969).

      The story is told in songs, montages and disconnected scenes – in a stream-of-consciousness style which collapses past and present, as Rita Joe recalls her youth on the reserve during her arraignment in court on charges of prostitution. Events and characters are presented from her point of view. Ryga effects this collapsing of time through the set design – a circular ramp that encloses the present, with a cyclorama to evoke the past. Lighting effects isolate characters and cast shadows of prison bars across Rita Joe as she sleeps, creating a mood of fear and claustrophobia. This "expressionist" style and form projects the state of mind of the protagonist, externalizing feelings through action and image. (Charlebois and Nothof)

      Grace further argues that "If I were to remount it today ... I would stage it as Major Walsh's expressionistic nightmare" ("Imagining Canada," 137).

7   Commissioned by Alberta Theatre Projects, *Generations* opened on 28 October 1980, at the Canmore Opera House. It had a previous incarnation as the CBC Radio drama *Generation*, which aired on CBC in December 1978.

8   Commissioned by Theatre Calgary, it opened on 10 February 1983, under the title *Whiskey Six* and was subsequently nominated for the Governor General's Award for English Language Drama upon its publication in 1987.

9   *Doc* premiered at Theatre Calgary in April 1984 and won the Governor General's Award for English Language Drama (1986) upon its publication.

Works Cited

Bessai, Diane. "Introduction." *Blood Relations and Other Plays*. Ed. Diane Bessai. Edmonton: NeWest, 1981. 7–9. Print.

———. "Sharon Pollock's Women." *Sharon Pollock: Essays on Her Works*. Ed. Anne F. Nothof. Toronto: Guernica, 2000. 44–67. Print.

Charlebois, Gaetan, and Anne F. Nothof. "The Ecstasy of Rita Joe." *Canadian Theatre Encyclopedia*. Athabasca University, 15 Sept. 2009. Web.

Chong, Corinna. "Sharon Pollock." *New Brunswick Literary Encyclopedia*. St. Thomas University, 2011. Web.

Council of Ministers of Education of Canada. *Canadian Literature: A Guide*. 1986. Print.

Grace, Sherrill. "Imagining Canada: Sharon Pollock's *Walsh* and *Fair Liberty's Call*." *Sharon Pollock: Critical Perspectives on Canadian Theatre in English*. Ed. Sherrill Grace and Michelle La Flamme. Toronto: Playwrights Canada P, 2008. 133–50. Print.

———. *Making Theatre: A Life of Sharon Pollock*. Vancouver: Talonbooks, 2008. Print.

Knowles, Ric. *The Theater of Form and the Production of Meaning: Contemporary Canadian Dramaturgies*. Toronto: ECW, 1999. Print.

Much, Rita. "Sharon Pollock Interview." *Fair Play: Twelve Women Speak*. Ed. Judith Rudakoff and Rita Much. Toronto: Simon & Pierre, 1990. 208–20. Print.

Nothof, Anne. Introduction. *Blood Relations and Other Plays*. New ed. Edmonton: NeWest, 2002. Print.

———. "Staging the Intersections of Time in Sharon Pollock's *Doc, Moving Pictures* and *End Dream*." *Theatre Research in Canada* 22.2 (2001): 139–50. Print.

Nothof, Anne F. "Crossing Borders: Sharon Pollock's Revisitation of Canadian Frontiers." *Sharon Pollock: Essays on Her Works*. Ed. Anne F. Nothof. Toronto: Guernica, 2000: 81–99. Print.

———. "Interview with Sharon Pollock." *Sharon Pollock: Essays on Her Works*. Ed. Anne F. Nothof. Toronto: Guernica, 2000: 167–79. Print.

Nunn, Robert C. "Sharon Pollock's Plays: A Review Article." *Sharon Pollock: Essays on Her Works*. Ed. Anne F. Nothof. Toronto: Guernica, 2000: 26–43. Print.

Page, Malcolm. "Sharon Pollock: Committed Playwright." *Sharon Pollock: Essays on Her Works*. Ed. Anne F. Nothof. Toronto: Guernica, 2000: 12–25. Print.

Pollock, Sharon. "Blood Relations: Afterword." *Plays by Women*. Vol. 3. Ed. Michelene Wandor. London: Methuen, 1984: 123–24. Print.

———. *Doc. Sharon Pollock: Collected Works*. Vol. 2. Ed. Cynthia Zimmerman. Toronto: Playwrights Canada P, 2005. 125–97. Print.

———. "Designers, Dramaturgy and Production." Annual General Meeting of the Associated Designers of Canada. University of Calgary. 17 June 2012. Roundtable Discussion.

———. *Generations. Sharon Pollock: Collected Works*. Vol. 1. Ed. Cynthia Zimmerman. Toronto: Playwrights Canada P, 2005. 275–335. Print.

———. *The Komagata Maru Incident. Sharon Pollock: Collected Works*. Vol. 1. Ed. Cynthia Zimmerman. Toronto: Playwrights Canada P, 2005. 97–137. Print.

———. "Reflections." *Sharon Pollock: Collected Works*. Vol. 3. Ed. Cynthia Zimmerman. Toronto: Playwrights Canada P, 2005. 15–24. Print.

———. *Walsh. Sharon Pollock: Collected Works*. Vol. 1. Ed. Cynthia Zimmerman. Toronto: Playwrights Canada P, 2005. 29–95. Print.

———. *Whiskey Six Cadenza. Sharon Pollock: Collected Works*. Vol. 2. Ed. Cynthia Zimmerman. Toronto: Playwrights Canada P, 2005. 35–124. Print.

Ringer, Delores. "Re-Visioning Scenography: A Feminist's Approach to Design for the Theatre." *Theatre and Feminist Aesthetics*. Ed. Karen Laughlin and Catherine Schuler. Madison, NJ: Fairleigh Dickinson UP, 1995: 299–315. Print.

Salter, Denis. "(Im)possible Worlds: The Plays of Sharon Pollock." *Sharon Pollock: Critical Perspectives on Canadian Theatre in English*. Ed. Sherrill Grace and Michelle La Flamme. Toronto: Playwrights Canada P, 2008. 13–32. Print.

Walker, Craig Stewart. *The Buried Astrolabe: Canadian Dramatic Imagination and Western Tradition*. Montreal: McGill-Queen's UP, 2001. Print.

Wallace, Robert and Cynthia Zimmerman. *The Work: Conversations with English-Canadian Playwrights*. Toronto: Coach House, 1982. Print.

Zimmerman, Cynthia. "Anatomising the Question." *Sharon Pollock Collected Works.* Vol. 1. Ed. Cynthia Zimmerman. Toronto: Playwrights Canada P, 2005. 1–13. Print.

———. "Sharon Pollock: The Making of Warriors." *Playwriting Women: Female Voices in English Canada.* Ed. Cynthia Zimmerman. Toronto: Simon & Pierre, 1994. Print.

Listening is Telling:
Eddie Roberts's Poetics of Repair in Sharon Pollock's *Fair Liberty's Call*

Carmen Derkson

Let me find my talk / so I can teach you about me.

—"I Lost My Talk," Rita Joe,
Mi'gmaq Poet Laureate

In a recent *Canadian Literature* review (2011), Terry Goldie claims Sharon Pollock's 1995 play *Fair Liberty's Call* is as "tired as its title" (205). Of the play, he writes,

> the conflict between rebels and loyalists in the American Revolution could rise above the material, but it doesn't. In the early seventies such revisionist representations of Canadian history seemed of value in themselves but those days are past. When at the end the cross-dressing soldier known as Eddie and Wullie, the ex-slave, seem ready to go

off together, it is just too cute. All that disruption of gender and race so nicely resolved. (205)

I disagree with Goldie's glib reading of a rather complex play that brings much to mind beyond epithets of "tired," "past," and "cute" (205). Goldie's critique does not seem attuned to the residual effects of the American Revolution within Canadian history, or the conflicts that often find an echo in our current political landscape. Goldie fails to mention or recognize Pollock's counter-play and subtext about indigenous presence and identity in *Fair Liberty's Call*. In a play about exile, civil war, and settler-land disputes, Pollock presents an alternative script and history, one often forgotten by settlers: the indigenous rights to land and identity prior to settler land claims. Rather than performing a "straightforward" reading of the script, I read against the grain to examine the "othered" histories at the core of this play, which has also been consistently overlooked by critics.

This essay examines how Pollock brings indigenous identity to the spectator's attention. By engaging the audience's auditory senses, Pollock subverts the importance of the most significant performers in the play in favour of those who perform behind the scenes, often unheard and unrecognized. Pollock's stage directions, used as a performative strategy, emphasize sound and its relationship to listening practices in order to foreground indigenous presence. An auditory reader will note the connection to "hearing" (10), the "heart" (10), and the displaced eye (10), along with the reappearance of the "red woman" (11) throughout the script. Theorizing a reparative practice, this essay demonstrates how listening functions as an active, intersubjective, rather than passive mode. Further, a reparative practice positions listening in acoustic exchange as the antidote for miscommunication between histories. While the gaze may act as a witness, auditory recognition exposes what the gaze passes over and so allows: listening is not passive activity. An auditory-recognition practice requires a shift in the privileging of the visual and kinetic senses in order to participate fully and experientially in sound-traces that recognize the sound patterns that define us, whether past or present.

Pollock's counter-play challenges the passivity of the gaze, whether of performer, audience, or reader, to show how sound and listening practices prompt a different kind of recognition in *Fair Liberty's Call*. According to poet Rae Armantrout, recognition manifests as a complex act. In a recent poem, Armantrout discusses the benefits of misrecognition when she writes, "I was trying to tell myself / what I must have known before / in a form / I wouldn't recognize at first" (58). Similarly, Pollock's mistellings (9) allow other voices, spaces, and histories to emerge from misrecognition. Similarly, Siobhan Senier offers compelling material on the differing gradients between mere acknowledgement and recognition. In a recent article, Senier writes, "by recognition I mean the formal, colonial, governmental processes that acknowledge indigenous territories, identities, and self-governance" (15), but acknowledgement differs from recognition because mere acknowledgement, no matter how hard won, retains a hollow ring: it does not mean much of anything. Senier indicates how "recognition affects Native people's self-representation" (2); depending on the federal government's relationship with the tribe, it can provide visibility and delimit identity and resources. By theorizing a tripartite reparative practice based on listening, auditory recognition, and acoustic exchange, I examine how acknowledgement, in primarily visual contexts, through "formal, colonial governmental processes" (15) is not enough to repair relations for disenfranchised groups, especially First Nations. Visibility also promotes negative acknowledgement, which often generates *interference* and mistranslation along with a refusal to actually see, a willful blindness that auditory-recognition and listening practices displace.

Eve Kosofsky Sedgwick coined the term "reparative critical practices" (128), which scholars and writers began to take up in their work recently.[1] Reparative reading critiques paranoid, fear-based, and suspicious reading and/or reading strategies in order to propose a shift not only in practice, but also in thinking and writing. The term I use, reparative *practice*, pays homage to Sedgwick's "reparative critical practices" (128), yet extends the definition to include and focus primarily on listening and sound, such as performative reading. Sedgwick draws on a range of writers, theorists, and scholars such as Sigmund Freud, Judith Butler, Melanie Klein, and D.A. Miller to refigure paranoid strategies and define reparative critical practices. She destabilizes oppressive epistemological systems ensconced in the paranoid by unraveling the mimetic, and further suggests that "paranoia refuses to be only either a way of knowing or a thing known, but is characterized by an insistent tropism toward occupying both positions" (131). As paranoia imitates and embodies knowledges and practices, the challenge to destabilize its systems relies on naming it as a "theory" (134) in order to classify and recognize it as a theory. Once paranoia is recognized as a theory, another theory such as reparative practice works to mitigate the mimetic effects of paranoia.

Reparative practice as a listening praxis or theory of sound and auditory-recognition traces the affective dissonances and dis/assemblings of articulate nonverbals, sounds, and memories, instead of relying only on descriptions of verbal patterns or sound images. Reparative practice examines how the body listens or how the body's syntax or neutrality feels sound, beyond a general hearing within a community of spaces or places, to function as an act of repair in language, theory, and literature. "Music entreats the listener to hear that which the ear cannot perceive" (60), writes Alexander Stein when he references the late German pianist Wilhelm Kempff's observations on Beethoven's Piano Sonata, Op. 111. Similarly, this essay entreats the reader to listen to Pollock's counter play as sonic scripting, noted in and between the performers' utterances, spatiality, and presence within *Fair Liberty's Call* – to examine not only caesuras, but the sensory traces, which provide tangibility and voice to the seeming silences of objects or shadows as well as the tensions, whispers, and interiorities within bodies, objects, and spaces.

Pollock's play registers *listening* as a reparative form of speech – not a speech act – but a reparative speaking raised from almost indiscernible sound-traces. Sound provides another story, a play within the play, or counter to the play most readers read or audiences visualize. In the play, sound is not background or accompaniment; instead, Pollock emphasizes its significance in the play's prelude in a separate, distinct stage direction: "*all sound is impressionistic, even surrealistic, rather than realistic*" (9). With this positioning, sound functions as a cultural intervention in and between verbal exchanges or dialogue, as impressions and dis/assemblings. Sound, as cultural intervention, occurs because it does not cater to one kind of representation or economy; rather, sonification's ephemeral qualities situate boundaries within often overlapping yet specific contexts (Supper 258). Thus, the play is not just about "the conflict between rebels and loyalists in the American Revolution" (Goldie 205); by contrast, the play "rise[s] above the material" (Goldie 205) to explore an often overlooked terrain such as the First Nations' relationship to the Revolutionary War in 1785 New Brunswick and its effects upon them.

Complicating a seemingly straightforward play about American Loyalists exiled in New Brunswick, their land rights, and the definition of home, Pollock threads a counter-sonic narrative throughout the script of Aboriginal presence to provide an *acoustic exchange* between the exiled Loyalist family, the soldiers, the ex-slave, and the indigenous people already residing in New Brunswick: the "red woman stands in the glade of trees, and she watches" (18) as the Americans listen; their new-found lives, their survival, may depend on how well they listen. The play within the play begins, after a collaborative lyric chant, with a re-memory and telling by Joan Roberts of finding a "feather on the doorstep" (11) at this new place. Joan Roberts, the wife of George and mother to four children, grieves because her two sons, one a rebel and the other a loyalist, died as a result of the civil war. The feather, a seemingly small detail, symbolizes the gap in versions of the Roberts family's story about their arrival in New Brunswick from Boston and how Joan's sons died. However, Annie, Joan's oldest daughter, challenges Joan's version:

> JOAN: When first we come here after the revolution, when first we come . . . I saw a woman in the woods. A red woman. I saw her watchin'. Watchin' with a babe on her back. I saw her carryin' it like that, like—packed in moss, like—like nothin' I know. One mornin' I found a feather on the doorstep.

> ANNIE: We don't have a doorstep, Mama. We haven't had a doorstep since Boston. We may never have a doorstep again. (11)

Both women insist on their own version of events; Annie refuses not only to see the feather, but the possibility of a doorstep too, even though Joan asserts, "the feather was there. And in the sky a bird was circlin'. A bird like no bird I know. The colours were wrong, and the size" (11). For Joan, the feather represents all that is not home for these would-be settlers from Boston. The feather on Joan's imaginary doorstep is not only a fleeting image in the present, but an evocation of a language of listening – an object of repair, an ephemeral offering as it flutters to conjure and situate an undoing of home (a plot of land in New Brunswick) and the silence of never again home (Boston) – in a new but "barren" (11) place.

Although Joan sees the feather, even acknowledges its presence, she refuses, in this opening moment in the play, to engage in auditory-recognition and acoustic exchange. She refuses, like Annie, to recognize another version, to listen to an offering of difference: the "colours were wrong, and the size" (11). Annie, however, does more than simply refuse to listen – she refuses to see or acknowledge any kind of possible opening for exchange in this new place. Rather, Annie prefers to disengage from past memories of their lives in Boston, her lost brothers, and the new home she must now inhabit. Annie refuses recollection and so recognition.

Pollock uses sound to show the systemic gaps embedded in Revolutionary War narratives and the colonization process. In Act

CARMEN DERKSON

One, Joan glimpses the feather, its potential for repair, but does not pick it up; Annie refuses any kind of self-repair, repair for her family, or the people who already reside in New Brunswick, the Mi'gmaq and Maliseet First Nations. Pollock layers these acts of refusal to show the ruptures, the missed chances for repair, and emphatically demonstrates how a refusal to engage in recognition of another person, place, or object undermines any kind of reparation. To drive home her point, Pollock provides a visual image of an act of refusal – a colonial act. After the verbal exchange between Joan and Annie, George Roberts *"gets out a neatly folded English flag"* (11), while Eddie, Joan's cross-dressing soldier-"son" helps George, her father, *"guid[e] a white birchbark pole into place so the English flag may be attached and flown . . ."*(11). Neatly and smoothly, the potential for engagement in a new place and life, the possibility to repair from the war, is lost as the English flag unfolds.

Thus Pollock's script is not just a re-visioning of a played-out historical event (if historical events are ever played out); instead, *Fair Liberty's Call* shows us a different way of performing reading for those who *listen* closely: *Listening is telling* in Pollock's play. *Fair Liberty's Call* has a new resonance today due to its emphasis on the potential of reparative practice, if it is taken up, recognized, and engaged with. Pollock shows how listening, auditory-recognition, and acoustic exchange can occur or be missed within systemic gaps or hierarchal relationships, as George demonstrates with his statement of belief: "you can't have people without you have some kind of relationship between people, some kind of rankin', some kind of value put on their contribution and placement" (63). Joan, however, acknowledges the feather, the potential for engagement in a new place, but she, too, refuses to listen, to begin an acoustic exchange between the "red woman" and herself, or to discover how the found object, the feather, may speak to her.

If listening is telling, then sound becomes central rather than peripheral in *Fair Liberty's Call*. Sound is no longer marginalized; it becomes the performing aesthetic or a new way of reading the performed gaps between the authoritative and internal voices in a systemic discourse. According to Salomé Voegelin, "we cannot see to make sense but hear to understand, contingently, the meaning of [our] place" (133). She adds that the meaning of place, the value of our distinctions between relationships, whether between people, land, or history, depends upon *how* we hear and how we *listen* to who speaks to us and through what sounds. A reparative practice identifies, as Alexander Stein suggests, the parts of us that will not or cannot speak with words (61): "we are all that we have ever heard" (83). Stein's article explores how the "sound environment of earliest life plays a profound formative role in psychological development [to] assert inimitable ongoing influences throughout the life cycle" (59). I refer to this article because Stein's case studies show how sound affects relationships, past and present, while making precise distinctions between the definitions of hearing and listening (63). Following Peter H. Knapp, Stein defines *listening* as a "more developmentally advanced and usually conscious attempt to apprehend acoustically" (63); *hearing*, the more technical mode occurs as the "reception of stimuli over auditory pathways" (63). Listening requires an involvement of all senses with a specific concentration on audition. It is, therefore, a learned practice, which differs from modes of hearing. Pollock's play pivots on the acuity of the listening performed by the audience and performers. Hildegard Westerkamp, a soundscape composer and lecturer on listening, environmental sound, and acoustic ecology, writes that the strongest memory of her experience of crossing the Rajasthan Desert on a camel occurred through listening (19, 133), not watching. Westerkamp's example shows that although we may be displaced to a different time and place, where listening becomes more of a means of survival than a pleasure, we do not truly know how to listen or how we listen to a place or person, unless we move beyond the mode of *hearing* to the practice of listening.

Pollock makes a similar connection about listening beyond hearing in order to *unknow* or displace the visual. In Act One, after the distorting sound of a fading anthem, *God Save the King* (10), and the audience hears the "*sounds of a horrific battle: gunfire and cannon; men yelling encouragement and despair mixed with the cries of the wounded and the thunder and screams of horses*" (10), a silence follows. The three

Roberts women step into the *"dappled light"* of a *"glade in a stand of hardwood trees with sunlight filtering through the leaves"* (10); their voices intermingle to repeat in a *"taped montage . . . the following words"* (10): "you want to know where / where / where to put your eye / eye/ eye so you can hear the / heart / beat" (10). The chanted montage of words displaces the fixity and authority of the visual, the easy positioning of knowing through looking; instead, Pollock poses a question about "wanting to know where" to "put your eye so you can hear" (10), not only in the exterior sound of the body, but the interior beat of the body's heart (10). The opening of the play and the lyrical chant speak of a different need for recognition. Here, Pollock suggests a shift in practice to emphasize auditory-recognition rather than the intricacies and dilemmas often posed by relying on visual recognition between peoples: listening is telling.

In 1784, New Brunswick was a "country comin' into bein'" (10) for the British Parliament; however, then, as now, for the indigenous people, the Mi'gmaq and Maliseet First Nations, New Brunswick was already a country, a place called home. How did their *gi'g* (home) sound before it was named New Brunswick? How did the Mi'gmaq and Maliseet listen, and what sounds did they lose after the Dutch, French, British, and Americans arrived? What sounds did they listen for? What sounds disappeared from 1784 to the present? And then, as now, who listened?

According to Mela Sarkar and Mali A'n Metallic, in the spring of 1784, when the American Loyalists began to appear on the St. John's River keen to leave behind the despairs and losses of the American Revolution, the Mi'gmaq people, "forced to first inhabit land and communities with settlements by the Acadian French and English Colonists, co-existed with Euro-descended Canadians in such intimate quarters that their language, Mi'gmaq was already at risk" (53).[2] I raise the concern of the threatened Mi'gmaq language because Pollock's play suggests some basic reading and listening of indigenous languages before a performative understanding of *Fair Liberty's Call's* structure and scripting can occur. Sarkar and Metallic's article demonstrates two important points which relate indirectly to a reading of the play and performing of the script: all Mi'gmaq nouns fall into one of a two-category system, animate or inanimate (60); and the third person is gender-neutral in Mi'gmaq (67).

Although these two points are linguistic facts, when juxtaposed or read alongside *FLC*, the reading of the script becomes ironic. The scripted performers listen to the living to hear the dead while the script circles between the living and the dead and determines who is willing to die for whom, and in what kind of exchange. Secondly, Eddie Roberts performs as a gender-neutral catalyst, a third person, between the living and the dead; a girl-boy soldier who "talk[s] like a Rebel" (39) about exchange, and who raises freedom of rights as the Committee of Fifty-Five Families decides who will be given land and who will not. Throughout the script, the balance between the animate and inanimate circulates as the family members and soldiers, including Eddie, recount their tales of the battlefield in a ritualized re-memory of the missing and the dead. Joan recounts the memory of her son Edward's suicide upon his return home from fighting in the Cherry Valley (14). She remembers "first the noise, and after the noise, the sound of the gun as it fell to the floor. A small kind of noise, not like the other, and then . . . no noise at all. I stood there . . . holdin' my breath, not breathin' and knowin'" (14–15).

However, it is Emily, Joan's youngest daughter, who picks up her brother's gun to re-animate him, and in so doing, slips between genders to perform as Eddie. I refer to Emily as Eddie or s/he because when Eddie takes up her dead brother's soldier-vocation, s/he does not have a fixed identity, but enacts historical disguise by living in between genders: she lives as a man, as Eddie, taking her dead brother Edward's name and donning his army jacket after he commits suicide, but she remains Emily – Eddie is a performance. Eddie performs as an ex-Captain for one of the most well-known Loyalist units, the Tarleton's English Legion, which is known for Lieutenant Colonel Banastre Tarleton's brutality at Waxhaws against the Americans. Eddie challenges the empty Loyalist promises of land for the colonial-born soldier, and this criticism of the Loyalists' reneging on agreements over land rights results in accusations against her by Majors Williams and Anderson. These accusations depict Eddie as a traitor for betraying the Loyalists with "seditious and scandalous libel" (23). However, Eddie recognizes the doubleness involved in these kinds of language games because of her relationship with Wullie, a former scout with the Tarleton Legion, who resides in Birchtown, a Loyalist community of free blacks. Wullie's freedom is hampered by a shortage of food rations which, as he says, means there is "most often, nothin' left" (48) after the "molasses and meal, and that give out after White rations" (48). Although Wullie cannot read and hence requires Eddie's assistance, he is forced to sign "indentured service" (59) documents. The irony of this situation, wherein the white soldiers' struggles over land claims and title by those in power belies the serious basic rights issues blacks and indigenous populations confront over needs like food, along with the fight for their land claims and title.

Pollock, ever the provocateur, writes about the ironic stance taken by the Loyalist soldiers who fight for land rights on land that does not rightfully belong to them. Pollock's stage directions show how this irony occurs through sound with the reoccurring dry rattles, faint birdcalls, and ghostly moans in between the soldiers' escalating arguments and the Roberts family's memory threads. Although often read as "background noise," the frequent sound-traces evoke a presence, symbolically, perhaps, of those First Nations' voices unheard and unrecognized by Loyalists within a 1785 New Brunswick. Eddie's gendered "disguise" allows her to read and listen between the lines, whether Loyalist or Rebel, and hence to challenge the authoritative version circulated in her family, the army, the Committee of Fifty-Five, and the land in which s/he now resides. Eddie exposes the double rhetoric circulated by the soldiers and her father because s/he listens, as Mikhail Bakhtin might suggest, to the "internal persuasiveness that is denied all privilege" (342). Bakhtin, in his writing on the construction of ideological consciousness – how we become scripted and perform our scripting – shows how, unless auditory-recognition is practised, the interrelationship between the authoritative and internal version becomes inseparable, and how listening practices become thwarted. He writes,

> It happens more frequently that an individual's becoming, an ideological process, is characterized precisely by a sharp gap between these two categories: in one, the authoritative word (religious, political, moral; the word of a father, of adults and of teachers, etc.) that does not know internal persuasiveness, in the other internally persuasive word that is denied all privilege, backed up by no authority at all, and is frequently not even acknowledged in society (not by public opinion, nor by scholarly norms, nor by criticism), not even in the legal code. The struggle and dialogic interrelationship of these categories of ideological discourse are what usually determine the history of an individual ideological consciousness. (342)

Ideological consciousness (the "scriptedness" of our accounts, memories, and speech) develops due to a refusal of the "internal persuasiveness" (342) usually denied all privilege, authority, or recognition by family members, friends, or in a larger context, society. The refusal of the internal voice, our own sounds, manifests as scripted, performative responses until we no longer know our own voice or our own sounds.

Eddie retains a sound of her own, similar to Bakhtin's concept of "internal persuasiveness" (342), as does Wullie, which is why Eddie and Wullie work together against Loyalist interests *even as Loyalists*. Both Eddie and Willie perform reparative practice as listening, auditory-recognition, and acoustic exchange because they are attuned to their own internal sounds. Eddie's and Wullie's unscripting of the Loyalist project creates discomfort among those such as the Committee of Fifty-five who support the Loyalist script because they may benefit from its spoils. The rupture in the script, at least for Eddie, occurs when s/he realizes the double play of the colonial game, and she states, "I served as a soldier, Loyalist soldier, colonial born, bloodied my hands and my arms, waded in gore, in the name of a King who condoned his enemies' namin' me traitor. What does that tell you?" (18). When Eddie performs this speech, "*addressing a crowd*" (18), there is no clear response to her words. However, the "*sound of [a] dry rattle*" (19) occurs at the end of Eddie's speech, a possible acknowledgement from an as yet unrecognized presence.

Later, Eddie confronts Major Anderson to ask, "is dissent sedition?" (70), while Anderson plays roulette in a calculated attempt at revenge against the Loyalists in the glade; however, Anderson also plays roulette in order to assuage the pain he feels for his lost child-soldier brother (70). Pollock's ironic gesture surfaces again with the Major's willingness to sacrifice anyone, even those who are innocent of his brother's death, and yet persists in the blind refusal to listen and examine why one person may be, wrongly, valued more than another. After all, Major Anderson's anger toward Eddie stems from his investment in "patronage and preferment" (70) wherein he has opportunity to devalue those who do not fit into his preferred hierarchy of relationships; Anderson admonishes Eddie's lack of reverence for authority, stating, "you got no respect for position or placement!" (62). Again, Eddie listens, and so recognizes the unsound rhetoric of conflict scripted into the Majors' words. How perplexing then, the doubleness of Major Anderson's comment to Annie, Joan's eldest daughter, about her recognition of a tune sung by Loyalists that may be a "Rebel ditty" (36). Major Anderson responds to Annie by stating, "I'd say it depends on your angle of observation, ma'am" (36). However, as this essay shows, recognition also depends on the characters' angle of listening.

Listening in *Fair Liberty's Call* pivots between historical and place memory threads. Angles of listening require attentive acoustic exchanges between the small group of people gathered in a clearing to perform a remembrance ceremony for the dead, those lost in the American Revolution. The gathering consists of the remaining members of the Roberts family, the Majors Williams and Anderson, and ex-Corporal Wilson. However, in the periphery, beyond the woodland glade wherein Joan and Annie Roberts prepare and cook food, a variety of sound-traces reoccur. These sound-traces are interspersed between pieces of dialogue and frequently occur whenever one member of the group alludes to a broken promise, a missing or lost person, or an act of oppression. Although members of the group frequently notice the sound-traces, they rarely investigate the source of the sound, or note the repetitive, looping qualities, almost as though the sound-traces signalled some kind of warning.

As Joan and Annie prepare food for the ceremony, Joan recalls through various memory threads the circumstances surrounding the deaths of her two sons. While she speaks, she hears a "*faint bird call followed by a dry rattle*" (18) at random intervals. After the bird call, Joan begins discussion of an unknown burial mound: "up in the woods where I saw the red woman, there are bones. [. . .] Disarranged" (18). As Joan recounts her discovery of a First Nations' burial mound, she states, "they aren't our Dead" (18). Pollock situates Joan's monologue between two sound descriptions in the script: "*gunfire and voices and voices resonate and fade as Joan speaks*" (18); and "*a faint bird call followed by a dry rattle*" (18). The sound-traces evoke a signal and a warning or a possible intervention between gunfire and the memory of the dead. Joan speaks about her memory of the burial mound or grave to no one in particular, for who is listening? She recounts that,

> when you stand there, you feel your feet restin' on top of the soil. You could slip. You could fall. Empty eye sockets catch your eye tellin' you somethin'. Your feet carry you back to the house but they leave no trace of your passing . . . This isn't home. They aren't our dead. The red woman stands in the glade of trees, and she watches. (18)

The past and the present collide with Joan's recollection of the disassembled dead; her possible slip or fall into the grave with the already dead registers the absence of the unrecognized people who perform behind the scene, in the wood, the glade, and who lie buried at her feet.

CARMEN DERKSON

Joan's resistance and refusal to recognize the dead as her own is a sign of her arrogant cultural blindness; there is "no trace of [her] passing" (18) because there is no auditory-recognition or acoustic exchange. Joan seemingly speaks to no one, yet sees the frequent reappearance of the "red woman" in the woods (18) in various temporalities. Joan first notices the red woman in the past tense "watchin' with a babe on her back. I saw her carryin' it like that, like – packed in moss, like – like nothin' I know" (11). Joan also refers to a presence near the burial mounds "up in the woods where I saw the red woman, there are bones" (18). Later, near the end of the play, Joan refers to the red woman in the present tense: "I see the red woman with the babe on her back step out of the glade of trees" (73). The temporal shifts, or shifts in tense, indicate Joan's developing practice and sense of auditory-recognition through acoustic exchange. At first, Joan's silence shows a refusal to even witness the red woman's presence, and this act of refusal denies the red woman and her baby their identity; it is a refusal to acknowledge presence. Joan buries the dead once again at the burial mound due to her refusal to once again acknowledge or recognize who lies "disarranged" (18). Instead of seeking to repair the disinterred body and disrupted burial ground, Joan slips away, leaving the unknown dead man laid-out, bare, out of the earth, visible, but not recognized, spoken of, or heard.

Cultural theorist Joseph Roach discusses the "diseases of American memory" (273) and notes disease reappearing over time in continual conflict between the visual and the embodied. The disturbed First Nations' burial ground, or the possible depiction thereof, shows not only a disrespect for the dead but also a betrayal and silencing of the living to whom the dead belong. Roach concludes that in such "*lieux de mémoire* [...] whiteness and rights reappear as interdependent domains, the self-dramatizing defenders of their contingent frontiers can never allow themselves to forget the obvious: they must always keep alive the specter of the others in opposition to whom they reinvent themselves" (273). Early in the play, Joan situates the red woman as spectral; however, once she engages in attentive, active listening practices, her "angle of observation" (36) also shifts and the red woman loses her spectral quality and becomes human after all. In *Fair Liberty's Call*, Pollock reinvents the usual "specter of the others" – kept alive by the Americans in their struggle for the past in the present – "your feet carry you back to the house but they leave no trace of your passin'" (18); instead, the Americans, the soldiers, and the Roberts family begin to, as Roach might put it, "surrender their version of the past and lose control over the totality of the future" (273–74).

However, Pollock dismantles the "theatre of war" by disrupting the planned ceremony and showing Wullie and Eddie packing up the souvenirs and trophies: "*Wullie and Eddie begin clearing the space during the dialogue; they will take down the war and Rememberin' paraphernalia*" (71). Further, as Wullie and Eddie perform the erasure of the ritualized glorification of war, as the ceremony was intended, Eddie destroys Wullie's "indenture papers" (72). The last gestures in the play offer strategies for reinvention and peace against a persistent re-memorialization caused by a continuous re-enlisting in war. Instead, in the last moments of the final act, Pollock emphasizes the relationship between listening as reparative practice to generate auditory-recognition and acoustic exchange: Joan whispers directly to George, "I can hear you" (72). Meanwhile Eddie/Emily and Wullie laugh together as they stand side by side by "*the birchbark pole with their rum*" (73), celebrating their refusal to return to the army. Each performer listens in recognition and exchange with each other.

The final scenes trace the poetics of repair in and through the performance of the land, in what British performance scholar Mike Pearson might claim to be an agent of reconstitution (28). The land, not just the people, perform intersubjective connection through acts of listening:

> JOAN: I feel my feet pressin' flat 'gainst the surface of the soil now. I kneel readin' the contours of the skull and listenin' to the words spoke by the man with the missin' jaw-bone. The caps of my knees make a small indentation in the

dirt. I see the red woman with the babe on her back step out from under the glade of trees. She holds out a bowl. She offers a bowl full of dirt. (73)

Joan's last piece of dialogue indicates the palpable and sensory shift from visual-recognition to auditory-recognition. Joan's body language shifts from a descriptive, visual mechanics into an acoustic sensorium relying on touch and listening. Joan's feet and knees meld into the surface of the soil to show the interrelationship between sound, body, and land, wherein indentations and impressions become a kind of listening-speaking, or an acoustic exchange between the trace and the body, the earth and the senses. As Joan *listens* to the "words spoke by the man with the missin' jawbone" (73), she "see[s] the red woman with the babe on her back" (73). The interrelationship between listening and seeing, or auditory-recognition, cannot be mistaken. Through auditory-recognition, Joan sees differently. Joan does not render the child as a foreign object dehumanized through her speech: the red woman's baby is no longer an "it" (18); likewise the red woman is now human, someone to listen to rather than to merely speak of or name, a person offering precious sustenance (73). The red woman is no longer a spectral threat. Instead, she offers sustenance they both can share: "Eat, she says. Swallow. And I do" (73). Thus listening as reparative practice fosters coexistence through sustenance and shared experience as a gathering together, a collaborative experience. However, surveillance remains: the hearing practices invested in theories of paranoia and fear within cultural discourses do not easily fade away. Theorizing as reparative practice interferes with and exposes the surveillant narratives we still grapple with today.

NOTES

1   To begin to trace the multiple circuits of reparative reading, see Ellis Hanson, "The Future's Eve: Reparative Reading after Sedgwick," *South Atlantic Quarterly* 110.1 (2011): 101–19.

2   Mela Sarkar and Mali A'n Metallic examine how Mi'gmaq, an Algonkian language of North Eastern North America, is one of nearly fifty surviving indigenous languages in Canada usually not considered to be viable into the next century. "Only the Inuktitut, Cree, and Ojibwe currently have enough younger speakers to provide a critical mass for long-term survival" (49). See also Bonita Lawrence's "Gender, Race, and the Regulation of Native Identity in Canada and the U.S: An Overview," *Hypatia* (2003): 3–31.

Works Cited

Bakhtin, M.M. "Discourse in the Novel." *The Dialogic Imagination: Four Essays.* Ed. Michael Holquist. Trans. Caryl Emerson and Michael Holquist. Austin: U of Texas P, 2008. Print.

Goldie, Terry. "Playing with the Margins." *Canadian Literature.* www.canlit.ca. 8 December 2011. Web.

Pearson, Mike. "Village-Performance." *'In Comes I': Performance, Memory, and Landscape.* Exeter: U of Exeter P, 2006. Print.

Pollock, Sharon. *Fair Liberty's Call.* Toronto: Broadview, 2002. Print.

Roach, Joseph. "Carnival and the Law." *Cities of the Dead: Circum-Atlantic Performance.* New York: Columbia UP, 1996. 239–81. Print.

Sarkar, Mela, and Mali A'n Metallic. "Indigenizing the Structural Syllabus: The Challenge of Revitalizing Mi'gmaq in Listuguj." *Canadian Modern Language Review* 66.1 (2009): 49–71. Print.

Sedgwick, Eve Kosofsky. "Paranoid Reading and Reparative Reading, Or You're So Paranoid, You Probably Think This Essay Is About You." *Touching Feeling: Affect, Pedagogy, Performativity.* London: Duke UP, 2003. 1–34. Print.

Senier, Siobhan. "Rethinking Recognition: Mi'kmaq and Maliseet Poets Re-write Land and Community." *Melus: Multi-Ethnic Literature of the U.S.* 37.1 (2012): 15–34. Print.

Stein, Alexander. "The Sound of Memory: Music and Acoustic Origins." *American Imago* 64.1 (2007): 59–85. Print.

Supper, Alexandra. "The Search for the 'Killer Application': Drawing the Boundaries Around the Sonification of Scientific Data. *The Oxford Handbook of Sound Studies*. Ed. Trevor Pinch and Karin Bijsterveld. New York: Oxford UP, 2012. 249–70. Print.

Voegelin, Salomé. "Time and Space." *Listening to Noise and Silence: Towards a Philosophy of Sound Art*. New York: Continuum, 2010. Print.

Westerkamp, Hildegard. "The Local and Global 'Language' of Environmental Sound." *Sonic Geography: Imagined and Remembered*. Ed. Ellen Waterman. Oshawa, ON: Penumbra Press and the Frost Centre for Canadian Studies and Native Studies, 2002. 130–38. Print.

Loss and Mourning in Sharon Pollock's *Fair Liberty's Call*

Kathy K. Y. Chung

Sharon Pollock's *Fair Liberty's Call*[1] is a rich and complex play, which Sherrill Grace describes as "an allegory of Canada and as a treatment of contemporary issues and timeless, if not universal, ideas about liberty, human rights, war and injustice, and many kinds of violence" (287). To Grace's observation, I would add that the play offers an exploration of loss and mourning, subjects which have attracted limited critical attention. One of the few scholars to examine these subjects is Cynthia Zimmerman. In "Transfiguring the Maternal," she considers Joan as the last in a series of increasingly positive representations, from the daughter's perspective, of the lost maternal figure. In her biography of Pollock, *Making Theatre: A Life of Sharon Pollock*, Grace also emphasizes the influence of the life and death of Eloise Chalmers (*née* Roberts), Pollock's mother, throughout Pollock's large body of work. Both of these approaches highlight the mother–daughter relationship. However, *Fair Liberty's Call* contains multiple deaths that represent loss from a broader communal perspective. Pollock also expresses loss and mourning through symbolic and structural elements, specifically those associated with liminality. These are aspects of the drama I wish to explore in this paper.

While the absence of persons can be profound, other forms of loss are equally powerful and significant. In "Mourning and Melancholia," Freud writes: "Mourning is regularly the reaction to the loss of a loved person, or to the loss of some abstraction which has taken the place of one, such as one's country, liberty, an ideal, and so on" (243). Undoubtedly, abstractions such as home, country, liberty, as well as promises and hopes, honour and justice, are desired, lost, and mourned in *Fair Liberty's Call*. In fact, often the loss of a beloved person and the loss of an abstraction are intertwined. For example, for the Roberts family, the loss of home and country (real and ideal) cannot be dissociated from the loss of family members Richard, Edward, and Emily.

Freud's definition of mourning emphasizes the internal mental state of an individual. However, there is a more public facet to mourning, in which it is commonly understood as the outward *expression* of grief and loss and associated with customary ceremonies, rituals, dress, and behaviour. As such, there are elements of the social and the performative in mourning, including performers, performance spaces and contexts, conventions, standards, and audiences. There is also an ambivalent duality associated with the mourner. As Gail Holst-Warhaft notes, on an individual level, bereavement often places the mourner in a vulnerable emotional and psychological state. However, on the collective level, the outward expression of bereavement can unite a community into concerted political action or chaotic unrest (*Cue* 2). Pollock's account of her mother's funeral explicitly highlights her awareness of the vulnerable and performative aspects of mourning:

> Then came the funeral: My father was weeping, my brother was weeping, my grandmother – who didn't forgive my father for years; she was convinced it was all his fault – was weeping. It was the most hysterically *embarrassing* event I had ever known. I said to myself, "I won't cry in front of all these people if it kills me, I won't show my grief before this

audience," the people who had packed the church. (qtd. in Hofsess 52, emphasis in original)

Her description of being seen by an "audience" and her judgement of her family's weeping as "embarrassing" reflect an awareness of mourning as a performance. In addition, her refusal to cry and to show her grief to those present suggests a sense of her emotional vulnerability and an attempt to protect herself.

While the living in Pollock's drama struggle with their grief and the process of mourning itself, they do not always act solely as independent agents. The dead themselves seem to require actions of those who remain. In the poignant words of Annie Roberts, "Sometimes I feel his name fillin' my head and pressin' hard on my lips to be spoke" (75). Here, Annie is referring to Major John Andre, the British spy she betrayed to the Rebels, but her words apply equally to the other dead and other mourners in the play. And while the dead place demands on the living, so too do the living "press" upon the dead, the absent, the past, choosing whether or not to speak their names and tell their stories. And if so, how? To whom? When? Where? Which stories?

While *Fair Liberty's Call* is about beginnings – *"a country comin' into bein'"* (20) – as Eddie, Annie, and Joan tell us in the verbal montage at the start of the drama, it is also very much about endings and loss, the choices they necessitate, and the mourning they provoke. The play opens with a reunion of members of Tarleton's Loyalist Legion to participate in what Pollock's stage directions call a *"Remembrance Ritual"* (37) complete with *"totems"* (37), ceremonial objects, and memory aids – flags, dress, war trophies, music, song, and storytelling. The veterans celebrate their battle victories and mourn their dead comrades. The play also contains the remembrance of more particular deaths: the Roberts children (Richard, who died fighting for the Rebels; Edward, who fought for the Loyalists but committed suicide rather than return to battle; and Emily, who is supposed to have died of smallpox); the Rebel John Anderson's younger brother, killed at the battle of Waxhaws; Major Andre, the British spy caught and executed by the Rebels; the Legion's drummer boy Charlie Meyers, who died on the exodus ship to Nova Scotia; Frank Taylor, murdered in the forest just before the play opens; and the Aboriginal Dead, represented by the human bones Joan sees in the forest.[2]

Prior to the veterans' Remembrance Ritual, Pollock creates a context that allows an interpretation of *Fair Liberty's Call* in terms of loss and mourning on a broader symbolic basis. Her opening set description and stage directions state:

> *A bare stage, the floor of which radiates in a dark-hued swirl of colour, represents the "virgin" land.[2] Although this space appears empty and uncorrupted, it projects an aura of foreboding, a sense of the unseen. A subtle sound fills the space as if the air itself is vibrating just below the level of conscious hearing. There are several lightning-like flashes, each followed by a split second of darkness.* JOAN *and* ANNIE, *each carrying a large bundle of belongings, and* EDDIE, *carrying a long gun, appear at the edge of the stage. They are followed by* GEORGE, DANIEL, *the* MAJOR, *and* WULLIE. DANIEL *pulls a wagon, piled high with barrels, trunks and rough pieces of wood.* GEORGE *has a trunk lashed to his back, and carries a keg. The* MAJOR, DANIEL, *and* WULLIE *carry long guns.* JOAN, ANNIE *and* EDDIE *step further into the space.*
>
> *Following the lightning comes the sound of a rolling rumble of thunder, or of what might be thunder, for all sound is impressionistic, even surrealistic, rather than realistic.[3] (19)*

While the land is physically stationary and inert, Pollock's description, with its many verbs, is one of intense outward energy and activity. The solid and fluid, the seen and unseen, the heard and unheard, the dark and the light, coexist in this threatening, elemental space, which is empty and full, inert and alive. The characters, clearly on a journey, appear poised on *"the edge of the stage"* before *"step[ping] further into the*

KATHY K. Y. CHUNG

space." Here, Pollock has created an ambivalent and mysterious setting to frame her drama.

This nebulous space is not only a familiar representation of the past in the "mist of time," but following the ideas of Arnold van Gennep in *The Rites of Passage*, it is also the liminal, sacred, transitional space of loss and mourning. Gennep identifies three stages in the passage from one social status to another: separation, transition, and incorporation, each with its associated rites. He adds, "in certain ceremonial patterns where the transitional period is sufficiently elaborate to constitute an independent state, the arrangement is reduplicated" (11). Furthermore, he writes that mourning "is a transitional period for the survivors, and they enter it through rites of separation and emerge from it through rites of reintegration into society (rites of the lifting of mourning)" (147). In fact, Gennep envisions both survivors and deceased as embarking on parallel passages. Following a death, both groups separate from the world of the living and enter a transitional, liminal zone. If all goes well, after a period of time, the deceased continue onward to be incorporated into the world of the dead. The living survivors, in their mourning, also enter a transitional zone but, at the end of mourning, they return to the world of the living (147).

Gennep continues with a description of transitional or neutral spaces. He writes, "the neutral zones are ordinarily deserts, marshes, and most frequently virgin forests where everyone has full rights to travel and hunt" (18). In addition, Victor Turner observes that liminal or transitional people, without or between categories, are socially undefined or less well defined and thus are both vulnerable and powerful. They are vulnerable because they lack the rights and protections associated with any stable status or community; they are also powerful and dangerous because they are not bound by such rules or laws (27). In *Fair Liberty's Call*, Eddie/Emily and Joan are examples of such unbounded, vulnerable, yet powerful, individuals. They are also women who mourn the loss of loved ones and parts of their own identity.

The licence "to travel" certainly prevails in the "virgin forest" of *Fair Liberty's Call*.[4] The Roberts family and their guests, gathering for the Remembrance Ritual, all travel through the wilderness. The freedom to "hunt" also exists in the drama. Frank Taylor is ambushed and killed. Anderson arrives intent on killing the Loyalist responsible for his brother's death. Hearing a mysterious moaning cry, George prompts the men to move into the forest to stalk the wild cat he believes made the noise (40). Later, Eddie takes aim and fires her rifle at Major Williams (46).

This liminal freedom of movement, and of the exercise of power and violence, provides an additional perspective on the play's fascinating carnival and grotesque elements, which combine life and death. Rather than signs of madness, one can hear Joan's background muttering of "pink porker, pink, pink porker, pink porker" while she is "engaged in repetitive slicing of bread, cheese and sausage" (28–29) and her apparently incongruous but startling and powerful outburst during the Major's assault on Annie, "like a bullet-hole in his head, like a rope catchin' you under the chin, like a narrow ravine, a depression, a dip, like a Valley! Like saltwater runnin' out of the bay, like the tide rushin' in through the gorge!" (31), as eruptions of free speech, black humour, and liminal violence. The play's song and dance are also elements of the liminal. For example, Daniel sings to Annie (39); he improvises a dance and song to the English boots he took off a Rebel corpse (37, 39); and he dances with both the Major and with Annie (54–55).[5] In addition to revealing his clown-like and life-affirming character, his behaviour adds to the potential for unrest and disorder, which can be both destructive and productive. Indeed, Turner identifies the grotesque, play, and disorder with liminal space as the seedbed for positive change and cultural creativity (27–28), conditions to which the hopeful conclusion of the play aspires.

Pollock's New Brunswick forest is a liminal space of loss and mourning as well as change; it is a symbolic, psychological, and physical space, which the characters, mourners all, enter, inhabit, and pass through on a journey from one identity to another. Such formal elements resonate on symbolic and subliminal levels. They contribute to the depth and power of the drama and the "timeless[ness]" (287)

KATHY K. Y. CHUNG

which Grace finds on the thematic level. This interpretation of the landscape as the transitional zone of mourning in turn sheds new light on Pollock's depiction of Joan's changing physical relationship to the land. Initially, Joan describes the land where she encounters the red woman and the bones of the Aboriginal dead as unfamiliar and she leaves no mark upon it:

> When you stand there, you feel your feet restin' on top of the soil. You could slip. You could fall. Empty eye sockets catch your eye tellin' you somethin'. Your feet carry you back to the house but they leave no trace of your passing ... This isn't home. They aren't our Dead. (27)

Clearly Joan is sensitive to the cultural presence and entitlements of the Native peoples. Her words also provide a formulation of home related to familial loss: home is where your "Dead" are buried.

At the end of the drama, Joan completes her narrative of encounter with the red woman and of home:

> I feel my feet pressin' flat "gainst the surface of the soil now. I kneel readin' the contours of the skull and listenin' to the words spoke by the man with the missin' jawbone, and the caps of my knees make a small indentation in the dirt.
>
> [. . . . .]
>
> And the red woman with the baby on her back steps out from under the glade of trees and she holds out a bowl, she offers a bowl full of earth.
>
> [. . . . .]
>
> Eat, she says. Swallow.
>
> And I do. (79–80)

It is possible to attribute Joan's new ability to make an impression upon the land to her learned ability to read and to listen to the signs and words of Native culture and her reception of the red woman's gift. But Pollock's provocative image is reminiscent of Gennep's comment regarding ceremonies in which an individual is carried above the ground by others. Such practices, he claims, are also transition rites.[6] Accordingly, Joan's passage leaves no traces on the ground because, as a mourner grieving the loss of home and her children, she inhabits a transitional zone removed from the world of the living, the earth. Her feet and knees later pressing upon the soil and leaving a mark suggest that she has been able to express her loss sufficiently to Anderson and her family to enable her to leave the liminal zone and be reincorporated into the world of the living.

Finally, Joan's enactment of the red woman's instruction to eat the soil is also a ritual act of incorporation, the stage which follows transition and completes the passage from one state to another. Incorporation occurs on two levels: between Joan and the land, and between Joan and the red woman. In being ingested, the earth is literally incorporated into Joan; the land and Joan become one body. In addition, sharing a meal is also a rite of incorporation, and the symbolic significance of the soil as food relates to the ethos of gifts and their circulation. Lewis Hyde points out that food is a nourishing but perishable gift that cannot be hoarded (8).[7] Hence, the red woman's gesture signals to Joan the nature of the relationship she intends – between the two women, between the women and the land, and, by extension, between the two cultures and their relationship to the land.[8]

However, the fulfillment of mourning is not easily achieved by Joan or other characters in *Fair Liberty's Call*. I see at least two obstacles to the mourning process in the play: they are flaws in the act of remembering and disenfranchised grief. Freud and subsequent researchers identify a meticulous testing of every memory related to the lost object as a major part of mourning. By comparison, then, the Loyalist veterans' determined refusal to remember and acknowledge their war crimes, combined with their focus exclusively on their heroism and victories, are forms of incomplete mourning. For example, during the Remembrance Ritual, Eddie and Anderson remind the veterans of "Tarleton's quarters," their dishonourable behaviour of continuing to kill Rebel soldiers after their cries of surrender at the battle of Waxhaws. Daniel's repeated refusal to talk about Waxhaws and Eddie's grim acknowledgement of its brutality (38–39) demonstrate differing responses in Tarleton's Legion to the loss of their sense of self and purpose as purely honourable, heroic, and just.

Another example of a refusal to remember and to mourn lies in George Roberts' willed forgetfulness in disowning his elder son, Richard, who chose to join the Rebels. George insists, "I had no son with the Rebels! I cut that boy out of my heart" (34). He also prevents Joan from speaking about the loss of their sons, of Emily, and their home in Boston (23–24). In contrast, Joan and Annie defy George's will by speaking of Richard to John Anderson. From this perspective, Joan, Annie, and Eddie, who attempt to remember more fully by acknowledging all their actions, heroic and shameful, and all their dead (sons and brothers, comrades and enemies), are the more successful and healthy mourners in the drama.

In addition, Kenneth Doka's discussion of disenfranchised grief highlights other social dimensions to mourning relevant to Pollock's work. Doka defines disenfranchised grief as occurring when "a person experiences a sense of loss but does not have a socially recognized right, role, or capacity to grieve" (3). This concept points out that societies have norms which try "to specify who, when, where, how long, and for whom people should grieve" (4), standards which may differ from an individual's actual experience. Doka gives three possible reasons for disenfranchised grief: the *relationship* is not socially recognized (for example, non-kin or non-traditional relationships); the *loss* is not recognized (for example, the death of a pet or criminal); or the *griever* is not recognized (as capable of grief, such as the very young or the mentally ill) (5–6). Jeffrey Kauffman notes that "Community is the natural support network in which one's basic sense of *identity* and *belongingness* are realized . . . Communities that sanction and support the grief of their members, that have norms that are flexibly responsive to the needs of their members by recognising and sanctioning the suffering that exists within the community – these are sane and healing communities [emphasis in original]" (29).

The best example of a character experiencing disenfranchised grief is Joan, who encounters social obstacles in mourning the loss of her children. Edward's desertion from the Loyalist forces and his suicide are socially shameful acts. Therefore, from the perspective of Joan's Loyalists community, his death does not merit mourning. In addition, due to the family's deception and replacement of Edward by Emily, she cannot even publicly acknowledge, much less mourn, his death. Joan's loss of Richard is another example of disenfranchised grief. Because Richard chose to join the Rebels, the Loyalists see him as an enemy traitor, and his death, like Edward's, as not meriting mourning; thus her loss is not recognized as significant. In addition, how can she adequately mourn for a son her husband publicly disowned? In this case, Richard, her husband, does not recognize her relationship to Richard as his mother. Finally, Joan also struggles with mourning the loss of Emily, who is, in Eddie's words, "changed" (78) and, in the minds of her community, deceased. Of course, all the living members of the Roberts family must, to a degree, experience any grief they may feel over the loss of Edward, Richard, and Emily as disenfranchised by their Loyalist community. It is through the course of the drama that their loss and grief find adequate expression and acknowledgement.

Another common loss experienced by the community in *Fair Liberty's Call* is the loss of faith in an ideal, which is both an abstraction and a defining component of the characters' self-conceptions. For example, Eddie Roberts loses faith in her former idealism and moral identity, as well as in the political honesty of her Loyalist leaders and her father. She acknowledges that she has murdered in battle, having disregarded calls of surrender at the battle of Waxhaws, and that she is capable of murder and deceit in civil society to achieve her goals. She killed Frank Taylor to protect Wullie's freedom and she is prepared to "remove" (77), in other words "to kill," Major Williams. There are few

KATHY K. Y. CHUNG

within Eddie's community who would recognize and sanction her losses and any sense of grief she may have. The Major refuses to consider Tarleton's quarters as dishonourable; Daniel, overwhelmed with guilt, refuses to remember Waxhaws at all; Eddie's civilian father is unaware of the real brutalities of war; and his/her mother vehemently calls her a "murderer" (25), linking her actions to her dead brothers and the Rebel dead. Even the peripheral characters, such as Wullie and the red woman, must contend with losses; for example, their freedom and equity are threatened by the white community's racism. Wullie, in his relationship with Eddie, and the red woman in her exchange with Joan, both demonstrate the willingness to risk the loss, or another loss, of their faith and trust in the hope of creating the "better world" (75) Annie wishes for them all.

Despite the many obstacles, mourning does eventually take place, but there are clear differences in the form and the context in which it occurs. The Loyalist veterans perform an elaborate ritual of remembrance with memorial objects and ceremonies to help verify and reinforce their identity as brave soldiers and loyal citizens. However, it is the deeds and character of the group, Tarleton's Legion, which dominate over those of the individual. In fact, when recollections of individuals do surface, such as the description of Frank Taylor's duplicity or Charlie Meyers' un-heroic death (38–39), they disrupt the ritual and fracture the unity of the group. In contrast, the women, Joan and Annie, remember their war dead without props or ceremony, in relative privacy. Their personal stories of Edward, Richard, and John Andre, confided quietly to John Anderson, focus not on heroism and glory but on loss, suffering, guilt, and death.

This contrast between the mourning practices of the veterans and the women can be considered within two separate but related frameworks: gender and socio-political differences in mourning forms. Holst-Warhaft argues that men and women mourn differently, and that in traditional cultures it was women who composed and performed laments.[9] Focussing on Western, particularly Greek, development, she argues that the power of women's funeral laments is dangerous to the city or state because it "can be used as a means of inciting an uncontrolled sequence of reciprocal violence (a potential which the state may conceivably co-opt to its own advantage). Secondly, by focusing as it does on mourning and loss rather than praise of the dead, it denies the value of death for the community or state, making it difficult for authorities to recruit an obedient army" (*Dangerous* 3). She argues that women's lament as a public expression of grief was gradually replaced by men's funeral oration. In the case of the war dead, this meant that a mourning whose tone commonly stresses "pain, loss, emotions, resulting economic and social hardship" was replaced by one that "makes a virtue of death, provided it is death in the service of the state" (*Dangerous* 5). The forms of mourning performed by the Loyalist veterans and by Joan and Annie reflect the masculine and feminine modes of mourning Holst-Warhaft describes. The veterans' Remembrance Ritual focuses on funeral orations, and tales of heroism and fortitude, which make death in the service of the Loyalist cause a virtue, while the tone of the women's mourning is a more passionate expression of grief that focuses on loss, pain, and hardship.

While the frame of gender is useful, it is worth pointing out that Pollock's work has always courted a feminist perspective while resisting any absolute placement within its boundaries. John Bodnar offers a socio-political approach to mourning that is different from, but complements that of, a gender perspective. Bodnar identifies an "official" and a "vernacular" mode of mourning in the realm of public memory, modes which represent the conflict between national and personal interests. He characterizes official culture as that sanctioned and promoted by "political and cultural leaders" interested in "social unity, the continuity of existing institutions, and loyalty to the status quo" (75). Bodnar states that official culture presents "reality in ideal rather than complex or ambiguous terms" and "desires to present the past on an abstract basis of timelessness and sacredness." Thus, official commemorations speak "the ideal language of patriotism rather than . . . the real language of grief and sorrow" (75). Alternatively, vernacular culture is associated with groups within a whole and "reality derived from first-hand experience in small-scale communities rather than the 'imagined communities' of a large nation" (75). It tends to express what "social reality feels like rather than what it should be like," and its commemoration tends toward an expression of loss and suffering (75). Bodnar also notes that individuals can participate in both official and vernacular cultures.

Clearly, the Remembrance Ritual of Tarleton's Loyalist Legion, with its focus on and support of nationalist group identity, military valour, and glorious sacrifice, exemplifies official culture. Likewise, the women's stories of familial loss, which focus on individual deaths, personal relationships, and personal suffering, express vernacular culture. Thus, with Bodnar's framework in mind, we can see that Joan's and Annie's modes of mourning are marginalised because they are vernacular in addition to being feminine. Bodnar's formulation also allows us to better understand actions that a strictly gendered typography might overlook, such as the conflict between Daniel and the Major during the veterans' Remembrance Ritual over remembering Charlie Meyers (53–54).

Both official and vernacular communities make moral and political judgements about who is worthy of being remembered and mourned. Major Williams, the chief representative of official culture, excludes Charlie Meyers from remembrance because he did not die heroically in battle, but of illness and starvation following the Loyalist defeat. For Daniel, who participates in both communities, Charlie has a personal significance; the boy's integrity and bravery touched him. Daniel tells the Major: "He was a good boy and would have been . . . an asset! to this god forsaken place . . . had he got here!" (54). Charlie was "a good boy" who embodied a promise of the future and he died in Daniel's arms. Pollock shows Daniel struggling to find a testimony that would give the boy meaning in the language of official culture and stumbling on the objectifying, legal, and financial term "asset."

Interestingly, while Daniel seeks the participation and support of Eddie to tell the story of Charlie's death, she remains silent, reluctant to participate fully in the men's Remembrance Ritual and unable to publicly join in the women's more feminine and vernacular mourning.[10] It is Annie who answers him in a shared act of narration and testimony, which is both a means of community building and a validation of grief. In fact, the call and response, question and answer structure of their exchange exemplifies antiphony, which Susan Letzler Cole identifies as a ritual feature of mourning. Cole writes that "antiphony, dialogue, refrain – some of the oldest features of Greek lament – survive in the modern Greek *moirológia*" (22). Margaret Alexiou explains this is "because antiphony is still imbedded in the ritual performance, with more than one group of mourners, sometimes representing the living and the dead and singing in response to each other" (qtd. in Cole 22). In fact, Pollock uses this vocal technique near the start of the drama in a scene where Joan, with Annie's assistance, describes Edward's suicide (23–24). The women's question and answer recitation publicly establishes and validates Joan's loss of Edward and her reality in an act of ritualistic communal storytelling.

We therefore come full circle to the formal structures and ritual symbolism of mourning. Despite attempts at silence and forgetfulness, the secrets and losses of the community in *Fair Liberty's Call* are eventually revealed, remembered, and recognized, as Joan describes Edward's suicide, Emily's disguise, and Richard's departure. While Daniel insists that he does not want to remember Waxhaws and Tarleton's quarter, the men discuss both events. They also expose Frank Taylor's brutality in battle and his greed, deception, and racism in civilian life. Anderson reveals his Rebel identity and speaks of his brother's death. Annie recounts the personal price she paid to visit Richard in the prison ship and her betrayal of "Sweet Major Andre." Eddie admits to murdering Frank Taylor and voices her angry loss of faith in the honesty of her leaders. George finally acknowledges his rejection of Richard and coercion of Edward and Emily. Remembrances of love and bravery, as well as expressions of shame, pain, loss, and grief – in other words, a more complete mourning, both individual and communal – take place.

Pollock has written a symbolic play about national origins that is hopeful, yet permeated with loss, remembrance, and mourning. This combination of national beginnings with loss resonates with Ernest Renan's observations about nations and nationalism. He states that "historical enquiry brings to light deeds of violence which took place at the origin of all political formations, even of those whose consequences have been altogether beneficial. Unity is always effected by means of brutality" (11). In addition, "the essence of a nation is that all individuals have many things in common, and also that they have forgotten many things" (11). He also claims that "suffering in common unifies more than joy does. Where national memories are concerned, griefs are of more value than triumphs, for they impose duties, and require a common effort" (19). Thus, violence, loss, and suffering often accompany the beginning of a new country, as they do the passage from one social state to another.

In *Fair Liberty's Call*, Pollock highlights the historic brutality and injustices at the origins of Canada. She alerts us to our choices and our responsibilities, past, present, and future, and asks which common things we – as individuals, communities, and as a nation – will choose to keep in remembrance and mourn and which we will choose to forget. In addition, recalling the words of Kauffman, we can see that Pollock also suggests that the health and sanity of a community and a nation are dependent not only on its wealth and power, but also on its responsiveness to the needs of all its members, including the recognition and support of their losses and suffering. In this sense, while some scholars characterize Joan as a mother driven insane by grief,[11] it is equally possible to see her behaviour as the result not of grief, but of an unhealthy community that refuses to recognise the losses and permit the mourning of all its members.

Finally, while Renan does not elaborate on what "duties" and "common effort" grief imposes, Pollock dramatizes several possibilities. Anderson's desire for revenge, George's rejection of Richard, the Roberts's concealment of Edward's death, and the Legion's "disowning" of Tarleton's quarter exemplify destructive "duties" and "common efforts," as well as failures in mourning. Alternatively, Annie provides a more hopeful and compelling response. Near the end of the drama, she reveals to Anderson that she betrayed the British spy John Andre, leading to his capture and execution by the Rebels, and withheld from the British forces the plans to West Point he had given her for safe-keeping. Anderson tells her the plans were unimportant.

> ANDERSON: They [the plans] wouldn't have made any difference to the war.

> ANNIE: Maybe they would. Maybe they wouldn't. I know it changes nothin' for Richard. Or Edward. Sweet Major Andre. I wonder if he thought of me at the end . . . Sometimes I feel his name fillin' my head and pressin' hard on my lips to be spoke . . . There's nothin' I can do for him now. There's nothin' I can do to put paid to my brothers or you to yours. We oughta be lookin' to a better world for our children. That's the only way to serve our brothers. (75)

Here, then, in its final articulation in *Fair Liberty's Call* – an exchange between two people grieving the destructions of war, the loss of home, and the deaths of their siblings – mourning encompasses the individual and the communal, private emotions and public actions; it becomes an obligation to create "a better world for our children," a service to the past, the present, and the future.

NOTES

1   Throughout this paper, unless where noted, my quotations of *Fair Liberty's Call* come from the 1995 publication. The 2006 publication contains revisions, which I point out when they are relevant. I chose the original text because it contains elements that contribute to the play's symbolic depth. I would argue that the omission of some of these elements in the later text cloaks one source of the power and resonance in the drama. The earlier text allows us to see more clearly what is invisible, but no less present, in the later version.

2   The reference to the land as *"virgin"* is absent from the 2006 play text, although the direction, at the end of the drama, that Eddie and Wullie return *"the stage to some semblance of its virgin state at the beginning of the play"* (78), remains the same in both texts.

3   Also absent in the 2006 version are the *"lightning-like flashes"* and the sound of *"a rolling rumble of thunder, or of what might be thunder . . . impressionistic, even surrealistic, rather than realistic."* These elements are replaced by the sounds of *"a horrific battle, gunfire and cannon, men yelling encouragement and despair mixed with the cry of the wounded and the thunder and scream of horses"* (365). These changes reduce the abstract and ambiguous feel of the opening and focus more on the specific horrors of war and the recent past.

4   Pollock herself used the term *"'virgin' land"* (19) in her 1995 set description.

5   The juxtaposition of Annie (life) with the boots (death) is also a liminal dissolution of categories.

6   Gennep writes that such actions are "intended to show that at the moment in question the individual does not belong either to the sacred or to the profane world; or, if he does belong to one of the two, it is desired that he be properly reincorporated into the other, and he is therefore isolated and maintained in an intermediate position, held between heaven and earth, just as the deceased on his bier or in his temporary coffin is suspended between life and death" (186).

7   Hyde writes, "A gift that cannot move loses its gift properties . . . Another way to describe the motion of the gift is to say that a gift must always be used up, consumed, eaten. *The gift is property that perishes* . . . Food is one of the most common images for the gift because it is so obviously consumed. Even when the gift is not food, when it is something we would think of as a durable good, it is often referred to as a thing to be eaten [emphasis in original]" (8).

8   Zimmerman suggests an alternate but complementary reading in which Joan's words "I do" echo those spoken in a marriage ceremony, thereby signifying a union between Joan and her new country (158).

9   While laments are mainly sung for the dead, Holst-Warhaft notes that they are also composed for other forms of departure and loss such as emigration and marriage (where women leave one family for another [1]).

10   Eddie stays on the periphery of both forms of recollection and mourning. She helps construct the set for the Remembrance Ritual but does not participate in the military storytelling. She speaks to Anderson of a boy with the Loyalist Rangers who went home after Cherry Hill and killed himself; obviously a reference to her brother Edward, but she does not identify him as such (41). In the second half of the drama, Eddie joins the men in their deliberations rather than her mother and sister in their sharing of familial loss with Anderson.

11   For example, Walker describes Joan as "a middle-aged woman who, through grief and despair, has become mentally disordered" (191) and Zimmerman describes her as "half-crazed by grief" (157).

Works Cited

Bodnar, John. "Public Memory in an American City: Commemoration in Cleveland." *Commemorations: The Politics of National Identity*. Ed. John R. Gillis. Princeton, NJ: Princeton UP, 1994. 74–89. Print.

Boss, Pauline. *Ambiguous Loss: Learning to Live with Unresolved Grief*. Cambridge, MA: Harvard UP, 1999. Print.

Cole, Susan Letzler. *The Absent One: Mourning Ritual, Tragedy, and the Performance of Ambivalence*. University Park: Pennsylvania State UP, 1985. Print.

Doka, Kenneth J. "Disenfranchised Grief." *Disenfranchised Grief: Recognizing Hidden Sorrow*. Ed. Kenneth J. Doka. Lexington, MA: Lexington Books–D.C. Heath, 1989. 3–11. Print.

Freud, Sigmund. "Mourning and Melancholia." *On the History of the Psycho-Analytic Movement, Papers on Metapsychology and Other Works*. Gen. ed. James Strachey et al. Vol. 14. *The Standard Edition of the Complete Psychological Works of Sigmund Freud*. London: Hogarth Press and the Institute of Psycho-Analysis, 1981. 237–58. Print.

Gennep, Arnold van. *The Rites of Passage*. Trans. Monika B. Vizedom and Gabrielle L. Caffee. Chicago: U of Chicago P, 1960. Print.

Grace, Sherrill. *Making Theatre: A Life of Sharon Pollock*. Vancouver: Talonbooks, 2008. Print.

Hofsess, John. "Sticking Together . . ." *Homemaker's Magazine* 15.2 (1980): 41–44, 48–49, 52, 54, 58, 60. Print.

Holst-Warhaft, Gail. *The Cue for Passion: Grief and Its Political Uses*. Cambridge, MA: Harvard UP, 2000. Print.

———. *Dangerous Voices: Women's Laments and Greek Literature*. London: Routledge, 1992. Print.

Hyde, Lewis. *The Gift. Imagination and the Erotic Life of Property*. New York: Vintage–Random House, 1983. Print.

Kauffman, Jeffrey. "Intrapsychic Dimensions of Disenfranchised Grief." *Disenfranchised Grief: Recognizing Hidden Sorrow*. Ed. Kenneth J. Doka. Lexington, MA: Lexington Books–D.C. Heath, 1989. 25–29. Print.

Pollock, Sharon. *Fair Liberty's Call*. Toronto: Coach House, 1995. Print.

———. "Fair Liberty's Call." *Sharon Pollock: Collected Plays*. Vol. 2. Ed. Cynthia Zimmerman. Toronto: Playwrights Canada P, 2006. 359–418. Print.

Renan, Ernest. "What Is a Nation?" Trans. Martin Thom. *Nation and Narration*. Ed. Homi K. Bhabha. London: Routledge, 1995. 8–22. Print.

Turner, Victor. *From Ritual to Theatre: The Human Seriousness of Play*. New York: Performing Arts Journal Publications, 1982. Print.

Walker, Craig Stewart. *The Buried Astrolabe: Canadian Dramatic Imagination*. Montreal: McGill-Queen's UP, 2001. Print.

Zimmerman, Cynthia. "Sharon Pollock: Transfiguring the Maternal." *Theatre Research in Canada/Recherches théâtrales au Canada* 22.2 (2001): 151–60. Print.

Questions of Collective Responsibility in Sharon Pollock's *Man Out of Joint*

Tanya Schaap

> *The artist constantly lives in such a state of ambiguity,*
> *incapable of negating the real and yet eternally bound to*
> *question it in its eternally unfinished aspects.*

> —ALBERT CAMUS, CREATE DANGEROUSLY

In *The Political Unconscious,* Marxist literary theorist Fredric Jameson accredits the political interpretation of literary texts "not as some supplementary method . . . but rather as the absolute horizon of all reading and all interpretation" (17). There is no working distinction for Jameson between political and apolitical literary texts; explicitly or symbolically, all texts operate as doctrines of political consciousness. For Jameson, mysteries of our cultural past "can recover their original urgency for us only if they are retold within the unity of a single great collective story; only if, in however disguised or symbolic a form, they are seen as sharing a single fundamental theme" (19). In such a context, the process of working through certain historical and cultural events – that is, the demystification, reconsideration, and re-evaluation of events that confound or confuse a social collective – demands a representation of those events within the confines of a single collective narrative form. Based on her extensive body of work over the last forty years that repeatedly engages with the political and the historical, playwright Sharon Pollock must agree.

In many of her plays, such as *Walsh* (1973), which examines the relationship between Sioux Chief Sitting Bull and James Walsh of the North West Mounted Police; *The Komagata Maru Incident* (1976), which dramatizes the plight of 376 British subjects aboard a Japanese steamship denied access into Canada in 1914 due to their Asian descent; *One Tiger to a Hill* (1980), which dramatizes a 1975 hostage taking at a British Columbian prison; *Fair Liberty's Call* (1993), which recounts the story of a Loyalist family in 1785 fleeing from Boston to New Brunswick during the American Revolution; and most recently *Man Out of Joint* (2007), a drama that examines the controversy over 9/11 conspiracy theories and the prisoner abuse at Guantanamo Bay, Pollock consistently weaves the political consciousness of a particular historical moment into a single great collective story. As theatre critic Jeff Kubik asserts, Pollock is an "agitator in her own right," politically, socially, and artistically engaged with the notorious, the controversial, and the politically charged (n.p.).

In *Man Out of Joint*, Pollock chronicles the detainee abuse at Guantanamo Bay as well as the controversies surrounding 9/11 conspiracy theories, which are based on the case of Delmart Vreeland, a man who claims to have warned the Canadian embassy of possible attacks on New York City and the Pentagon. Pollock stages aspects of the torture and abuse as a kind of framework, or emblematic context, for the central story line of the play's protagonist, Toronto lawyer Joel Gianelli, a character based on Rocco Galati, Vreeland's real-life lawyer. Pollock is careful, however, to pay attention to the ways in which these events should be represented, not as mere subject matter, or as a retracing of the events as they happened, but rather as narratives that go beyond simple storytelling, and which raise questions regarding collective responsibility and cultural memory. In an interview with Kubik, Pollock states, "I don't want to write a tract, I want to tell a story . . . And inherent in the story some questions arise, and to me that's politics in theatre. I'm not interested in those opinion pieces, which tend to be more about the person writing the piece than the opinion, so I can't imagine doing anything except theatre in terms of that politic" (Kubik n.p.). In *Man Out of Joint*, Pollock seeks to expand audience awareness by directing their attention to the experience of various victims, witnesses, bystanders, and perpetrators in the aftermath of the attacks on 11 September 2001, and the years of reported abuse at Guantanamo Bay that followed. On the surface, *Man Out of Joint* functions as an artistic representation of the disturbing and controversial incidents at Guantanamo Bay. On a deeper level, however, the play challenges audiences to question their collective responsibility to incidents such as (but not limited to) the torture and abuse of detainees at Guantanamo Bay. I am concerned here with the ways in which *Man Out of Joint* invites audience members to contemplate their collective response in the context of historically painful and culturally discomforting incidents such as public reports of the detainee abuse at Guantanamo Bay. This essay will examine the play through a theory of trauma – specifically, the ways in which Pollock's play operates as a trauma narrative. A consideration of *Man Out of Joint* in this context allows for a serious reflection on the ways in which Pollock aims to awaken and provoke our collective memory of such incidents. In staging these disturbing events, Pollock strives to bear witness to those that suffer, to avert the process of social indifference, and to persuade audiences to consider their own culpability.

As Donna Coates explains, *Man Out of Joint* stemmed from Pollock's intense interest in the reports of detainee abuse at Guantanamo Bay that were released by the American Center for Constitutional Rights (CCR), and which eventually led her to the lawyer for the Toronto terror suspects, Rocco Galati (254). Much of the play's dialogue is taken from actual conversations with detainees in the CCR report (Kubik n.p.). In this way, Pollock's play might be read as docudrama or verbatim theatre, theatre that takes as its subject matter actual historical events, often transcribed word for word from archival documents. Contemporary theatre critics Will Hammond and Dan Steward explain that in verbatim theatre, the playwright takes the words of real people as they are recorded in an interview or archival document, and edits, arranges, and recontextualizes them for dramatic presentation (9). For Pollock, this meant resourcing the actual reports from the detainment of prisoners at Guantanamo Bay (specifically the case of Omar Khadr, the fifteen-year-old Canadian detainee charged with murdering American combat medic Christopher Speer in Afghanistan in 2002), as well as the documented interviews with Toronto lawyer, Rocco Galati, on whom the lead character Joel is based.[1] According to Hammond and Steward, there is a claim in verbatim theatre for veracity and authenticity: "When this claim is made, theatre and journalism overlap . . . we turn to verbatim theatre because we feel that it is somehow better suited to the task of dealing with serious subject matter" (10–11). Pollock reminds us that it is never her intention to create biography, docudrama, or documentary: "I think of biography as an aspect of my research, a means to some other end in which the life and times provides bits or chunks of raw material" ("Playwright" 297). The verbatim method allows Pollock to use the documentary material as a springboard from which to explore the larger political and cultural dilemmas, while still remaining tethered to the actual events around which the play is written.

I raise these issues of genre and classification to suggest that *Man Out of Joint* is docudrama, or verbatim theatre, but with a difference. Not only does Pollock draw from actual reports regarding detainee abuse at Guantanamo Bay, she also includes highly contested, controversial information relating to 9/11 conspiracy theories. Throughout the play, Joel continually questions the legitimacy of certain 9/11 reports that have come to his attention through his dealings with his client, Ed Leland. After Joel interviews Ed, the stage directions read:

TANYA SCHAAP

> Sound of a click. "QUESTIONS SURROUNDING 9/11
> (www.whatreallyhappened.com)" bleed up on the cyc. They roll
> fairly quickly, are not intended to be read. They might begin
> with "Did Delmart Vreeland warn Canadian Intelligence in
> August 2001 about possible terrorist attacks on New York and
> the Pentagon?" (283)

Pollock deliberately blends real names and news stories into the fiction of her play in order to blur the distinction between truth and fiction. The "facts" of this play, with regards to existing 9/11 conspiracy theories, may be fiction; the actual information she uses in the play is both real and imaginary, depending on whom you talk to, and depending on whom you believe. In using verbatim techniques in a play of this sort, which takes as its principal subject matter a topic that is not only highly controversial but also highly contested for its truthfulness, Pollock raises more questions than she answers, which is, I would argue, her overriding intention.

In *Trauma and Survival in Contemporary Fiction*, Laurie Vickroy explores the ways in which contemporary fiction narratives represent trauma, defined in her words as "a response to events so overwhelmingly intense that they impair normal emotional and cognitive responses and bring lasting psychological disruption" (ix). For the abused and tortured detainees, their experiences at Guantanamo Bay were psychologically and physically traumatic. As sociologist Sherene Razack explains,

> Shortly after 9/11, men and some children rounded
> up from the villages and battlefields of Afghanistan were
> herded into shipping containers . . . Many died . . . Those
> who survived typically were taken to prisons at Bagram
> and Kandahar, Afghanistan . . . or to the U.S. base at
> Guantanamo, Cuba, where they were detained on the basis
> that the president, as the commander-in-chief, possessed the
> unilateral authority to arrest and detain anyone. Detainees

were declared "enemy combatants," a designation that left them in a no man's land of rights, neither prisoners of war nor criminals. (29)

Convicted of no crime, many of the detainees were detained with an "unquestioned absence of evidence," on the basis that they were "'Islamic terrorists,' men who come from a culture in which religion, not rationality, produces individuals with an *inherent* capacity for violence" (Razak 29). The CCR reports "accounts of torture and cruel, inhuman, and degrading treatment," based upon detainee statements, public unclassified sources, and government documents released through a Freedom of Information Act (CCR 2) request.

In June 2008, CBC News published an interview between the Associated Press and Dr. Allen Keller, one of the doctors who conducted medical and psychological tests on some of the (now-released) detainees at Abu Ghraib and Guantanamo Bay. Keller claims: "We found clear physical and psychological evidence of torture and abuse, often causing lasting suffering" ("Guantanamo"). He goes on to report that "the treatment the detainees reported were 'eerily familiar' to stories from other torture survivors around the world. He said the sexual humiliation of the prisoners was often the most traumatic experience." The medical and psychological evidence obtained through examinations of the detainees, most of whom have since been released, suggest that due to the intensive abuse and torture to which they were subjected, many of these individuals suffer from post-traumatic stress disorder.

Thus, Pollock's staging of the abuse experienced at Guantanamo Bay in *Man Out of Joint*, which draws attention both literally (through the re-enactment of the abuse) and symbolically (through the use of sound, light, and props) to the abuse of power that occurred at the Cuban prison, can be classified as a trauma narrative. Within the context of trauma theory, we might consider the various ways in which Pollock's play effectively functions as trauma fiction, that is, as Vickroy puts it, how it "poses a number of thought-provoking questions and dilemmas for writers and readers, ranging from the potentially ethical function of literature [or in this case, theatre], to reconsidering our cultural assumptions about identity, relationality, and intentionality" (ix). Not only does Pollock's play personalize the experience of detainees at Guantanamo Bay, and in so doing invite audiences to embrace a more meaningful connection with victims, but it also challenges dominant ideologies and certain socio-political assumptions that may have led to the abuse of power.

Through the use of sound, "*a loud cacophony of disorienting music and sound,*" the onstage presence of hooded, shackled detainees in those now-identifiable orange jumpsuits, strobe lights, brief blasts of sound, and a voice-over asserting: "This place is a place beyond the law . . . In this place, we are the law," Pollock begins by positioning her play within a disorienting context of torture and abuse (259–60). This stylistic approach corresponds with the implicit aesthetic of trauma narratives. As trauma theorist Roger Luckhurst suggests, "Because a traumatic event confounds narrative knowledge, the . . . narrative form . . . must acknowledge this in different kinds of temporal disruption. . . . Disorders of emplotment are read as mimicking the traumatic effect" (88). In other words, trauma narratives defy logical, progressive, conventional narrative technique. Instead, they embrace avant-garde and experimental techniques in their attempt to mimic or mirror the effects of trauma; as a trauma narrative, the play exposes and illuminates the traumatic experience of the victims of torture and abuse at Guantanamo Bay through artistic inventiveness and non-linear narrative sequencing. In order to mirror the disorienting psychological takeover of the detainees, Pollock abandons conventional storytelling, and disorients her audience by mimicking the uncertain rhythms and processes of traumatic experience.

This technique of disorientation or rhythm of uncertainty, as I paradoxically call it, is woven throughout the play even while the chief narrative thread, the story of Joel Gianelli, and the most conventional part of the play, is developed. Examples of this rhythm of uncertainty include the voice of "K," described in the list of characters as "*a voice-over with power and formality,"* who continually interrupts and disrupts dialogue between characters; Scrolls of Bill C-36, the Anti-Terrorism Act, which appear periodically up on the CYC; murmuring voices, incoherent dialogue, and disorienting sounds in the background; the ghost-like presence of Joel's deceased father, Dominic Gianelli, who often makes an appearance in the middle of conversations between principal characters; soldiers who appear in the background assaulting the detainees; and the dissociative aspect of Joel's character, who often appears onstage as "Joe," played by a different actor. In the staging notes, directors are told that all the characters, whether or not they are directly involved in the scene, *"are always present, perhaps in shadows or 'out of focus' although they remain engaged by what transpires and may subtly react to it"* (258). In other words, there is a sense of interconnectedness between all that goes on in the play in spite of the multiple "storylines" operating independently. On their own, some of these disorienting techniques, such as the presence of a ghost (Dominic) and the twinning or splitting of Joe/Joel's character, render *Man Out of Joint* a paradigmatic trauma narrative. Taken together, however, these aspects point to a definitive rhythm of uncertainty in the play, what Luckhurst calls the "disarticulation of linear narrative" (91) and what Toni Morrison describes as "compelling confusion," a narrative technique she employs in her novel, *Beloved*, a paradigmatic trauma narrative (qtd. in Luckhurst 90).

While the principal trauma in question, and the one by which Pollock seems most disturbed, is the torture and abuse of detainees at Guantanamo Bay, other traumatic (or at least psychologically and emotionally disturbing) incidents are layered throughout the play. Through the development of the character Dominic, for example, Pollock illuminates the (often-unheard-of) internment of Italians in Canada in the 1940s, in which over 600 Italian-Canadians were interned across the country as soon as Mussolini joined forces with Nazi Germany. As Dominic says: "'Defence of Canada Regulations,' that is how they can do it. The Ottawa man, the big one. June 1940. Before he opens his mouth, we are citizens. He speaks a few words. He closes his mouth.

Now we are enemy alien" (288). Dominic recalls how, in a matter of moments and with only a few government-sanctioned declarations, his entire identity shifts. Pollock is, of course, drawing a parallel between the abuse of power at Guantanamo Bay and the prejudice, discriminatory actions and declarations of the Canadian government during World War II; Canadians are also guilty of abuse and bigotry. She is also creating a conjunction between those victimized by socio-political biases and intense abuses of authority. A more subtle parallel, however, could involve her questions around collective responsibility and social responses. We might ask, how did Canadians respond to the Italian (not to mention the Japanese) internment during World War II? Does this part of Canadian history remain a dark secret? In the same context, how have we responded to the torture and abuse of detainees at Guantanamo Bay or Abu Ghraib? Should we stick our heads in the sand and hope it will all just fade away? Or should we speak up, act, object, and protest? Incidentally, to encourage audience members to write their government representatives about the issue, the playbill for *Man Out of Joint* provided names and contact information for local members of parliament.

Another example of psychological or emotional anguish that plays a large role in the play is the drowning death of Joel's three-year-old son, Spencer. Joel accuses his wife, Suzanne, of standing idly by when Spencer falls in the river after chasing their dog down to the water. Instead of jumping in to rescue him, Suzanne does nothing: "I'm sorry," says Suzanne. "I should have done this and done that and this and the other, I should have done something, I know that. But I didn't. I just froze and I'm sorry" (295). In this same scene, Pollock intermingles multiple stories or "traumas," one on top of the other, without pause or interruption: Dominic interrupts to recall an instance of bigotry and prejudice by a woman on the street directed toward him and a three-year-old Joel; Suzanne recalls with anguish her inability to jump in after Spencer; and Joel becomes distracted and begins describing waterboarding, "interrogation technique, number six," a torture tactic which simulates drowning by holding down the victim, covering his mouth with a towel, and pouring water in his mouth until panic sets in. In using this technique of layering multiple emotionally disturbing stories upon each other, Pollock is engaging in what Luckhurst might describe as a "disorder of emplotment." This technique enables Pollock to mimic or mirror the effects of trauma, the confounding, confusing, and disorienting consequences of a psychological wound so intense it overwhelms the normal processes of memory and identity. In so doing, Pollock invites the audience to connect on some level with the experience of the traumatized; by layering multiple narratives upon each other, Pollock reminds us that these experiences are not limited to one particular time or place (Coates 234).

As Vickroy suggests, one of the principal aims of trauma narratives is to thwart societal disregard for painful, uncomfortable, often-controversial historical events: "they enact the directing outward of an inward, silent process to other witnesses, both within and outside the texts. Such reconstruction is also directed toward readers, engaging them in a meditation on individual distress, collective responsibilities, and communal healing in relation to trauma" (3). According to Vickroy's model, trauma narratives accomplish two things: they publicly reconstruct the private, psychological experience of the traumatized individual, directing readers (or in this case audiences) into a sobering contemplative examination of the individual, psychological suffering of witnesses/victims; and they invite the public (readers/audiences) to reflect upon their own collective responsibility with regards to the trauma at hand. According to Vickroy, trauma narratives raise "important questions about the value of cultural representations of trauma and if they provide simplistic solutions or easy consolations. Truthful trauma narratives avoid this by often critiquing oppressive forces" (xiii). I use Vickroy's model here to emphasize that it is precisely the aim of trauma narratives to ask questions, to avoid simplistic solutions, and to refuse to provide consolatory answers.

Within this context, *Man Out of Joint* further qualifies as a trauma narrative: first, as we have already seen, through the reconstruction of the traumatic experience of Guantanamo Bay detainees and the disorienting rhythm of the play; and second, by not yielding to the temptation to provide easy answers or simple explanations for these particular events. Instead, Pollock uses the play as a platform to counter or challenge the abuse of power, and to question the public's response to political interpretations and assessments of such incidents. According to Vickroy, effective trauma narratives, which are often centred on traumatic situations imposed by human beings in positions of power, provide "implicit critiques of the ways social, economic, and political structures can create and perpetuate trauma" (4). In other words, narratives that deal in some way with the testimony or experiences of those victimized by oppressive human forces challenge audiences/readers to question the socio-political aspects of such incidents, and force them to evaluate their own reaction to the abuse(s) of power. Instead of screening the public from traumatic events, such as the abuse at Guantanamo Bay, and in so doing, distancing the public from having to evaluate their response to the abuse, plays such as *Man Out of Joint* aim to bring the public close, intentionally staging an uncomfortable and disturbing environment from which they are forced to consider their own response to issues such as government-endorsed abuse and torture.

Through the development of the characters Joel, Suzanne, and Joel's law partner Erin, none of whom are directly involved in the torture or abuse at Guantanamo Bay, Pollock invites audiences to reflect upon their own collective responsibility with regards to these issues. As neither perpetrators nor victims of the torture and abuse, these three characters offer Pollock a vantage point from which to consider the public's role and response to such atrocities. These characters represent a continuum of responses to political, social, and ethical dilemmas; Pollock presents audiences with a representational trajectory of responses here to question dominant political, social and cultural ideologies, and to question the politics of cultural memory and the public understanding of controversy. In support of this theory, Pollock articulates her motivation for writing the play as follows:

Really, I don't think it's important what I believe . . . I didn't write the play to get [those ideas] out there. If you are confronted with that kind of information, which may or may not be valid, do you take a path of willful ignorance, or what is an appropriate action? That to me is the dilemma . . . Do we indulge in a willful ignorance, or are we compelled to say, "I'm going to do something about it?" (Kubik n.p.)

Pollock's goal is not to provide an opinion or explanation that will serve to justify or condemn historical acts of violence and abuse. Rather, Pollock is concerned here with collective responses and actions to such atrocities.

On the continuum of social responses, Joel represents agency, or action. He is, as his law partner Erin suggests, not afraid to "open this can of worms" (278). Despite his initial reluctance, Joel buries himself deeper and deeper into the unpopular case of Ed Leland. Erin questions his pursuit as follows:

ERIN: You're getting a reputation, Joel.

JOEL: So we should throw these "unpopular defendants" to the wall, is that it?

ERIN: That's not what I'm saying.

JOEL: So what are you saying?

. . .

ERIN: . . . But you'll be targeted and I'll be targeted.

JOEL: When did that start to concern you?

ERIN: I'm saying things have changed since 9/11 and I just don't think we want our names on a list.

JOEL: That's not like you.

ERIN: Yeah, well proximity to you has given me a touch of paranoia. (271–72)

While Erin is not in complete opposition to Joel, she does represent something of a "middle-of-the-road" response; she represents neither action nor inaction, but instead adopts a self-protective posture. She tells Joel that he is "taking on too many of these terrorist detainee cases," that he should just "forget Guantanamo North," and leave "Omar Khadr and Gitmo to the Yankees" (267). Erin might have good intentions, but she remains inactive, concerned more about personal consequences than social justice. When Joel asks if she is running out on him, she responds, "Not running, but I am walking" (273). Adopting a stance of indifference, Erin represents collective apathy or cultural complacency – a quiet, passive social response to events such as the abuse at Guantanamo Bay; these are individuals who may know the facts, offer a mildly antipathetic response, but who ultimately choose to walk away, too concerned about potential repercussions if they were to act or respond in any broad or bold way. Erin, like so many others, is not content with abandoning these controversial issues entirely, yet she is also too afraid to speak up.

In contrast to Joel (at one end) and Erin (somewhere in the middle), Suzanne represents the other end of the spectrum in terms of social response and collective memory. From the beginning of the play, the stage directions focus our attention on Suzanne's alienation from Joel: "*Suzanne is isolated literally and metaphorically from Joel*" (261). Joel and Suzanne's relationship throughout the play remains suspended, on the edge of total collapse, stunted after the drowning death of Spencer a year prior. Unlike Joel, who becomes increasingly obsessed with finding answers to the perplexities around him (9/11 conspiracy theories, the torture and abuse of detainees, the death of his son), Suzanne is inclined to avoid these issues entirely, and uses humour, anger, or ignorance to colour her response. Responding to Joel's explanation of one of the torture tactics used at Guantanamo called "Long

Time Standing," a term used by the CIA to describe one of the "alternative methods" of interrogation, Suzanne appears uninterested:

> SUZANNE: What're you reading that's possibly more important than us?
>
> JOEL: (*reads from the file*) "Long Time Standing."
>
> SUZANNE: (*smiles finding the term a bit funny*) "Long Time Standing?"
>
> JOEL: Do you know what that is?
>
> SUZANNE: A Japanese print of a crane on one leg?
>
> JOEL: (*reads*) "Enhanced Interrogation Techniques. Number four: Long Time Standing: Forced to stand, handcuffed, feet shackled to an eyebolt in the floor for excess of forty hours. Exhaustion and sleep deprivation is effective in yielding results."
>
> SUZANNE: I think I prefer my Japanese print. (288–89)

Suzanne "doesn't care to dwell on that kind of thing"; she doesn't want to "talk about this"; she "doesn't feel anything"; it's "not our problem," she says (289–90). When accused of being uninterested in things that matter, Suzanne responds: "Does that make me a bad person? Because I don't care to dwell on the kind of thing that you're reading?" (289). Furthermore, Pollock characterizes Suzanne as prejudiced and discriminatory; when Joel explains that one of the detainees is a Canadian boy (Omar Khadr), Suzanne responds, "First of all, he's not Canadian, he's Muslim" (289). Taken together, all of these examples depict Suzanne as an individual content with living her own life, protected from the atrocities that occur in the world, and ignorant of – or unconcerned with – how to respond appropriately.

Similar to Erin, although more active in her avoidance of controversy, Suzanne can be read as representational of a collective response, that is, social ignorance, socio-political biases, and an evasion of cultural atrocities and controversies. Suzanne's avoidance of the issues so central to Joel is tragically and symbolically echoed in her role in Spencer's death. When discussing Spencer's drowning, Joel makes it clear that he holds Suzanne responsible, which he describes as follows:

> [Spencer] turns and he trips and he falls. Into the water, not – a fucking disaster, if maybe, you'd run, maybe you'd – jumped – into the water – maybe you'd grabbed him – maybe you'd, you'd saved him – maybe you'd done some fucking thing instead of standing there like a statue, like a, like a – if you'd done something, anything, done anything except stand there and watch. Watch while the river took Spencie away. You stupid . . . nothing. Just – nothing. (296)

Suzanne's failure to save her son from drowning is emblematic of her lack of interest or critical concern over the human suffering and exploitation of power that occurred at Guantanamo Bay. There is an implicit, yet distinct, parallel between Suzanne's failure to save Spencer and her refusal to become emotionally or intellectually invested in the complex cultural and political dilemmas that haunt Joel. In characterizing Suzanne as complacent, ignorant, and apathetic, Pollock holds a mirror up to audiences, and invites them to consider existing collective behaviour that demonstrates prejudice, ignorance, or avoidance of human suffering caused by oppressive forces. Incidentally, at the end of the play, Pollock depicts both Erin and Suzanne reading: "ERIN *begins by picking up paper but is caught by information on one and starts to read. SUZANNE draws closer. She too starts to pick up and read documents*" (319). This reflects Pollock's optimism, that despite previous behaviour, we can and will pay attention once awakened from complacency.

Does the character of Suzanne in *Man Out of Joint* model the "innocent" tourist of history – one who is more comfortable evading issues of trauma, avoiding the suffering of others, and misreading cultural crises? In *Tourists of History: Memory, Kitsch, and Consumerism from Oklahoma City to Ground Zero*, Marita Sturken examines how certain practices and tendencies in American culture (often media-generated) relate to a national tendency to see the United States as somehow detached from and un-implicated in the troubled global strife of the world (4). She takes aim at the American public as *tourists of history* and questions those aspects of American culture, such as consumerism and media-induced paranoia, which encourage such a posture. She writes, "the tourist is a figure who embodies a detached and seemingly innocent pose. In using the term 'tourists of history' I am defining a particular mode through which the American public is encouraged to experience itself as the subject of history through consumerism, media images, souvenirs, popular culture" (9). She goes on to explain that "tourism is about travel that wants to imagine itself as innocent; a tourist is someone who stands outside of a culture, looking at it from a position that demands no responsibility" (13). She examines how the practices of tourism and consumerism "both allow for certain kinds of individual engagement with traumatic experience yet, at the same time, foreclose on other possible ways of understanding national politics and political engagement" (13). Does Suzanne's apathetic disposition epitomize this narrative of innocence, a narrative so important, as Sturken claims, to the US national identity throughout much of American history? (15) Just as the tourist stands innocently outside of the culture she finds herself in, Suzanne continually repositions herself outside of Joel's principal humanitarian concerns. Unlike Erin, who represents complacency, Suzanne represents detachment, privilege, status, and ignorance. She is someone capable of reshaping the truth to suit personal need or desire; she even changes Joel's name to suit her own desires:

SUZANNE: . . . We were introduced and I swear I
heard "Joel" and it was months before you corrected me. By
then it was too late.

JOEL: You heard a name you preferred.

SUZANNE: Preference had nothing to do with it. I
heard Joel, I called you Joel, you answered to Joel and now
you are Joel. (292)

Suzanne is content, without apology or justification, to reshape history as she desires, disregarding the truth to suit a personal preference.
Perhaps Pollock is drawing a parallel here to the collective reaction to
cultural tragedy and atrocity.

In presenting these three characters as a trajectory of social responses, with Joel at one end as action, Suzanne at the other end as detachment, and Erin somewhere in the middle as complacency, Pollock
encourages her audience to identify with one or perhaps more of these
characters. In *Man Out of Joint*, Pollock respects both the complexity
of the issues at hand and the myriad of collective and social responses that can, and often do, occur. In so doing, she invites audiences to
reconsider their own cultural assumptions, and to encourage what
Vickroy describes as "a necessary public understanding of complex
psychosocial quandaries that continue to haunt us all" (xvi).

To this end, *Man Out of Joint* becomes a working model of what
theorist and historian Dominick LaCapra calls "empathic unsettlement." LaCapra argues that the role of empathy is critical toward
authentic historical understanding, and that a "working through" of
trauma involves the articulation and representation of that experience
(42). He asserts,

Being responsive to the traumatic experience of others,
notably of victims, implies not the appropriation of their
experience but what I would call empathic unsettlement,
which should have stylistic effects or, more broadly, effects

in writing which cannot be reduced to formulas or rules of method. (41)

LaCapra cautions us against over-identification with victims and argues instead for empathetic reactions triggered through the representation of unsettling narratives. He explains that these unsettling representations often appear in disarticulate, unconventional narrative form, a claim echoed by Luckhurst and Vickroy, as outlined earlier. Empathic unsettlement allows others to associate, and yet not over-identify, with a victim's experience, and thus "poses a barrier to closure in discourse" (40–41). As LaCapra explains, the role of empathy and empathic unsettlement creates attentive secondary witnesses. He writes that "opening oneself to empathic unsettlement is . . . a desirable affective dimension of inquiry" (78). Empathic unsettlement thus creates thoughtful, conscientious responses to trauma, and at the same time, prevents us from adopting easy answers, simple solutions, and sentimental sympathies toward human suffering. Vickroy agrees, suggesting that trauma narratives try to make readers "experience emotional intimacy and immediacy, individual voices and memories, and the sensory responses of the characters" (xvi). When they succeed, she argues, they function as important contributions to a necessary public consideration of trauma, and they "elucidate the dilemma of the public's relationship to the traumatized, made problematic by victims' painful experiences and psychic defenses that can alienate others, and by the public's resistance" (2). In other words, trauma narratives such as *Man Out of Joint* work to arouse public empathy toward the victims of trauma, which in this case includes (but is not limited to) the victims of abuse at Guantanamo Bay. In so doing, they open up a space for identification and emotional intimacy between the traumatized and others, a space often closed due to fear, ignorance, and resistance.

A number of obstacles plague the artist who engages with history, especially controversial and contested "history." We might ask, what is the relationship between history and art, between "truth" and fiction, between the real and the imagined? How does the artist locate a

TANYA SCHAAP

space of interrogation or contemplation within the problematic space of represented history, perhaps especially when this history is difficult, unsettling, and controversial? In other words, how does the artist work to condense the levels of representation when dealing with real, historical events? In a keynote address in 2004, Pollock provides an answer when she compares herself to the demon-possessed child in the 1973 horror film, *The Exorcist*:

> Whenever I sit down to draw my thoughts together for an address like this . . . an image comes to me. It's from *The Exorcist*. The priest is sitting by the bedside table of the physically transformed and possessed child. The priest asks, "Who are you?" A deep frightening voice answers, "I am legion."

> Well, I am legion. I am many competing thoughts and voices, and No Theories . . . I open my mouth and speak. Before the sentence, phrase, or word is out, internally I'm hearing three or four conflicting statements: "This can't be right"; "True today, what about tomorrow?"; "What a load of crap." And "Oh, shut up!" . . I know it's impossible to find out *what is, what isn't*, and *why* but that in no way diminishes my desire or need to continue the search. (Pollock "Playwright" 295)

In many ways, the analogy between the demon-possessed child and the writer encapsulates a *postmodern* challenge; as Linda Hutcheon explains, "Postmodern fiction suggests that to re-write or to re-present the past in fiction and in history is, in both cases, to open it up to the present, [and] to prevent it from being conclusive and teleological" (110). But while an artist like Pollock may surrender to the impossibility of knowing anything with certainty, the "conclusive," the "teleological", the "*what is, what isn't* and *why*," she does not necessarily abandon her desire to ask these questions. As Albert Camus suggests in a speech from 1957: "Remaining aloof has always been possible in history. When someone did not approve, he could always keep silent or talk of something else. Today everything is changed and even silence has dangerous implications. The moment that abstaining from choice is itself looked upon as a choice and punished or praised, the artist is willy-nilly impressed into service" (249). Indeed, narrative representation of difficult, discomfiting history has the capacity to become an agent of change not in its ability to provide answers, but in the subjective way it asks questions, assesses possibilities, and contemplates potentials.

NOTE

1   After spending almost a decade imprisoned at the detention facility at Guantanamo Bay, labelled an "illegal enemy combatant" by the US government, Khadr pleaded guilty to murder, attempted murder, spying, conspiracy, and material support for terrorism. In September 2012, he was extradited to Canada; the terms of his plea deal allow him to serve out the majority of his eight-year sentence in a Canadian security facility. He is currently serving his sentence at a medium-security penitentiary north of Calgary, Alberta.

Works Cited

Camus, Albert. *Resistance, Rebellion, and Death: Essays*. New York: Knopf, 1961. Print.

Coates, Donna, and Sherrill Grace, eds. *Canada and the Theatre of War*. Vol. 2. Toronto: Playwrights Canada P, 2009. Print.

"Guantanamo Detainees were Tortured, Medical Exams Show." CBC News. 18 June 2008. *Cbc.ca*. Web.

Hammond, Will, and Dan Steward, eds. *Verbatim, Verbatim: Contemporary Documentary Theater*. London: Oberon, 2008. Print.

Hutcheon, Linda. *A Poetics of Postmodernism: History, Theory, Fiction*. New York: Routledge, 1988. Print.

Jameson, Fredric. *The Political Unconscious: Narrative as a Socially Symbolic Act*. Ithaca: Cornell UP, 1981. Print.

Kubik, Jeff. "Confronting Injustice through Story: Downstage Debuts New Sharon Pollock Play, *Man Out of Joint*." *FastForward Weekly*. FFWDweekly.com. 3 May 2007. Web.

LaCapra, Dominick. *Writing History, Writing Trauma*. Baltimore: Johns Hopkins UP, 2001. Print.

Luckhurst, Roger. *The Trauma Question*. London: Routledge, 2008. Print.

Pollock, Sharon. "Man Out of Joint." *Canada and the Theatre of War*. Vol. 2. Ed. Donna Coates and Sherrill Grace. Toronto: Playwrights Canada P, 2009. 251–320. Print.

———. "Playwright: Parasite or Symbiont." *Theatre and AutoBiography: Writing and Performing Lives in Theory and Practice*. Eds. Sherrill Grace and Jerry Wasserman. Vancouver: Talonbooks, 2006. 295–300. Print.

Razack, Sherene H. *Casting Out: The Eviction of Muslims from Western Law and Politics*. Toronto: U of Toronto P, 2008. Print.

Vickroy, Laurie. *Trauma and Survival in Contemporary Fiction*. Charlottesville: U of Virginia P, 2002. Print.

Equal-Opportunity Torturers in Judith Thompson's *Palace of the End* and Sharon Pollock's *Man Out of Joint*

Donna Coates

In 2007, two of Canada's best-known, Governor General's Award-winning playwrights, Judith Thompson and Sharon Pollock, produced brave new works inspired by real-life persons and events on the subject of institutional torture. In her "Playwright's Notes," Thompson describes the triptych of monologues that comprises *Palace of the End* as follows: the first, "'*My Pyramids*' was inspired by the media circus around Lynndie England, the American soldier convicted of the sexual torture of Iraqi detainees in Abu Ghraib prison" [Thompson refers to her as Soldier]; the second, "'*Harrowdown Hill*' was inspired by the well-publicized events surrounding the public life and solitary death of Dr. David Kelly, the British weapons inspector and microbiologist"; and the third, "'*Instruments of Yearning*' was inspired by the true story of Nehrjas Al Saffarh, a well-known member of the Communist party of Iraq, who was tortured by Saddam Hussein's secret police in the 1970s. She died when her home was bombed by the Americans in the first Gulf War" (n.p.). Similarly, in *Man Out of Joint*, Pollock draws attention to the torture and abuse of detainees at Guantanamo Bay, and specifically to Omar Khadr, the fifteen-year-old Canadian child soldier captured in Afghanistan and charged with murdering an American army medic in 2002.[1] Interspersed with the detainee stories are those about Joel Gianelli, based on Toronto lawyer Rocco Galati, and his American client Ed Leland, based on Delmart Vreeland, who appears to have accurately predicted the attacks on the World Trade Centre. As a result of his association with Leland, Gianelli becomes increasingly concerned with inconsistencies in reports about 9/11. But Gianelli is also preoccupied with the recent drowning death of his son, as well as haunted by the hardship his family endured after his Italian father and grandfather were unjustly interned during World War II. Taken together, these interlocking narratives track how multiple systems of oppression come into existence and how they are connected. As Pollock tells Stephen Hunt, "the structure of [the play] makes its own statement about how the past impacts the present, how different arenas that you work in affect other arenas. In other words, you can't really ignore what is happening outside of our safe little cocoon that we have here" ("Downstage").

In my essay, I want to concentrate, however, on Thompson's and Pollock's representations of "torture chicks," a phrase coined after three white women – Sabrina Harman, Megan Ambuhl, and Lynndie England – were caught and charged with torturing prisoners at Abu Ghraib. I will examine Thompson's Soldier's role as sexual interrogator at Abu Ghraib and Pollock's Soldier #1's (Pete) and Soldier #2's (Lolly) roles as "guards" at Guantanamo Bay prison ("Gitmo").[2] In writing about torture, neither Thompson nor Pollock is doing anything especially new because, as American critic Coco Fusco observes, "torture is not a new element of war. Interrogation has invariably been crucial to military efforts to thwart insurgencies, and rare are the instances in which information is obtained from captured enemies without some degree of physical or psychological violence" (33). Nor is the torture of women and children new, as recent events in Bosnia, Rwanda, and the Democratic Republic of Congo remind us, although novels and plays about the subject have only recently begun to be written and produced.[3] What is new, however, is that in February 2005, the Pentagon deliberately instigated a program which employed women as "sexual aggressors" (Fusco 26). According to Fusco, even "high ranking female intelligence officers in Iraq and Afghanistan authorized the use of coercive interrogation strategies – in other words, torture" (19). Like most of us, Cusco learned about the "torture chicks" when she saw those now-infamous photos of England leading a naked prisoner on a leash (a photo Susan Sontag claims depicts "classic dominatrix imagery" ["Regarding"]); giving the thumbs-up sign with one hand and with the other pointing her finger in a cocked gun position at a prisoner's genitals; and standing arm in arm with Specialist Charles Graner (with whom she had an affair and subsequently a child) both grinning and offering the thumbs-up sign while perched behind a cluster of several Iraqis piled awkwardly atop one another in the shape of a human pyramid.

When Fusco realized that "the media frenzy over the Abu Ghraib photographs focused on the questions of the soldiers' culpability," she determined to figure out "how they got there, how many of them there were, who came up with the idea to do such things to prisoners and why" (26). Over the course of her research, Fusco learned that

> there are now more American women waging war these days than there are those who try to prevent it . . . [The United States'] high rate of unemployment, the demand for troops, and the absence of a draft have led to the unparalleled involvement of American women in the making of war. [The country's] active duty armed forces have more women in them than ever before in history [they comprise about 15 percent of the military population], and American women soldiers are closer than they have ever come to combat. (18)[4]

As the number of women in the US military grows, Fusco observes it is not surprising that the military would want to transform women's "particular assets" (47) into weapons and "exploit their presence strategically and tactically" (18). But what the Pentagon hoped to achieve by making women perpetrators of sexual torture is not so readily apparent. Fusco posits they may have wanted to "humanize" the US military occupation of Iraq because most assume torture cannot be "bad" if performed by members of the "'weaker sex'" (39); moreover, women are viewed as "much less intimidating than the over-sized Special Forces commandos in black ninja suits and masks who preside over interrogations in those notorious so-called black holes and secret prisons that are managed by the CIA" (20–21). Fusco notes that even the language used to describe what female torturers do sounds harmless: "when male interrogators perform sex acts on non-consenting subjects it is understood as sexual assault, but when women do it, it can be authorized as an invasion of space" (Fusco 33). But as she further argues, to employ women in military interrogations specifically "to provoke male anxiety, and to then label it 'Invasion of Space by a Female'. . . is testimony in itself of the state's rationalization of its exploitation of femininity" (41). Fusco then suggests that women's presence in the prisons creates the impression that American institutions engaging in domination are "actually democratic, since they appear to practice gender equity" (41). Moreover, some feminists, reluctant to place women in the role of victims, have argued that "female sexual assertiveness should be understood as a form of freedom of expression" (Fusco 50).

Canadian critic Sherene H. Razack also attempts to come to terms with why the military decided to use female torturers: echoing Fusco, she suggests that the practice marked Americans as "modern people who do not subscribe to puritanical notions of sex or to patriarchal notions of women's role in it. The Iraqis, of course, remained forever confined to the premodern" ("Kill" 223). She adds that those who attempt to justify these "new methods of interrogation" ("Kill" 220) assert they are dealing with a "culturally different enemy": "unlike the Cold War, the war on terror and the occupations of Iraq and Afghanistan have produced conditions where military interrogators need cultural help" in dealing with the Arab enemy, who is "more ideologically driven and more religious" ("Kill" 220). But declaring these prisoners "culturally different enemies" means that few have questioned the "Orientalist underpinnings" of these strategies, which infer that "unlike us, the Arabs/Muslims are sexually repressed, homophobic, misogynist and likely to crack in sexualized situations, particularly those involving women dominating men or those involving sex between men" (Razack, "Casting," 65). She stresses that this "clash of civilizations" approach to torture "reinforced the idea of the detainees' barbarism at the same time that it enabled the West to remain on moral high ground. First, through the idea of cultural difference, sexualized torture became something more generic – torture for the purpose of obtaining information, something that was not even torture at all. Sexualized torture, then, was devised simply "to attack the prisoners' identity and values" ("Kill" 222). But Razack further asserts that "such methods would in fact humiliate men of all cultures both because they are violent and because they target what it means to be a man in patriarchy" ("Casting" 65).

Several feminist critics have identified the role that training plays in the racist indoctrination of soldiers. Eve Ensler notes that "brainwashing" teaches soldiers to view Iraqis as "less than human" (18), and Ilene Feinman points out that "military boot camp is far from gender-neutral training. . . Women are now being trained to respond equally to their male counterparts with a racialized, patriarchally constructed tool kit of behaviours" (71). Clearly, Thompson's Soldier has been handed the "tool kit" and taught to objectify and dehumanize the enemy as she carries out what she declares she is "trained to do, which is SERIOUS – INTELLIGENCE – WORK" (155). Soldier insists that those under her command are not "men, they are terrorists" who "look exactly alike" (159); the "RAKEES" are not humans but "APES," "monsters in the shape of human beings" (160); they are pigs to "slaughter" and cattle to "herd" (160). Although Thompson does not suggest that Soldier was racist before she joined the military,

Coleen Kesner, a resident from England's home town, certainly suggests that England was: "If you're a different nationality, a different race, you're sub-human. That's the way that girls like Lynndie England are raised. Tormenting Iraqis, in her mind, would be no different from shooting a turkey. Every season here you're hunting something. Over there they're hunting Iraqis" (cited in Razack 77). While Thompson's Soldier admits that she and the others abused the detainees in much worse ways than the pictures showed –"What YOU seen is tiddly-winks," she states (161) – but none of what they did, whether laughing "at a man's willy" or forcing him to masturbate, was torture: it was merely humiliation. But as Sontag insists, "all covenants on torture specify that it includes treatment intended to humiliate the victim" ("Regarding").

But why women (like Soldier) should agree to work as sexual interrogators is also not so obvious. Fusco points out that given the recent increase in enlistment, it appears that many women consider "the military as an exceptional educational and work opportunity and as an economic solution. They characterize it as a structure that challenges them and enhances personal characteristics such as assertiveness that enable them to advance professionally and eschew limiting traditional female roles and modes of address" (61). Accordingly, both Pollock's and Thompson's female soldiers stem from the ranks of the under-privileged and view joining the military as a positive career move. In spite of having been fired several times by the Dairy Queen, Soldier is working there again when the recruiters come calling: she signs up because there is "no way in hell [she is] going back to [the night shift] at the chicken factory" (149) and claims she wants to do "whatever it takes to protect [her] country" (149). Similarly, Pollock's Soldier #2 confesses that she was "poor white trash," that she "grew up in a fuckin' trailer full of empties and dog shit," that the "smartest thing" she ever did was to join the military, which she claims has given her a "family," a "place," a "home" (302). She is prepared to do whatever they ask of her: "I get orders / ... I follow orders. I know what I'm to do and I do it ... I'm like a machine ... The military counts on me and I can count

DONNA COATES

on it" (302–03). When Pollock intersperses Soldier #2's emphatic declarations – that she is "proud of who [she] is today" (302), "proud of what [she has] become / . . .and "proud of what [she] can be" (303) – with the detainees' descriptions of the torture she subjects them to, it becomes apparent that, like Thompson's Soldier, she regards herself as culturally and racially superior to what she perceives of as her innately barbaric and primitive victims.

Thompson's Soldier is also "proud" she has "fitted in," that she did not "wussy out" in the "hardest ass prison" when her male counterparts insisted she should be "cleanin' or cookin'" (161) and then reinforced their patriarchal objections to her presence by subjecting her to what might be considered "torture lite": they did not talk to her (isolation); they "stole" her food (starvation); they "hung [her] upside down" (hanging gestures); and "poured water on [her] in the night" (waterboarding). Nevertheless, she is proud that she gained their acceptance by being "as tough and as bad assed as they were" (161). But she also takes pride in her "serious intelligence work": as she tells the audience, "So, there I was, little me, in ABU GHRAIB, . . . and I was the BIG boss of these BIG DEAL TERRORISTS, guys who had KILLED AMERICANS. GUYS WHO WERE PLANNING ANOTHER 9/11 dude" (162). As Lila Rajiva argues, women [like Soldier] "exulted in their power, both in the voluntary submission of their fellow soldiers to their sexual power . . .as well as in the coerced submission of the male prisoners. The triumph of the women lay in eliciting a response from men who did not want to give it. It was just this reduction of human beings to objects without their own wills that made them gloat" (228).

But according to Thompson, it was not this reversal of the male–female power dynamic that attracted public attention to England. During an interview with Anne Holloway, Thompson stated that when she "googled" England and discovered there were "66,000 sites" on her, she naively thought that people "really care[d] about the situation," but closer inspection revealed that the comments were "sexually violent, pornographic, misogynistic things," worse than anything she'd "ever seen in her life" (140). Thompson lamented that not a "single one mentioned the prisoners, and the injustice, and [England's] obviously acting out the will of the Pentagon and the will of America" (140), an observation that I will argue Thompson herself ironically failed to act on. In that same interview, Thompson stated that she thought it would be "fun" to write about England and admitted that she found herself "laughing at [England's] lack of education" (141). Because she and Holloway "have advantages and the resources of education, affluence and intellect," Thompson argued, they might have been able to "step out" and say what they were involved in "isn't right" and think about "reporting" it, but she reiterated that England couldn't do that because she's "just a product – a product of American society" (143). When Holloway asked if she thinks "Lynndie's a monster," if "there is something psychologically wrong with her," Thompson replied that she's "absolutely typical," that she is a "symptom of Western society," which she agreed has a lot to do with "capitalism" (142). In an interview with Martin Morrow, Thompson again insisted "*[England] has been strung up in the public square as a monster, but that monster was created by American society*" (Morrow). But in spite of these repeated references to "American society," Thompson offered no serious indictment of it: Soldier makes frequent references to junk food (Thompson told Holloway that she chose Dairy Queen because "'that's American culture'" [139]), to late-night American television talk shows, to Disney movies and Hollywood film stars. The naively patriotic and superficially religious Soldier also declares that she hates "liberals," "feminists," "gays," "PEACE PINHEADS," and the terrorists who caused the collapse of the Twin Towers. But instead of depicting a female soldier acting out the will of the Pentagon and the will of America, Thompson dwells on Soldier's rank ignorance, her moral deficiencies, and turns her into a bimbo, an object of derision, a depiction which thereby reinforces the military's description of those who were eventually charged (none above the rank of sergeant) as "the seven bad apples" who had to be punished for embarrassing the military and the administration.

Several critics have pointed out the problems with blaming only a few low-ranking personnel for what happened at Abu Ghraib. Razack claims that "the failure to more closely examine the actions of rank and file soldiers, and to insist on a deeper and broader public accountability secures for Americans a national innocence. If the only problem about Abu Ghraib was a few bad leaders, then there need not be any sustained confrontation with the facts of empire, both then and now" ("Kill" 218). Feinman also asserts that "the insistence on the 'few bad apples' theory following the release of the Abu Ghraib photos served to exonerate the rest of us from culpability, and served the administration by keeping the 'authority' for carrying out the torture among the lowest-ranked officers in the U. S. military – in itself contradictory, given the hierarchical command structure of the forces" (5). She adds that to concentrate on "the function of women as the focus of the torture revelations, disproportional to their actual presence in either the military or the group of soldiers convicted of torture, serves to both anomalize the incidents of torture, and to discredit 'unintelligent and incapable women,' while ignoring the very rank command structure that authorized the torture in the first instance" (58).

Although it is difficult to divorce Thompson's imaginative construction of Soldier from what we already know about England, nevertheless, I find it troubling that Soldier feels occasional twinges of remorse. While she reserves the most sympathy for an American (of course) "friend" she helped torture as a child, she is also plagued by the refusal of an Iraqi man to "amuse" the torturers by obeying their vile orders. This sounds a false note, for as Joanne Laurier remarks, "England and the other 'seven bad apples' were utterly devoid of an awareness of the depravity of their actions" ("*Standard*"). In Errol Morris and Philip Gourevitch's documentary *Standard Operating Procedure*, England seems especially unrepentant when she speaks so belligerently about the treatment of detainees: "'We didn't kill 'em . . . We didn't cut their heads off. We didn't shoot 'em. We didn't make 'em bleed to death. We did what we were told, soften 'em up [for interrogation]'" ("*Standard*"). As Razack argues, torturers like England express no shame or moral outrage or sorrow because they have not confronted "what torture *is*: a systematic dehumanization of the Other" ("Kill" 225). Moreover, as Richard Weisman and others assert, "expressions of remorse have to include an unconditional acknowledgement of responsibility, sincere self-condemnation and, most crucially, an awareness that the victim has suffered" (cited in Razack, "Kill," 228–29). Razack declares that "without these components, we are not being invited into a moral community in which torture is wrong. If no one thinks that the acts of torture at Abu Ghraib were really wrong or regrettable, then are Muslims/Arabs full members of the human and political community?" (229). Thus, although self-pity and self-justification run throughout Soldier's monologue, she remains delusional, certain that the "higher-ups" will eventually exonerate her from all charges against her.

Similarly, Pollock's Soldier #2, arguably as physically forceful and sexually threatening as Thompson's Soldier, feels no sense of guilt or shame, because Pollock recognizes, as does Barbara Finlay, that "just as men can become torturers given the 'right' conditions, so can women" (211). Pollock also understands that women's exclusion from power "has not necessarily made them immune to its seductive qualities or critical of the use of force" (Fusco 17); nor has it led them to use power differently from men. But at the same time, she suggests that because women like Soldier #2 have fewer employment opportunities than men, they are less likely to question orders and more likely to do whatever the military asks of them. Hence Pollock's Soldier #1, who has not made the military his "home," his "place," or his "family," looks forward to going home because he has become increasingly horrified by the violence of the duties he is required to perform (Pollock hints at an authorized and condoned chain of command). Unlike Thompson's Soldier, he has become aware of the detainees' courage and resilience in spite of their suffering (he hears them "knocking their heads 'gainst the walls and doors" (303); "sees eyes that are beggin' like, pleadin' and full of pain" [308]); and begins to understand that he wishes to inhabit a "moral community" where torture is "wrong." He concludes that while the detainees are "caged," everyone at Guantanamo, including him and Soldier #2, are "prisoner[s]" (304).

The play holds out partial hope for Soldier #1, who joins Gianelli's partner Erin and his social-climber wife Suzanne (both of whom are content to remain willfully blind to the torture and abuse taking place at Guantanamo) in reading the documents Gianelli has received from Leland. (In her "Staging Notes," Pollock indicates that "multiple dimensions of time and space are layered in the world of the play" [258]). As they read through the material, the stage directions indicate that they become *caught by information*" (319): Soldier #1, for example, offers the shocking news that Afghan president Hamid Karzai worked for Enocal, which Gianelli explains is a "consortium of companies to bring oil from Turkmenistan through Afghanistan to Pakistan" (317); furthermore, Condoleeza Rice was on the board, and Americans attacked Afghanistan in order to secure access to oil resources. But although Soldier #1 is becoming enlightened about the human cost of internment at Guantanamo, his future remains uncertain because he is experiencing classic trauma symptoms such as sleeplessness and recurring nightmares. As Finlay observes, "both men and women who participate in these horrors will carry the images in their minds throughout their lives, with unknown consequences for their mental, spiritual, moral, and physical well-being and that of those around them" (212).

But for now, Soldier #2 remains unmoved by the torment and anguish of the inmates. She calls Soldier #1 a "wuss" when he confesses he is affected by the suffering of the detainees, and claims that, unlike him, she has no trouble sleeping. Soldier #2 fails to recognize that women like her were, as Aziz Huq suggests, merely "instrumentalities to be taken down from the shelf and applied in the course of ritualistic abuse and torture" (131). Sadly, as Huq also suggests, the "events at Abu Ghraib [and by extension Guantanamo] are powerful evidence of the military culture's ability to absorb and integrate women and femininity without fundamental challenge to the Manichean logic that underwrites that culture" (131). Moreover, as Angela Y. Davis argues, "if success can be interpreted as obtaining access to hierarchical institutions and power structures that perpetuate male dominance, racism, and American political hegemony" (60), then we need to examine how these women's "induction and training is designed to make them identify with conservative power structures as legitimate entities, and to see the exercise of force within guiding regulations as moral and politically justifiable and salutary for a democratic order" (60).

Thus while Pollock's play introduces two soldiers who are products of "American society," instead of pointing to the flaws of the US capitalist system, she reveals, as Laurier puts it [in another context] "the ugly face of US imperialism" ("*Standard*"), and never lets us forget what "made in America" means –hypocrisy, duplicitousness, a desire for world domination at any cost. In *Man Out of Joint*, she stresses that the Bush administration believes the "war on terrorism" can only be won by disregarding legal constraints and drafting new rules of engagement, which she carefully lays out in the opening scenes. As Louis Hobson observes in his review, "Pollock and [director Simon] Mallett have created five distinct areas on stage, including an imposing prison backdrop where detainees are tortured and abused regardless of what is happening elsewhere on stage. It is a constant reminder this is a play that wants us to react not just while we're watching it, but after we've left the theatre" ("Play"). The play begins with a Blackout, followed by the words "Honour Bound to Defend Freedom," spoken by the disembodied voice of "K," a capital letter which puts us in mind of Kafka (although the name of the man in charge of Guantanamo began with the same initial). These words are followed by "*Sound: a loud cacophony of disorienting music and sound,*" and then a "*strobe light will reveal in the background a shuffling line of hooded men in orange jumpsuits, shackled hands and feet linked to a waist chain, herded by two soldiers . . . .The hooded detainees will each be placed in his "cell" – a barred square of light on the floor*" (259). Almost immediately, audiences become aware of the hypocrisy of the words "Honour Bound to Defend Freedom" as the "guards" subject one of the caged detainees to "sensory deprivation" (259), and the voice-overs continue to emphasize that all detainees' rights have been removed in "this . . . prison beyond the law" (260), a "law" which apparently gives "them" the right to torture anyone they deem suspicious. As Razack affirms,

> Torture has what we might regard as an almost built-in connection to race. Quite simply, torture is permissible against those whom we have evicted from personhood even as torture itself guarantees this outcome. Nothing committed against *homo sacer* can be regarded as a crime, commented Giorgio Agamben, since the law has determined that the rule of law does not apply . . . . Whether "enemy combatants" or inhabitants of a refugee camp, the legal distinction that marks who enjoys the rule of law and who does not, often thinly disguises that the camp's inmates are *already* regarded as a lower form of humanity . . . [and therefore] outside the law's protection. The Bush administration produced Arabs/Muslims in a state of exception in which the rule of law could be suspended in their case. ("Kill" 238–39)

She concludes that "torture talk and culture talk" often merge: "Cultural difference, the enemy's 'innate barbarism,' is an important element in the eviction of the tortured from the rule of law, and thus from humanity" ("Kill" 239).

Pollock has clearly designed the opening scenes to disturb complacent spectators, to remind audiences that, as Fusco asserts, America has a "dark history of doing extremely violent things to some people so that others here can be 'free' – and it is only through insisting on the hypocrisy of that double standard that democratic practices have been secured, protected, and expanded" (59). By making the torture and abuse of detainees at Guantanamo Bay visible throughout, frequently interrupting the action in Toronto between Gianelli and his client Leland or between Gianelli and his wife (the couple appears to be heading for a divorce partially as a result of Suzanne's failure to prevent their son from drowning), Pollock attempts to narrow the distance between viewer and perpetrator, for as Carrie A. Rentschler observes, "people may not feel obligated to act in the present if they associate atrocity with distant places and times" (300). As Fusco argues, "even though the idea of torture dominates the media sphere and public consciousness, we are compelled to imagine the full range of what it is through personal and collective factors, because most of us don't get to see the real thing" (35). Moreover, as Sontag writes, we make less from "harrowing photographs," which inevitably lose their power to shock, than from "narratives" which, she argues, can "make us understand" ("Pain" 80).

Thus in Pollock's play, we do get to see (and hear) "the real thing," or at least enactments of torture, and as John Durham Peters points out, if we witness torture, "we cannot say we do not know . . . To witness an event is to be responsible in some way to it" (708). His belief that "citizens have a duty to be informed about the events of the day" (723) is one Pollock certainly shares. Rentschler, like Peters, argues that "witnesses have a responsibility to react to acts of witnessing as something other than passive bystanders," but she also points out that "people may simply not know how to act or what to do with their vicarious experience of others' suffering, because they have not been taught how to transform feeling into action" (300). Aware that her audiences may not know how to transform "feeling into action" but hopeful that they do not remain "passive bystanders," Pollock included in the playbill a list of names of members of parliament and information on how to contact them. But she would also agree with Sontag's view that

> to designate a hell is not, of course, to tell us anything about how to extract people from that hell, how to moderate hell's flames. Still, it seems a good in itself to acknowledge, to have enlarged one's sense of how much suffering caused by human wickedness there is in the world we share with others. Someone who is perennially surprised that depravity exists, who continues to feel disillusioned (even incredulous) when confronted with evidence of what humans are

capable of inflicting in the way of gruesome, hands-on cruelties upon other humans, has not reached moral or psychological adulthood.

No one after a certain age has the right to this kind of innocence, of superficiality, to this degree of ignorance, or amnesia.[5] ("Pain" 104)

Sontag also insists that we allow the "atrocious images" to "haunt us," to let the images function so that we "Don't forget" (102), which is one of the reasons Pollock includes the story of the Italian internment and Gianelli's father, who often cautions his son, "Don't forget," and "Remember."

In presenting the atrocity on stage, Pollock also attempts to negate the notions (expressed by Gianelli's wife Suzanne) that Canadians need not pay attention because it's the "Americans, not us" who torture; that Omar Khadr is not "Canadian, he's Muslim" (290); that "he was a soldier, he was killing people" (289) by forcing us to watch torture enacted on stage (not in a faraway place), most of it executed by Soldier #2. For example, when Soldier #2 realizes that Soldier #1 is ignoring a detainee who paces about his "too-small cage," she immediately calls [the detainee] an "*asshole*," "*confronts*" him, "*knees him in the groin, and as he bends over in pain, cracks him on the back of his head*" (262). A few scenes later, in spite of the other detainees' attempts to attract the attention of the guards, a detainee hangs himself (one of three who die and are carried out on stretchers), an act of desperation that Soldier #2 appears to regard as merely a nuisance. So, too, does "K," who announces matter-of-factly that in 2003, there had been 350 reported cases of self-harm and 120 cases of "hanging gestures" – but he stresses that reliable figures after that were "'unavailable,'" as the military had no intention of keeping accurate records of this kind of abuse thereafter (281). We also watch the "guards" subject one detainee to "Long Time Standing"; they shackle his feet to an eyebolt on the floor for more than forty hours, and place a second detainee, naked, in a "Cold Cell" for extended periods of time and "intermediately" douse him with cold water (285). Significantly, we also witness Soldier #2 sexually assault a detainee: stage directions indicate that "*she slip[s] off her helmet, undo[es] a hair clip,*" and while they do not specify exactly what she does, the scene ends with her giving "*a squeeze to the testicles*" (274).

While the sexual assault is occurring, Soldier #1 immediately begins taking photos, which reminds us of Sontag's observation that "most of the torture photographs have a sexual theme," perhaps because "torture is more attractive, as something to record, when it has a sexual component" ("Regarding"). Furthermore, it appears that Soldier #2's gestures stem from her training, because as Kristine A. Huskey notes, the touching and "squeezing" of "devout Muslim men's" private parts was part of their "sexual harassment and abuse both in and out of interrogation" (176). During the shooting, however, Soldier #2 remains expressionless and makes no exhibitionist display of her sexuality: her lack of emotional engagement with the detainee indicates her desire to remain in control, and thus her manipulation of male anxiety seems especially monstrous, even grotesque. But as Basuli Deb points out, at Abu Ghraib (and presumably Guantanamo), "the camera itself became an instrument of torture, informing the tortured prisoner that this spectacle of humiliation and pain could be reproduced, amplified, and circulated indefinitely through circuits of consumption over which the detainee would have no control" (12). Moreover, according to Jasbir K. Puar, "these photos do not merely reflect the tortures committed; they also function as an integral part of the humiliating, dehumanizing violence itself: the giddy process of documentation, the visual evidence of corporeal shame, the keen ecstatic eye of the voyeur, the haunting of surveillance, the dissemination of the images, like pornography on the Internet, the speed of transmission an aphrodisiac in itself" (531). Puar further remarks that "as postcolonial scholars have aptly demonstrated, the sexual is already part and parcel of the histories of colonial domination and empire building; conquest is innately corporeal" (534).

Both Sontag and LaNitra Walker make a number of specific comparisons of these photos to American lynching photos. Sontag argues that

> if there is something comparable to what these pictures show, it would be some of the photographs of black victims of lynching taken between the 1880s and 1930s, which show Americans grinning beneath the naked mutilated body of a black man or woman hanging behind them from a tree. The lynching photographs were souvenirs of a collective action whose participants felt perfectly justified in what they had done. So are the pictures from Abu Ghraib. ("Regarding")

Walker observes that both African-Americans during the pre–Civil Rights era and the Iraqi prisoners were arrested and detained without any clear evidence that they had committed crimes, and just as the lynching of more than 4,700 African-Americans were documented in photographs, so, too, was the physical and sexual abuse of detainees (190). She notes that "images of torture from the Abu Ghraib prison were already part of America's visual vocabulary through the legacy of lynching photography. Both sets of images depict how gender roles reinforce perceptions of racial superiority; and by comparing them, it is possible to see how white American women have moved from the background to the foreground in committing politically motivated acts of violence" (190). The Abu Ghraib photos demonstrate that they have become "equal partners in the abuse of prisoners" (191). Walker also reminds us that two of those "equal partners" grew up in states – England in West Virginia, and Sabrina Harman in Virginia – where "at least fifty lynchings were recorded" (197). Walker also draws attention to several of England's actions that evoke images from lynching photos. For example, when England points her finger in a cocked gun position at a detainee's genitals, she reminds viewers that "castration was a common part of the lynching process with the ritual emasculation manifested in stripping a man of his sexual and political power"

(195). Walker adds that "photographing the event or simulated event connotes further social and emotional humiliation of the individual and the community, demonstrating their powerlessness in stopping the torture" (195). In *Man Out of Joint*, Pollock may be reflecting Sontag's suggestion that the lynching photos included "grinning Americans" in the background, because were Soldier #1 to take a wide-angle shot, he might include audiences in his photo. While we would not be "grinning" (although we might be in Thompson's "My Pyramids"), Pollock suggests that if we do nothing after witnessing these acts of torture, we become complicit in the action.

While *Man Out of Joint* demonstrates acts of torture on stage, it also imagines the anguish of the incarcerated and tortured and charts how their levels of discomfort and anger increase. In the opening scenes, the detainees *"shift slightly within their cells, extend a hand through the 'bars,' react minimally to heat or cold"* (260), but as they listen to evidence of cover-ups or sense something "ominous" (such as the detainees' suicides), they become increasingly agitated: when they read about Bill C-36, stage directions indicate that they begin to *"murmur,"* to *"express emotion (anguish, anger, childish frustration, madness)"* (268). Then, when they hear that Leland has obtained his information from Marc Bastien, a young and healthy Canadian attached to the embassy in Moscow who appears to have been murdered because "he knew too much" about the impending attacks on the United States, and that an autopsy, which would provide "proof," has still not been carried out, the detainees *"rock [. . .] back and forth; curl [. . .] into a fetus-like ball, pac[e], appeal[], smil[e] in conversation with no one"* (278). (Their distress evokes no response in the "guards," who are busy examining their photos.) But when "K" lays out the terms and conditions of the 2006 Military Commissions Act, which labels the detainees "unlawful enemy combatants" and effectively removes all of their rights and freedoms, stage directions indicate that *"a faint murmur of voices"* gradually *"grows in volume,"* until there is an *"increasing roar of multiple voices"* (299) which cannot be silenced, even though the *"soldiers"* move *"amongst them, attempting to control them, to shut them up"* (299).

Although all of "K's" words disturb the detainees, arguably, they might find the reference to them as "unlawful enemy combatants" the most offensive, because according to Donald Rumsfeld, who appears to have originated the phrase, "technically", this means they have "no rights under the Geneva Convention" ("Regarding"). But "technically," they are neither "unlawful," nor are they "combatants." Like Fusco, Pollock is aware that "one of the slickest and scariest elements of the current war machine is the effectiveness of the strategies used to distance most of us from it physically and psychologically" (Fusco 12). "Semantic subterfuge," which means that "the practice of torture can continue take place [sic] while the decision makers deliberate duplicitously about what it 'really' is" (37), is one of the most powerful strategies. Throughout the play, "K" refers to "'enhanced' interrogation techniques" such as "frequent-flier programs" or "waterboarding," neither of which sound like torture, nor does Thompson's Soldier's insistence that they were merely "softening up" the Iraqis. Several times in the play, "K" undermines his own point when he insists that the "balanced interrogation techniques" such as "extreme sensory deprivation" or "sensory overload" lead to "positive interrogation results," even when they have caused "personality disintegration," (303) which would obviously render any "results" useless. But as Fusco also suggests, "now that our involvement [in torture] has become visible, we continue the ruse [that we don't torture] by trying to call it something else, or saying we are not sure what it is" (34). According to Sontag, the Bush administration avoided using the word "torture" altogether: the most they "admitted to" was "abuse," and eventually "humiliation" ("Regarding"). Sontag further suggests that even using the word "detainees" for those "held in the extralegal American penal empire" is problematic: "'prisoners,' a newly obsolete word, might suggest that they have the rights accorded by international law and the laws of all civilized countries" ("Regarding"). According to Huskey, even "high-ranking U.S. officials" have admitted that "many were brought to Guantanamo by mistake and have no connection to terrorism" (178), and as Anne McClintock also observes, the detainees "were mostly unarmed non-combatant civilian populations – many of them innocent people . . . . Having no information to offer, they could do nothing to put an end to their agonies" (cited in Deb 10). Feinman notes, too, that "70–90 percent of the prisoners at Abu Ghraib were arrested by mistake through systematic roundups in neighbourhoods" (59). Pollock's detainees attest they have been captured as a result of the bounty plan, which purported to help *the anti-Taliban forces rid Afghanistan of murderers and terrorists* and would pay *millions of dollars* to anyone who aids them (299). Moreover, none of the IRF (Immediate Reaction Force) was a designated torturer, but detainees who attempted any kind of protest were "IRFed" – in other words, beaten by the Immediate Reaction Force, which was, writes Jeremy Scahill, known inside the walls of Guantanamo as the "Extreme Repression Force." But according to Michael Ratner, president of the Center for Constitutional Rights, "IRFs can't be separated from torture. They are a part of the brutalization of humans treated as less than human" (cited in Scahill). Nevertheless, as Huskey points out, even if any of the detainees in these prisons had had information that would have "prevent[ed] future attacks" on America, "their treatment went beyond [what] we might consider to be legal or even valid interrogation for known criminals" (178).

But *Man Out of Joint* not only gives a face to injustices and atrocities by demonstrating on stage the reality of what "'enhanced' interrogation techniques" consist of, it also informs audiences about the widespread geographical capture of detainees held at Guantanamo when hundreds of names from Libya, Saudi Arabia, Afghanistan, and the United Arab Emirates roll by on a screen for audiences to read. Additionally, Pollock also includes in her cast of characters the names of five "real detainees" who inform audiences about their experiences at Guantanamo. I refer to them as "real" because in her note to the script, Pollock writes that she "verified 'detainee abuse' with several Center for Constitutional Rights (CCR) publications" (n.p.). From these sources, she also presumably gained access to actual names and occupations of the detainees (social workers and hospital administrators, among other respectable occupations) and descriptions of the abuse they have been subjected to. Before describing their abuse, they signal their awareness that one of the goals of the prison is to remove "the inner comfort of identity" (307) by identifying themselves by name, not by number. Mirbati describes being beaten by the IRF (a large man wearing a lot of gear "jump[s] on his back" causing permanent injury to the vertebrae in his back [304]), but he receives no medical aid because he is told his injury is the "result of a degenerative disease" (305). Nechla is confronted by barking dogs whose breath is so close he is terrified of being bitten or killed (304), and he has good reason to be fearful, for as Feinman points out, there is "recent evidence that the dog handlers . . . were in fact given instructions to use their dogs in illegally violent ways" (62). The detainees also attest that any kind of protest (which ranges from writing "Have a Nice Day" on a Styrofoam cup to participating in a lengthy hunger strike) resulted in severe beatings, forced-feeding, and other types of increased torture for which no medical aid was provided. Although Pollock does not give Khadr a voice, Gianelli, who has become one of his lawyers, states that Khadr incurred "shrapnel wounds to the head and the eye" (305), was "shot three times" (306), interrogated and tortured with attack dogs at his chest at Bagram (307) before he was transported to Guantanamo, where he was then subjected to sustained torture. (Even though Gianelli has obtained proper documentation and permission to visit Khadr at Guantanamo, "K" prevents him from doing so.)

That Pollock presents the actual words of "real" detainees at Guantanamo is crucial, for according to Razack, the Americans have studiously avoided "*embodying*" torture at all: "it thus remains a particular policy or law. We seldom hear the voices of the tortured of Abu Ghraib, Guantanamo" ("Kill" 225). In the final scenes of the play, Pollock underscores that the use of torture was bound up with policies pursued by the Bush administration, which used the September 11 attack as a pretext to instigate a bogus war on terror. Even though they were warned by the Russians, the Iranians, and the Saudis, they did nothing, because they wanted another "Pearl Harbor." Pollock's play insists that any play about Guantanamo and Abu Ghraib must include an analysis of oil resources and other geopolitical factors as potential causes of conflict or, as Razack also stresses, the United States "is as heavily committed to securing territory and resources as it is to the reproduction of a society organized around white supremacy" ("Kill" 221). But Pollock also suggests that this kind of criminal behaviour which flies in the face of international humanitarian conventions has backfired and may now be serving as a recruitment tool for future enemies. Tellingly, one of the detainees, who declares he is an "educated" man, states these men are "foolish," because "someday, I will act" (309).

Undoubtedly, "torture chicks," who believe that they are becoming the equals of men by agreeing to perform as sexual interrogators, have played their own role in the creation of future enemies. But according to Deb, they are victims of what she terms *"liberal feminist thought,"* in which "the male remains normative, and patriarchy is undisturbed as the onus lies on women to enter structures of privilege. According to this theory, women who control male detainees have successfully reversed the power inequalities at least for themselves. Exercising power violently consolidates their status within patriarchal structures into which they have assimilated" (2). But Deb asserts that a "transnational" feminist response would "attempt to deter torture in the name of women's emancipation . . . attempt to stop imperialism from marching under the banner of women's rights, and . . . attempt to intervene in a liberal feminist politics that advocates for the unconditional empowerment of individual women" (4). She suggests that a transnational feminist ethics would insist that "women like Lynndie England would, at their own risk, resist patriarchal manipulation of military women by defying the chain of command that requires women to engage in torture" (3). Similarly, Barbara Ehrenreich argues that

> women do not change institutions simply by assimilating into them, only by consciously deciding to fight for change. We need a feminism that teaches a woman to say no – not just to the date rapist or overly insistent boyfriend,

but when necessary, to the military or corporate hierarchy within which she finds herself.

In short, we need a kind of feminism that aims not just to assimilate into the institutions that men have created over the centuries, but to infiltrate and subvert them. (4)

Davis, too, who asks why "the effort to challenge sexism and homophobia in the military [is] largely defined by the question of admission to existing hierarchies and not by a powerful critique of the institution itself" argues that "saying no" may be a positive aim: "Equality might also be considered to be the equal right to refuse and resist" (26). Eve Ensler finds that "feminism" is open to definition, but for her

feminism means reconstructing the world so that the mechanisms of dominance and violence are not the controlling factors. Rather than creating hierarchies based on abuse and submission, we would be creating partnerships based on equality and empowerment. In this world, women wouldn't hunger to be in the military at all. We wouldn't even have a military. (18)

Saying "no" might be harder than these feminists think, however, as several recent testimonies from "real" women in the military suggest. For example, Kayla Williams, who recounts her time in Iraq as a US Army sergeant serving in an intelligence company of the 101st Airborne Division in *Love My Rifle More Than You: Young and Female in the US Army*, had obtained a BA in English Literature from Bowling Green State University in 1997 and had also learned Arabic. Thus she had more agency than England, a low-level administrative clerk when she enlisted. Williams, by contrast, trained as an interpreter and then worked as an Arabic linguist/interpreter and operations specialist. Forced to take part in torture interrogations, she confesses that even though she initially *"enjoyed having power over this guy,"* she was *"uncomfortable with those feelings of pleasure at his discomfort"* (cited in Frost 143). But as Fusco suggests, Williams didn't "find fault with the order; she found herself to be lacking in ability to perform. In other words, she personalized an ethical and legal issue and thus avoided confrontation regarding the legitimacy of the practice" (49). Fusco's research led her to conclude that this is "not an uncommon position" among women in the military. Similarly, as I learned at a recent production in Calgary of Helen Benedict's unpublished play "The Lonely Soldier Monologues (Women at War in Iraq)," based on interviews with military women, any complaints about their treatment (such as sexual harassment or assault) or basic procedures went nowhere. In other words, saying "no" to the military has never been that easy. Pollock's solution (if she has one), would likely be to ensure that young women have many more and better opportunities to obtain decent educations so that they will never consider signing up for military duty a positive career move, but only a desperate last resort.

NOTES

1   Judith Thompson has also written about Omar Khadr. In the "Afterword" to *Omar Khadr, Oh Canada*, edited by Janice Williamson (Montreal: McGill-Queen's UP, 2012), Razack writes that Judith Thompson's play "Nail Biter" (165–73) offers "brilliant insight into the psyche of the *Canadian* subject who manages to live with torture through narratives that shield her character from seeing its horror" (431). The one-act play features a thirty-year-old CSIS agent who interrogated Khadr at Guantanamo. Razack adds that Thompson's "nail biter" is "Canada, the Canada that [Razack] once wrote about as anxious to prove itself as a grownup nation through participating in wars and peacekeeping ventures" (431).

2   I would like to thank Hollie Adams for her thoughtful paper on Pollock's *Man Out of Joint* (and other plays) which she wrote in my graduate seminar on Canadian War Drama in 2011. I drew upon several of her critical references and some of her clever insights about Pollock's use of photography in writing this essay.

3   In "The Misogynist Implications of Abu Ghraib," Lucinda Marshall asserts that although there is "ample evidence" that Iraqi women detained at Abu Ghraib have been sexually assaulted, the issue has received little attention because "quite simply, sexual abuse against men is considered torture; sexual abuse against women by men is business as usual" (*One of the Guys*, 55).

4   In "U. S. Lifting Ban on Women in Combat," Elisabeth Bumiller and Thom Shanker write that although the Pentagon claims to be lifting its ban on women in combat, in reality, more than 20,000 have served in combat in Iraq and Afghanistan: "as of last year, more than 800 women had been wounded in the two wars

and more than 130 had died." *National Post* 24 January 2013: A14. Moreover, "as recently as two months ago, four servicewomen filed a federal lawsuit against the Pentagon saying they had all served in combat in Iraq or Afghanistan but had not been officially recognized for it." (A14).

5   But Pollock's play also contains a number of history lessons that ensure that Canadians cannot claim to have a monopoly on moral virtue. Under the "Defence of Canada Regulations" invoked in World War Two, Italian-Canadians (like the Gianellis) who were assumed to pose a security threat were interned as enemy aliens without trial, even though most had no political affiliation and were captured as a result of mistaken identity or false accusations. Moreover, the Kingston Immigration Holding Centre, nicknamed Guantanamo North, located in the Millhaven Prison near Kingston, Ontario, incarcerates those determined to pose a risk to Canada's national security. Ironically, Omar Khadr was initially sent there to serve out his sentence, but after seven months, he was transferred to the Edmonton Institution for safety reasons. As Gianelli points out, the prison was put in place to hold "Muslim men . . . indefinitely without security certificates, without 'access to evidence against them' and with 'no judicial review of proceedings against them'" (290). Some have been held there for five or six years "without trial" and are "threatened with deportation to countries who torture" (290). The play also informs Canadians about Bill C-36, the Anti-Terrorism Act (268), which was passed in response to the 11 September 2001 attacks in the United States. The bill (now expired), which granted extensive powers of surveillance and control over anyone deemed suspicious, was widely considered incompatible with the Canadian Charter of Rights and Freedoms.

Works Cited

Davis, Angela Y. "Sexual Coercion, Prisons, and Female Responses." *One of the Guys: Women as Aggressors and Torturers*. Ed. Tara McKelvey. Emeryville, CA: Seal, 2007. 22–28. Print.

Deb, Basuli. "Transnational Feminism and Women Who Torture: Re-imag(in)ing Abu Ghraib Prison Photography." *Postcolonial Text* 7.1 (2012): 1–17. Print.

Ehrenreich, Barbara. "Foreword: Feminism's Assumptions Upended." *One of the Guys*, 1–5. Print.

Ensler, Eve. "I Still Don't Get How You Could Put a Leash on a Human Being." *One of the Guys*, 17–21. Print.

Feinman, Ilene. "Shock and Awe: Abu Ghraib, Women Soldiers, and Racially Gendered Torture." *One of the Guys*, 57–80. Print.

Finlay, Barbara. "Pawn, Scapegoat, or Collaborator? U.S. Military Women and Detainee Abuse in Iraq." *One of the Guys*, 199–212. Print.

Frost, Laura. "Photography/Pornography/Torture: The Politics of Seeing Abu Ghraib." *One of the Guys*, 135–40. Print.

Fusco, Coco. *A Field Guide for Female Interrogators*. Toronto: Seven Stories, 2008. Print.

Hobson, Louis. "Play Shines Light on Guantanamo." *Sun Media* 4 Dec. 2010. Web.

Holloway, Ann. "Hedda & Lynndie & Jabber & Ciel: An Interview with Judith Thomson." *The Masks of Judith Thompson*. Ed. Rick Knowles. Toronto: Playwrights Canada P, 2006. 138–46. Print.

Hunt, Stephen. "Pollock Heads Downstage: Small Group Takes on Icon's Risky New Play." *Calgary Herald* 9 May 2007: F1. Print.

Huq, Azia. "Bitter Fruit: Constitutional Gender Equality Comes to the Military." *One of the Guys*, 125–34. Print.

Huskey, Kristine A. "The 'Sex Interrogators' of Guantanamo." *One of the Guys*, 175–78. Print.

Kubik, Jeff. "Confronting Injustice Through Story: Downstage Debuts New Sharon Pollock Play, *Man Out of Joint*." *FastForward Weekly*. FFWDWeekly.com 3 May 2007. Web.

Laurier, Joanne. "*Standard Operating Procedure*: Images from a Neo-Colonial War." http://wsws.org/articles/2008/jun2008/sop-j17.shtml. Web.

Morrow, Martin. "From Hell." Review of *Palace of the End* and interview with Judith Thompson. http://www.subversivetheatre.org/productions/palace_end/related_thompson_interview.htm. Web.

Peters, John Durham. "Witnessing." *Media, Culture & Society* 23.6 (Nov. 2001): 707–23. Print.

Pollock, Sharon. "Man Out of Joint." *Canada and the Theatre of War*. Vol. 2. Ed. Donna Coates and Sherrill Grace. Toronto: Playwrights Canada P, 2010. 256–320. Print.

Puar, Jasbir K. "Abu Ghraib: Arguing against Exceptionalism." *Feminist Studies* 30.2 (Summer 2004): 522–35. Print.

Rajiva, Lila. "The Military Made Me Do It: Double Standards and Psychic Injuries at Abu Ghraib." *One of the Guys*, 217–28. Print.

Razack, Sherene H. "Afterword: The Mark of Torture." In *Omar Khadr, Oh Canada*. Ed. Janice Williamson. Montreal: McGill-Queen's UP, 2012: 429–37. Print.

———. "If It Wasn't For the Sex and the Photos: The Torture of Prisoners at Abu Ghraib." *Casting Out: The Eviction of Muslims From Western Law and Politics*. Toronto: U of Toronto P, 2008: 59–80. Print.

———. "'We Didn't Kill 'Em, We Didn't Cut Their Heads Off': Abu Ghraib Revisited." *Racial Formation in the Twenty-First Century*. Ed. Daniel Martinez HoSang, Oneka LaBennett, and Laura Polido. Berkeley: U of California P, 217–43. Print.

Rentschler, Carrie A. "Witnessing: US Citizenship and the Vicarious Experience of Suffering." *Media, Culture and Society* 26 (2004): 296–304. Print.

Scahill, Jeremy. "Guantanamo's Immediate Reaction Force Still Terrorizing Detainees." http://www.wikileaks.org /wiki/Guantanmo%27s_Immediate_Reaction_Force_still_terrorizing_detainees. Web.

Sontag, Susan. *Regarding the Pain of Others*. New York: Penguin, 2003. Print.

———. "Regarding the Torture of Others." http://www.southercrossreview.org/35/sontag.htm Web.

Thompson, Judith. *Palace of the End*. Canada and the Theatre of War. Vol. 2. Toronto: Playwrights Canada P, 2009. 147–82. Print.

Walker, LaNitra. "Women's Role in Mob Violence: Lynchings and Abu Ghraib." *One of the Guys*, 189–98. Print.

Williams, Kyla. *Love My Rifle More Than You: Young and Female in the US Army*. New York: Norton, 2005. Print.

Sharon Pollock and the Garry Theatre (1992-97)

Martin Morrow

The first time I encountered Sharon Pollock, she was in the middle of a fight.

It was early in January 1988, the year Calgary hosted the Winter Olympics, as well as its accompanying Olympic Arts Festival. As its contribution to the festival, Theatre Calgary had chosen to do a major revival of Sharon's 1973 play *Walsh*. The festival would garner national, if not international, attention, so the stakes were high. At the time, I was a young entertainment reporter at the *Calgary Herald*. I came into the newsroom one morning to be told something was amiss with the Theatre Calgary production. The company had abruptly removed the signs advertising the play outside the Max Bell Theatre. After an initially evasive response from TC, the company finally admitted there had been what it termed a "contractual disagreement" between Sharon and the theatre – in essence, they had locked horns over her input into the casting of the play – and she had demanded that her name be removed from the posters and all advertising ("Playwright").

That was my introduction to Sharon Pollock: a playwright with a fighting spirit who wasn't afraid to cause controversy and embarrassment in the middle of an international festival, if it meant defending the artistic integrity of her work. Within a few years, as the theatre critic for the *Herald*, I would watch her take on a much bigger fight, as she attempted to run a viable theatre company without public funding in a low-income neighbourhood a world away from the brass-and-brick "culture palace" then known as the Calgary Centre for Performing Arts – today's Arts Common.

This, of course, was the Garry Theatre. Or, as Calgary residents had known it for many years before, the Hyland International – a seedy porn cinema from the pre-video days, presumably frequented by men in slouch hats and trench coats, newspapers strategically spread across their knees. John and Oreal Kerr had bought the property in the Ramsay-Inglewood neighbourhood, on Ninth Avenue East, a strip otherwise occupied mainly by antique shops, dive bars and greasy spoons. It was a pocket of Calgary awaiting gentrification, and what better way to get it started than to open that most bourgeois of enterprises, a live theatre?

At the Kerrs' invitation, Sharon, multi–Governor General's Award-winning, internationally produced playwright, took over the old grindhouse and proceeded to transform it. This might seem like a task more suited to young, hungry artists than to a distinguished writer in her fifties – especially when you consider how hands-on the job was, but Sharon rolled up her sleeves and – along with her son Kirk, a.k.a. K.C. Campbell – did a lot of the work renovating and maintaining the building. You have to understand where she was coming from. By 1992, the year the Garry opened for business, Sharon had already been through two brief, unhappy stints as the artistic director of regional theatre companies: with Theatre Calgary in 1984–85 and with Theatre New Brunswick in her hometown of Fredericton in 1988–89. She had resigned from both positions when she found, in her view, that the boards of directors were unwilling to support her desire to produce serious and demanding plays. Disillusioned with the regional-theatre model and its pandering to the philistine tastes of a well-heeled elite, she was ready to run a company in which she was not beholden to a board and where she could realize her ideal of a theatre that reflected the whole community, not just its wealthy arts patrons. Her goals for the Garry Theatre were clearly populist. "We want to do affordable, accessible and entertaining theatre," she told me in an interview in October 1992, shortly before inaugurating the Garry's first season with that sure-fire Canadian hit, *Billy Bishop Goes to War* ("Billy").

Before creating the storefront Garry Theatre, she and Kirk did a dry run in what had been, literally, a store. They had set up the Performance Kitchen in a former Chinese grocery in Ramsay and presented performances and readings in its tiny front space. I recall going there to see Mark Lawes, future co-founder of Theatre Junction, give a dramatic recital of Tennyson's poem *Maud*. In theory, anybody could just walk in off the street and grab some theatre the way you'd pop in to buy a litre of milk. That idea extended to the Garry and I saw it in action the evening that I attended *Billy Bishop Goes to War*. Along with a typical opening-night crowd, there was a rough-looking old geezer who could have wandered in from the nearby fleabag hotel. I encountered him in the lobby during the interval. He came up to me, evidently excited by what he'd just seen, and asked if there was more. Yes, I told him, in a few minutes we're going to go back in for Act Two. I saw him again when the play was over, looking even more enthusiastic. So, was that it? he wanted to know. Or was there a *third* act? If there had been, he would have been front-row centre. This was Sharon's dream come true: theatre literally for the man or woman on the street.

At the time Sharon founded the Garry, Calgary's professional theatre scene was small but diverse. Theatre Calgary, the city's flagship organization, had been in a state of continual identity crisis during the late 1980s, but by the early 1990s was sticking resolutely to the mainstream. Alberta Theatre Projects had made the annual playRites Festival of New Canadian Plays its raison d'être, but relied heavily on a wrap-around season of recent New York and London hits to maintain its subscriber base. It and TC were in a constant, if unacknowledged, rivalry. One Yellow Rabbit, still under the radar for many Calgarians, was in the throes of creating its own signature brand of poetic physical theatre. Theatre Junction was just getting started in the studio space of the Jubilee Auditorium, where it was mixing off-Broadway fare with modern and nineteenth-century classics. Sharon, in fact, had directed its first show, a revival of *Look Back in Anger*. She had also directed a memorable and controversial playRites premiere at ATP in 1991 – *Final Decisions*, a political drama about torture by a then up-and-coming Argentine-Canadian playwright, Guillermo Verdecchia, which reportedly caused a well-known Calgary arts patron to exit the theatre in disgust. Theatre observers like me were eager to see what her Garry experiment would bring to the mix.

With no government grants and no agencies or boards to answer to, Sharon could program whatever she liked – as long as her company made enough to pay for itself. Its seasons came to represent Sharon's own tastes, which tended toward serious and intellectually stimulating drama. She did Miller, Shaw, and O'Neill, *Of Mice and Men*, *Equus* and *Agnes of God*. The Garry also became, as we'd expected, an outlet for her own plays, both premieres and revivals. With an eye to the box office, however, she also programmed a fair number of crowd-pleasers. There was a Canadian Christmas musical, *The Other Side of the Pole*, in the first season, and later on, productions of *Dracula*, *The Diary of Anne Frank* and the Harlequin Romance spoof, *Nurse Jane Goes to Hawaii*. The efforts at light-hearted fare were invariably disappointing; with the odd exception, like the acerbic *The Killing of Sister George* – in which Sharon played the title role of a gin-swilling lesbian soap-opera star – the Garry didn't do comedy well.

Aside from Sharon's work, there was a healthy serving of Canadian material. The Garry seasons included the revivals of *Billy Bishop*, Allan Stratton's *Nurse Jane*, Anne Chislett's *The Tomorrow Box* and David French's *Salt-Water Moon*; the Western Canadian premiere of Glen Cairns's *Danceland*; the remounting of a fringe play by K.C. Campbell called *Headin' Out*; and the debut of a docu-drama, *Highway #2*, written by Sharon, Paul Gélineau, and Janet Hinton, about the enduring Calgary–Edmonton rivalry. The work at the Garry that most interested me as a critic was Sharon's. Running her own company gave her an opportunity to revisit one of her earlier plays, *The Komagata Maru Incident*, as well as to premiere *Death in the Family* and *Saucy Jack*, and give her historical drama *Fair Liberty's Call* its first production after its 1993 debut at the Stratford Festival.

The first new Pollock play to be produced was *Death in the Family*, which closed the Garry's inaugural season in June of 1993. Although it starred Sharon – making her Garry acting debut – and was directed by former Theatre Calgary artistic boss Rick McNair, it was a decidedly minor affair. Originally written as a film script – and in fact later made into a television drama – it was a rural-set mystery thriller with elements of both Steinbeck's *Of Mice and Men* and Sam Shepard's *Buried Child*. (Interestingly, Sharon had directed Rick in a mid-1980s production of *Buried Child* and would later stage *Of Mice and Men* in the Garry's penultimate season.) If *Death in the Family* seemed like little more than an entertaining potboiler, what it did reveal for those of us who'd never seen her onstage was Sharon's considerable acting talent. Sharon played the troubled central character, Renée Havard, a middle-aged alcoholic living with her mentally challenged brother on a rundown Alberta farm. I described her Renée in my review as "gruff but glib, a colourful recluse staggering about her dilapidated homestead in gumboots and lumberjack jacket and guzzling straight rye from a jam jar" ("Pollock Play").

Sharon's next self-penned offering at the Garry, however, was a far stronger and more disturbing work. *Saucy Jack*, which made its debut early in the theatre's second season, was Sharon's take on the Jack the Ripper legend. In some respects, it was a sequel to *Blood Relations*, only this time the playwright was less concerned with the murderer's motives than with the lives of the victims. Using the same play-within-a-play conceit as *Blood Relations* (or *Hamlet*, for that matter), an actress is hired to impersonate the prostitutes brutally slain by the Ripper during his rampage. In the process, the identities of these poor, neglected women are reclaimed. Today, the play reminds one particularly of Vancouver's controversial Robert Pickton serial-killer case. It also anticipates Margaret Atwood's *The Penelopiad*, in which she gives a voice to the marginalized women victims of Homer's *The Odyssey*. At the time of *Saucy Jack's* debut, Sharon told me, "I think of all the women who die, whose names we never know. We have had a whole series of prostitute deaths in [Calgary] and their names are forgotten" ("Ripper").

Saucy Jack was terrific and I said so in my *Herald* review: "This is a haunting, gripping drama, abetted at the Garry by Pollock's skilled, understated direction ("Ripper"). I praised the bravura performance of Jarvis Hall as the semi-deranged scholar with royal connections, who may hold the key to the Ripper's identity in his shattered memory. I still remember his performance, along with the striking one by Rae Ellen Bodie as the actress who plays the prostitutes, and the subtly ghoulish set design by Kirk.

Sharon's third new play at the Garry, *Fair Liberty's Call*, also proved to be the company's last production. There was an odd symmetry in that; during the Garry's first season, she had simultaneously been preoccupied with preparing that play for its Stratford premiere. Now Calgarians finally got to see this new work by perhaps the city's best-known playwright, in what would turn out to be the Garry's swan song. *Fair Liberty's Call*, a historical drama about the United Empire Loyalists, was the kind of tough-minded examination of our country's past that Sharon does so well. In my review, I described it as having "the intellectual vigour of all her best plays, that determination to use history and legend as a key to the present." I called her writing "strong in irony and stinging insight" ("Pollock's Dark"). At the time this tale about the bloody birth of English Canada in the wake of the American Revolution, which pitted neighbour against neighbour, resonated with the recent atrocities of Bosnia and Rwanda. Even with the Stratford imprimatur, however, Sharon had a hard time getting it produced elsewhere. She told me in an interview at the time that the artistic directors of Canadian theatre companies tended to gently turn it down.

"They'd say to me, 'This is an important play . . . but no, I don't think there's room on my stage for it'" ("Play"). It was up to Sharon to stage it herself.

At this point you might be wondering how she was able to produce large-cast plays like this one – or indeed whole seasons of ambitious work – without subsidies. It was far from easy, although she and Kirk did their best to get the most out of their main asset – the theatre itself. From the outset, they offered competitive rental rates and sublet the place to everyone from touring companies to church groups. Quest Theatre, Calgary's young people's troupe, became a resident company for a time, and there were late-night and summer programs of fringe-style fare. Still, they quickly ran into trouble. In the Garry's first season, Sharon hired professional talent represented by the Canadian Actors Equity Association. While they were paid their Equity salaries, the Garry wasn't able to pay the benefit dues that were part of the contract. A portion was still owed by the end of the second season, at which time Actors' Equity put the Garry on its default list. Essentially blacklisted in the professional theatre community, the Garry ended up relying on non-Equity actors and even then was not always able to pay them. The Garry didn't discharge its debt until the fifth and final season, allowing *Fair Liberty's Call* to be produced as an Equity co-op.

That handicap was sometimes evident onstage. It led to actors being miscast – more often than not, playing roles they were too young for. And the lack of a production budget could be embarrassing – I have memories of some hilariously inept special effects for *Dracula*, and 15th-century knights wearing 19th-century sabres in *Saint Joan*. There were times when, frankly, had Sharon Pollock's name not been in the program, I might have thought I was watching a community theatre production. But Sharon also attracted some promising young talent and a few of the big ensemble shows, like *One Flew Over the Cuckoo's Nest* and *Of Mice and Men*, were surprisingly strong. Sharon herself could always be relied on to strengthen a show with her own not-infrequent performances.

In the end, though, running the Garry demanded too much of Sharon and Kirk and their collaborators. After *Fair Liberty's Call* – the high note at the end of a rough fifth season – it was time to call it quits. As Sharon later told me, the Garry "was sucking everybody dry" ("Pollock Feeling"). That it had lasted five seasons was remarkable. The Garry had been founded out of Sharon's bloody-minded determination to buck the subsidized theatre model and still create serious and significant work. Ultimately, it took the dedication of a small core of theatre artists to keep it going despite insufficient revenue. If its chances of success were always slim, the Garry did allow Sharon finally to run a theatre her way, while it provided training and opportunities for young actors in the Calgary community.

Despite the varying quality of the productions, my personal memory of the Garry is a fond one. The theatre really did have a folksy, welcoming feel to it. Sharon often worked the box office during shows, while I remember Kirk simultaneously stage managing and running the concession stand. The place also had a youthful vibe. Sharon had gathered round her a bunch of passionate young people, hard-working and, yes, sometimes hard-drinking, too. I knocked back more than a few pints with them after-hours myself. In June of 1993, when I sat down with Sharon and Kirk to assess their first Garry season, Sharon struck a rebellious note when she explained what she got out of the experience. Running the Garry, she said, kept her from ossifying into part of the theatrical establishment. "It's stimulating to work with people who, in a way, have nothing to lose in the theatre. I feel there's more openness and frankness and a more productive exploration of what we do in the theatre, and how we do it. It forces you to constantly reassess something that you would otherwise take for granted" ("Noted Canadian").

Professionally, as a theatre critic, my relationship with the Garry was generally supportive. I didn't pull any punches when it came to critiquing the productions – this was, after all, a company being run by one of Canada's major playwrights and deserved serious scrutiny. At the same time, I was quick to point out when a show was good and to urge people to head down to Inglewood and see it. Over the course of the Garry's life, I got to know Sharon a little better and spent some of that aforementioned drinking time with Kirk. I remember a number of intense discussions with both of them about what they hoped to achieve with the Garry and the state of Canadian theatre in general. I was aware that they relied on my *Herald* reviews to pull in audiences and I attended every play up until the final season. That season, 1996–97, there was plenty to pull focus from the Garry – ATP's controversial staging of *Angels in America*, Theatre Calgary's struggle back from the brink of bankruptcy. There was also the city's increasing theatrical activity in general. For me, the Garry ended up largely on the back burner. My lack of coverage may have contributed in some way to the theatre's demise at the end of that season, but I got the sense that by then it was already running on fumes.

However, I was left with tremendous respect for Sharon and what she had attempted to do. Certainly, as a mid-career playwright, she didn't need to plunge into such a risky and potentially embarrassing venture. Yet she did it wholeheartedly. Where she might have merely leant her name and prestige to the Garry, or stayed aloof as an artistic director, she got down-and-dirty in its day-to-day operations – from selling tickets to even cleaning the toilets when necessary. That last detail comes courtesy of Garry guest director Christopher Foreman, who then got annoyed with me when I repeated it in the pages of the *Herald*. But for me it illustrated Sharon's incredible dedication to the enterprise. Sharon may be a fighter, but hand-in-hand with that pugnacious spirit is a pure love for creating theatre.

Garry Theatre seasons:

1992–93: *Billy Bishop Goes to War; The Other Side of the Pole; The Tomorrow Box; Macbeth; Jack's Daughters; Death in the Family* (Pollock; premiere).

1993–94: *Come Back to the Five and Dime, Jimmy Dean, Jimmy Dean; Saucy Jack* (Pollock; premiere), *Agnes of God; Nurse Jane Goes to Hawaii; Headin' Out; Death of a Salesman.*

1994–95: *Loot; The Komagata Maru Incident* (Pollock, revival); *One Flew Over the Cuckoo's Nest; The Diary of Anne Frank; Saint Joan; Highway #2, the Great Divide.*

1995–96: *Gaslight; Salt-Water Moon; Dracula; The Killing of Sister George; Danceland; Of Mice and Men.*

1996–97: *The Lion in Winter; Equus; Scotland Road; A Moon for the Misbegotten; Fair Liberty's Call* (Pollock; western Canadian premiere).

Works Cited

Morrow, Martin. "Billy Bishop's Back: Canadian Classic Launches Calgary's Newest Theatre." *Calgary Herald* 16 Oct. 1992: G1. Print.

———. "Noted Canadian Playwright Sharon Pollock May Have to Sell Tickets at the Door, But at Least She Gets to Run a Theatre . . . Her Way." *Calgary Herald* 8 June 1993: D6. Print.

———. "Play Finally Comes to Town." *Calgary Herald* 23 April 1997: C8. Print.

———. "Playwright Pulls Name from Show." *Calgary Herald* 7 Jan. 1988: F4. Print.

———. "Pollock's Dark Drama Raises Audience: *Fair Liberty's Call* Pits Families Against Families Caught in the Bloody Fissure of our History." *Calgary Herald* 27 April 1997: C4. Print.

———. "Pollock Feeling Feisty Again." *Calgary Herald* 28 Jan. 1998: F1. Print.

———. "Pollock Play Better Suited to Big Screen." *Calgary Herald* 11 June 1993: C9. Print.

———. "Ripper a Chiller Under Pollock's Hand." *Calgary Herald* 29 Nov. 1993: C5. Print.

Sharon Pollock in Kosovo

Jeton Neziraj

In 2003, a few years after the war in Kosovo ended, some colleagues and I established the Centre for Children's Theatre Development (CCTD). Through our work, we aimed to aesthetically improve children's theatre in Kosovo, while using the theatre as a platform where we could address important social and political topics. However, we had very little experience, so it was necessary to seek other people's assistance. Thus we started by trying to create links with artists, theatre practitioners, and theatre institutions from different parts of the world.

Theatre in Kosovo had suffered from the country's ten-year period of war, repression, and isolation. During the 1990s it barely functioned. Albanian culture was a key target for the hegemonic politics of the Serbian dictator Slobodan Milošević. Theatre was unavoidably one of its casualties. Hence after Kosovo was freed, we wanted to connect culturally with the world. Just as space ships use frequent signals when trying to connect to Earth, we started sending messages to people and theatre institutions all over the world. We found it very encouraging that we immediately began receiving many positive responses. Some people offered to share their experiences, others sent books, and so on. Sharon Pollock, the distinguished Canadian playwright whom we had contacted by email, replied and offered to send us her next royalty cheque, which she was hoping to receive from one of her staged plays in the United States. We were thrilled by her response but asked her to send books instead of money since, at that time, we had few resources. We never did receive the books that Sharon sent us, though. Who knows where they ended up? Somehow, when I think of those books, I always imagine that they may come one day; those "lost books" make me think of the sentimental stories of letters mailed during the Second World War, which finally reached their destinations some forty or fifty years later.

From that time on, I continued to keep in touch with Sharon. She read one of my plays for children and offered some valuable comments. And every time I met someone from Canada, one of my first questions was, "Do you know Sharon Pollock?" I knew she was an important figure in the world of theatre, but I have since learned that she is legendary, one of the most prominent personalities in theatre.

After I visited Canada for the first time in 2008, Sharon again mailed me a generous package of books on theatre. Among these books were some of her plays. Finally, I could read her work! That same year, I started working as the artistic director at the National Theatre of Kosovo, and my colleagues and I decided that Sharon Pollock should be one of our first invited guests. On her first visit to Kosovo, she gave a lecture on Canadian theatre and facilitated a workshop designed for young playwrights. At that time, Sharon and I also initiated a Canadian–Kosovo cultural exchange project named "PlayLuaj." By then, I had read one of her best-known plays, *Blood Relations*, and as soon as I finished it, I was convinced that it should be made available to Kosovar audiences.

Blood Relations at the National Theatre of Kosovo

In 2010, the National Theatre of Kosovo decided that *Blood Relations* should be staged in the upcoming season, and that it should be directed by the well-known Kosovo director Fadil Hysaj. After he read the play, he said to me, "This is my play. No one in Kosovo can stage it better than me. It is made for me." I saw that his enthusiasm stemmed from more than just wanting a new theatrical adventure. The opening of *Blood Relations* took place on 17 December 2010, in Pristina, with all of the profits from the production allocated for humanitarian causes. We donated the money generated from ticket sales and sales of the published Albanian version of the play to Naxhije Deva, a pioneer actress of the Kosovo theatre, who was on the verge of poverty. In offering our funds this way, we felt we were embracing the same spirit of humanism and empathy that Sharon tries to evoke through her writing and through her intellectual engagements, evident in the support that she had so kindly offered us from the first time we were introduced to each other. We were also delighted that Sharon was able to attend the opening of her play in Pristina.

I have been asked many times in Canada why we decided to stage *Blood Relations* in Kosovo. My response is usually straightforward: this is an excellent play, which functions well in different cultural and social contexts. I believe that this is an essential feature of a good play – that audiences can easily find references in different social and cultural settings. Yet when I selected this play as a part of the theatre's program, I had something else in mind, too – something that I believed to be important, whether the audience could relate to it or not.

At that time (and still today), the UN mission in Kosovo was initiating trials against some of the former Kosovo Liberation Army soldiers who had fought against Serbian forces. These soldiers were being accused of murdering some of the traitors who had collaborated with the enemy. In the eyes of many people in Kosovo, especially those who had suffered at the hands of enemy forces, the killing of these traitors who had in turn killed mostly civilians was understandable, perhaps even justifiable.[1] Some also felt that justice might have been served had these traitors been arrested and jailed for their acts, but most were released for lack of evidence. This was the disturbing Kosovo political background at the time when the history of the American Lizzie Borden, the central character in *Blood Relations*, was introduced to the Kosovar audience.

This was the link I made between Sharon's play and what was happening in Kosovo. But at the same time, I was also convinced that the play would function even without this "contextualization." The director chose to treat the play solely in terms of its content, without making any overt parallels with other contexts. His decision, to use a symbolic and ritualistic approach (quite popular in Kosovo theatre), offered an unusual dimension, most likely different from the way it may have been staged in Canada or other countries. In my opinion, the play was staged very well and received a favourable response from the audience.

"The Hotel" Play

My collaboration with Sharon has continued since the staging of *Blood Relations*. As a part of our "PlayLuaj" project, Sharon and I have started working on a play tentatively titled "The Hotel." Our discussions on how to approach it have been extremely useful for me: as a young playwright, I have had the opportunity to observe Sharon's creative process, and at the same time, to be a part of this process. We have gathered a lot of the material necessary for writing the play, but there is still much work left to do. The topic we have chosen concerns a post-war location, a place like Kosovo, but not necessarily Kosovo. It is a place that has suffered through war and is trying to rebuild itself and find peace. The plot summary so far is as follows: a director (maybe Canadian) is invited by an international NGO to work on a short performance with actors who come from both sides of the conflict. The play is to be shown on the last day of the donors' conference, at the end of which the NGO hopes to gather sufficient funds in order to continue its activities in bringing reconciliation to this country that was destroyed by war.

As expected, many questions remain and we still have many unsolved issues. However, it is fascinating to see how two people with such different perspectives approach both the content and style of the play. Sharon writes, of course, from an outsider's perspective, as a "witness" to war, but at the same time she clearly discerns post-war problems, such as the emotional aspects of the characters and their inter-relations. By contrast, as an insider, as someone who has directly experienced war, I tend to be "overly involved." Obviously, bringing these two diverse experiences and perspectives together requires a great deal of understanding on both our parts. Although our collaboration remains unfinished, I hope that audiences in both Canada and Europe will one day be able to see this difficult and challenging work on stage. I also hope that the Canadian–Kosovar project "PlayLuaj" will continue. The distance between our two countries may be an obstacle, but with Sharon, anything is possible.

NOTE

1   For more background on Kosovar theatre during the war, see the following twenty-four-minute video, which includes an interview with Jeton Neziraj and clips from recent productions. nitenews.org/jeton-neziraj.kosovo-war-theatre.

Biography and *the* Archive

Sherrill Grace

> *The archive has always been a pledge, and like every pledge, a token of the future.*
>
> —DERRIDA, "ARCHIVE FEVER," 18

Biography

In a fascinating essay called "Poetry and Psychobiography," Phyllis Webb observes that,

> Biographers, bless them, have to make a good story out of a life, even an uneventful life, and they have to use all their resources as researchers, scholars, and writers to get things right. There are a lot of things to get right: drafts and manuscripts, letters, critical studies, recorded and printed

interviews, photographs, all kinds of data stored in attics and archives and libraries; in coat-pockets, in graveyards, in church and municipal records, in educational and mental institutions; on tapes and now on floppy disks.[1]

Webb continues her list with all the wives, husbands, lovers, psychiatrists and physicians, the travels, the literary influences, the quirks, the memorabilia, and she ends her observation on the resources of biography with a question: "The writer's work must surely be the reason for all this diligent activity – mustn't it?" (101).

Webb correctly identifies the main parameters and challenges of biography, and I especially appreciate her blessing and her recognition that biographers need to make good stories. I also agree with her that one writes a *literary* biography because of the literature, the *oeuvre*. But getting things right? That is for me the crucial question, the terrifying question, the black hole I fear when I tackle – or even read – a biography. What is right? How does one assert rightness over wrongness? What does one need in order to claim to be *right*? And finally – if anything can be final – what impact will rightness have when it finds its way into that good story about a life: for whom does this rightness matter and why? The same questions arise for wrongness. I will return to these fundamental questions because they accompanied me through the writing of *Making Theatre: A Life of Sharon Pollock* and they are returning to nip at my heels as I venture deeper into the resources for my current work – a biography of Timothy Findley. But before I make this return, I want to digress, first to Tiff and then to 1985 and the Canadian story of biography. Bear with me; this double detour will return me to Sharon and to my questions.

I have called this talk "Biography and *the* Archive." I stress *the* to capture the complexity of archives – not one archive, not *an* archive but something far larger, far less well defined. I could also have called it "biography IN the archive" or, more autobiographically – "my life as a biographer in archives" – because archives are my foundation, my repository, the resource of all biographical work. Archives are precious.

Archives help one get it right. But archives are fragile, vulnerable — subject to what Derrida calls "archive fever," the *mal d'archive*. They can also be dangerous and tricky; they can hide secrets — personal secrets, family skeletons, state documents sealed and classified so citizens will never know what happened or who did what to whom. Archives can be destroyed, and when they are, who knows what kinds of rightness are lost for ever — or maybe not lost because materials in an archive, when studied, must still be interpreted, woven into a story, made into a fiction. Which reminds me of that striking scene near the beginning of *The Wars*:

> You begin at the archives with photographs. Robert and Rowena — rabbits and wheelchairs — children, dogs and horses . . . Boxes and boxes of snapshots and portraits; maps and letters; cablegrams and clippings from the papers. All you have to do is sign them out and carry them across the room. Spread over table tops, a whole age lies in fragments underneath the lamps . . . The boxes smell of yellow dust. You hold your breath. As the past moves under your finger-tips, part of it crumbles. Other parts, you know you'll never find. This is what you have. (*The Wars* 5–6)

Where Webb described the resources of *the* archive and the imperative of rightness, Findley has made *an* archive come alive. He has inhabited it: you and I are there peering at these fragile documents, smelling the dust, settling down to do what we can with these fragments, knowing we will never find everything and therefore never get it *all* right.

But wait. There is another archive in Findley's work that I want to remind you about. Very near the end of *Famous Last Words*, the evil Harry Reinhardt, who has tracked Mauberley, our writer-protagonist and Second World War fascist sympathizer, to his hideaway in the Grand Elysium Hotel in the Austrian Alps and killed him by driving a pick axe through his eye, destroys the evidence he was hired to deal with — along with Mauberley. Here is what *we read*:

> Reinhardt's final act was to get the boy to help him burn the notebooks. All of Mauberley's journals and papers and letters, poured into the bathtub and covered with kerosene and set ablaze. It was marvelous to Harry's eyes. The complete destruction of the man he had been sent . . . to kill – and all his words. (*Famous Last Words* 388)

Such a scene is – for me – almost worse than the *spectacle* of Mauberley's corpse; my sympathies for him are mixed at best. Except that Reinhardt is only successful in part. He has killed Mauberley and silenced him and he has destroyed Mauberley's carefully guarded archive, his original documents, but he has not discovered the walls where Mauberley has written his version of what he witnessed and what others did before and during the Second World War. The original archive has been transformed into an auto/biography – that is, Mauberley's own story and the stories of many others – Ezra Pound, the Duke and Duchess of Windsor, Sir Harry Oakes, etc., and of an era – in the narrative that unfolds on the hotel walls. These are the famous last words that the two officers will find and argue over and that we, as readers, must try to interpret. This text is a version of *Mene Mene tekel upharsim* (Daniel 5), a warning, a challenge, an appeal to rightness: *you* will be tested and found wanting.

Fire has obliterated the archive but not before some version of a story is created from it. If Reinhardt had killed Mauberley before he began, let alone completed, his desperate confessional auto/biography, then we would never be able to read his words or know anything about what he took part in. We could not be warned. Getting things right, setting the record straight, putting his lands in order before he dies – all this would have been impossible. There are many other archive-like objects in Findley's works – Cassandra's photograph album in the play *Can You See Me, Yet?*, the secret state files on Ambassador Raymond in *The Stillborn Lover*, Vanessa Van Horne's journal and photographs in *The Telling of Lies*, the notebooks and memories that Will Shakespeare draws on to tell his story about the Queen in *Elizabeth Rex*. But in *The*

Wars and *Famous Last Words* Findley truly makes us see the value and vulnerability of records, photos, letters, journals, clippings, events witnessed and noted down – the archive – with which biographers, among others, must work. If Harry Reinhardt had succeeded, we would not learn about the fascist cabal involving the Duke and Duchess, the state secrets on both sides of the war, or the behind-the-scenes maneuverings of those in power. And we would not listen to the two soldiers, Lieutenant Quinn and Captain Freyberg (the intelligence officer), argue over human morality and guilt, or see over Freyberg's shoulder his scrapbook of photographs from the liberation of Dachau that he has so recently witnessed and will not forget.

In short, Findley insists that the archive matters. To deliberately destroy it is a crime; to carelessly damage it is serious. The archive holds keys to the future, to stories yet to be told, stories repressed perhaps by governments or the secret police; it is the custodian of evidence essential to the courts or simply to a family's awareness of their genealogy. Archives are the repositories of memory, identity and, to some degree, of getting it right.

But archives can be lost by accident. Think of those boxes in the attic that relatives toss out when granny dies and the house must be sold; those files ruined by water as they lie under a leaking roof or in a flooded garage. Or, those boxes lost to fire when old wiring in a house fails and flames whip through the rooms. In such a case – and the case in my mind is Sharon Pollock's – one does not fret over boxes. One gets out alive with one's pets, one's cell phone, and one's wallet.

So much for my first detour, which has returned me to the individual biography and personal archives. For my second detour, I want to reflect on the development of Canadian biography, by which I mean the national story that can be told through an accumulation of biographical stories. My contention is that biography tells us who we are. Us/we, as the people who live here now, who have arrived recently or generations ago, who have been here for millennia. And because I place such importance on biography, I do not accept the idea that only the life-stories of our politicians, generals and military heroes, hockey players, and business tycoons matter. If one begins from the assumption that biographies are composite narratives in an ongoing national narrative, then one must – it seems to me – open the door wide to include and stress the biographies of creative people – writers, as Webb reminds us, painters, composers, filmmakers, and performing artists – and so-called ordinary folks living among us.

In his 1985 essay on Findley's *The Wars* and *Famous Last Words*, George Woodcock reflected on the emergence of biography (and history) in the 1980s as an important contributor to Canadian literary culture.[2] By 1985 Findley had established himself as the major Canadian novelist to explore history in his fiction through the narrative lens of auto/biography – Robert Ross's biography, Mauberley's autobiography, and the auto/biography of Canada within the twentieth century's cataclysmic wars. By 1985, Sharon Pollock had established herself as the most important Canadian playwright to examine history in her plays – *Walsh*, *The Komagata Maru Incident*, *Blood Relations*, and *Doc*. Like Findley, she chose to frame history with biography and autobiography. Neither Pollock nor Findley were interested only in their own life-stories, although I would argue that those stories are there in their works. Each was, however, very curious about Canada's life-stories and about the ways in which such stories functioned to connect the private with the public, the individual man or woman, family or community, with the nation. Moreover, both Findley and Pollock challenged the national biography we'd been handed – in history books, in narratives of nation-building through railways or at Vimy Ridge; and both revisited key – originary, foundational – stories about who we were (and are) by exploring what and who was left out, misrepresented, or silenced.

I return to Woodcock here, himself a distinguished biographer, to identify a watershed moment in twentieth-century thinking about the role of biography and history within the literary life of the country. Canadians had written biographies prior to 1985, most notably about politicians, and we had some autobiographies/memoirs, again, usually by men in public life or the military. The *Dictionary of Literary*

Biography already existed as a reference resource; so did the *Canadian Who's Who* (now in its 112th year). And Hurtig began *The Canadian Encyclopedia* in the 1980s. But I would not claim that Canadians had a rich or varied corpus of biographical writing. Our examples of auto-biography were fewer still. Since 1985, however, this has changed. In this century, we are increasingly aware of and rich in both genres – so much so that one rarely opens the *Globe and Mail* (or reads it online) without finding a new Canadian biography just published. The 2005 biography of Alice Munro by Robert Thacker was updated and reissued in 2011, and I have recently read Charles Foran on Richler, Allen Levine on Mackenzie King, Brian Busby on John Glassco, Jane Lind on Paraskeva Clark, James Neufeld on Lois Marshall (a wonderful biography), Carol Bishop-Gwyn on Celia Franca and, most recently, *A Fiery Soul*, the 2011 biography of John Hirsch by Fraidie Martz and Andrew Wilson.[3]

Speaking of Richard Gwyn's new two-volume biography of Sir John A. (yes, another massive study of Macdonald) in his 10 December 2011 column in the *Globe and Mail*, Jeffrey Simpson stresses the aptness of the title *Nation Maker* and praises Gwyn's "recapturing [of] Macdonald's immense contributions to defining Canada" (F9). In short, Simpson understands – as Woodcock did over two decades ago – that biography tells a national story and that the biography of an influential person is also part of, a contributing element in, the production of the nation's biography. I was puzzled, therefore, to read Simpson's final remark to the effect that such biographical work doesn't fall on fertile ground in Canada. I was puzzled because I think the ground – readers, students, anyone interested in matters of identity – is very fertile right now. I also think that the writing of biography is a critically important activity – a responsibility to take very seriously. Where I diverge from Simpson or Levine or the long line of political biographers (John English on Trudeau, Denis Smith on Dief as rogue Tory, and so on) is in where I place my emphasis. I don't disagree that Macdonald was a nation maker, just as I don't quarrel with the nation-making story of Vimy Ridge (as long as it is self-reflexive and inclusive), but I do insist that biographies of our artists tell equally significant stories, that artists' lives and works are crucial identity-shaping stories. As Ted Chamberlin reminds us in his 2003 book *If This is Your Land, Where are Your Stories? Finding Common Ground*, we must have stories if we claim this land is ours. His title comes from a First Nations Elder who confronted white settler/explorers with this reality – you need stories to tell you who and where you are. And it is our artists who give us these stories and biographers who tell their stories, who get the story out there – as *right* as possible – on the walls before anyone messes with the archive. So I suggest that biographers should heed Woodcock (and even Simpson) and look beyond the accepted subjects for biography – politicians, generals, and the like – to the creative nation makers. This is what, I believe, we are increasingly witnessing in Canadian biography today, in our century. To do this, however, we must have resources, data, archives, and we must have access to these resources; hence my anxiety when a government destroys the records of the long-gun registry, abandons the long-form census, and makes crippling cuts to the budget of the National Archives.[4] Or when Michael Healey resigns from the Tarragon to protest its rejection of his play *Proud* because of its "potentially libellous" portrayal of a prime minister (see Brown).

The Archive

The archive, as Foucault and Derrida have told us, is as much a system (Foucault) and a concept (Derrida) as it is a physical place or collection of materials.[5] And for both thinkers it is a critically important socio-psychological-political-cultural repository or function of memory, life, and the future. These days it is also a feature on our email software and a verb: a box pops up (usually interrupting our work) to ask if we want *to archive* old messages now. I usually hit "yes," but given my allergy to technology I have never tried to "access" this archive. I prefer physical archives in real libraries, the kind that Findley describes in *The Wars*. These can be treasure troves of information for biographers and historians. They can also be traps, uncharted territory with hidden corridors, dead ends, and false floors. Everything about archives depends on who made the initial collection and why, on how the materials deposited reach the library, and on how and by whom they were catalogued. Moreover, there may be conditions placed on what can be consulted; access may be denied, as it was to Peter van Wyck when he tried to see the files of the Eldorado mining company for his book about the Second World War, uranium, and the highway of the atom.[6] If you go to an archive expecting to find Truth, you are almost certain to be disappointed or deceived. If you go expecting perfect order and continuity, then you will quickly realize you are in the wrong place looking for the wrong things. If you expect to find *all* the material you may need for a biography in an archive, then you have some dangerous illusions to discard. All these warnings add up to this: getting it right, as Phyllis Webb wants one to do, is very hard.

Although a professionally structured archive – Fonds – resides in an institution, cared for by highly trained professionals, *the* archive needed for a biography far exceeds such places of quiet, decorum, cleanliness, white gloves, and assistance. Biographers must be prepared to get dirty, to dig around, to inquire, beg, remind, travel (camera at the ready), and ask questions of as many people as possible. This questioning requires permission to interview people, time to sit down with them, to follow up, to persist; and it requires sensitivity and courtesy. Eighty-year-old Aunt Sally may well have a stash of letters in a dresser drawer underneath the woollies and the moth balls; John, the jilted lover or ex-partner, may have kept a lock of hair, photographs of happier days, and the note telling him it was all over. These casual, precious, intimate documents are part of *the* archive that a biographer gathers outside the professional precincts of an archive, and as physical documents they belong to Aunt Sally and John.

At best – with luck – you will find much to work with in and beyond an archive, but you will never find everything, and some materials may be off limits, classified. A lot of what you do find will be irrelevant, trivial, and of no use to your story. Sharon's shopping lists are of little interest; her veterinary bills are of passing interest; however, her records of books borrowed from libraries or a list of titles in her personal library are of potential value because they may shed light on her inner life, her interests, her own research in libraries and archives, and even on references, allusions, and echoes in her work. Of primary importance, of course, are manuscripts, letters, scrapbooks, diaries and journals, photographs, records of births, marriages, and deaths, and wills. But even these cannot be assumed to be right or reliable; never trust a diary; always treat letters as little narratives (the better the letter, the more likely it has been crafted); triple-check registries and wills; and handle photographs with the utmost caution. A picture may be worth a thousand words, but it can also lie.[7]

Let me briefly share with you some of my biographical adventures with archives and one or two examples from the work of other biographers. No one working on Malcolm Lowry can fail to be grateful for his voluminous surviving manuscripts of *Under the Volcano* or for the drafts (yes – drafts!) of his famous letter of January 1946 to Jonathan Cape. You will find these materials in the University of British Columbia (UBC) Lowry Collection. You will also find dozens of love notes that he wrote to his second wife, Margerie, and pinned to trees around their cabin. While these little ditties do provide a glimpse into his marriage, they provide diminishing returns: they quickly become embarrassing, cloying, and repetitive. I selected just a few representative ones for volume two of *Sursum Corda!* However, the Lowry archive extended far beyond UBC, as I discovered when I visited Lowry's first wife in California. She had, she claimed, many letters and some important manuscript material that scholars believed had been destroyed in a fire. Yes, indeed, a fire. I keep returning to fire.

Lowry was terrified of fire and with good reason. When his shack on the foreshore at Dollarton burned down on 7 June 1944, he lost most of his papers; Margerie saved the drafts of *Volcano*. A handful of charred fragments of the *lost* autobiographical novel manuscript were scooped up from the beach – a mere handful, pieces the size of a saucer or smaller – and they survive now, sealed in plastic, in the collection to tantalize and frustrate scholars. This woman – his first wife – was very gracious to me and generous. She was also adamant. I could see a few of her letters from Malc, but not all. And I would not see the *lost* (not really entirely lost) manuscript. I stayed in her home the night I was there but I scarcely slept. In the next room sat her archive, pulsing with secrets, glowing in the dark, whispering to me. I stayed in my room unable to imagine myself sneaking next door or surreptitiously opening files (damn, I hadn't thought to bring a flashlight or a camera). I have regretted my scruples, lack of preparedness, and cowardice ever since!

Occasionally, an archive will hold amazing items – like Mackenzie King's voluminous diaries, or a letter of such significance that it has a decisive influence on a biographer's interpretation of the life. When one happens upon such a document, I swear the earth moves under one's chair. I've been known to shriek with shock and delight and leap up to search for someone with whom to share my discovery. I had fervently hoped to find such a document when working on Sharon's biography and with her Fonds here at the University of Calgary, and you may be able to guess what that desired document was . . . the letter from her dead grandmother Chalmers, the one that grandmother wrote to her son, Everett (Sharon's father), and the one *he* (actor/character/father/son?) holds, unopened and unread, in *Doc*. As we know, Doc does not open or read this letter because he and his daughter agree to burn it (oh dear, fire again) at the end of the play. I understand that this is a theatre device and that it makes for good stage business, but that unopened, unread letter is also very eloquent, strategic, thematically important, and symbolic. So is that damn trunk sitting there on stage (in the attic, in a back room of the house), daring me to creep up and lift the lid. I will never be convinced there was not a *real* letter, by the way, not even if Sharon swears on a bottle of scotch that there wasn't.

And what about things Charles Foran found in the Mordecai Richler Fonds, also here at the University of Calgary? If you have yet to read *Mordecai: The Life and Times*, then I will not spoil the surprise. Suffice it to say that Foran found a letter – *the letter* that Richler wrote to his "Dear Maw" on 4 August 1976 in which he blamed her for all his pain, accused her of almost every selfishness and sin under the sun, made it clear that he disliked her, and dismissed her from his life – unless she were to be in financial need. In the published book, this epistle runs to seven pages; it is, therefore, a very long, as well as a very intimate, document. But I come away from reading it wondering why Richler's widow granted Foran permission to reproduce it. I wonder whose version of the life-story is at stake here? I certainly wonder if Foran has got it right. "Dear Maw" is long dead and cannot protest.

Tiff's archive is still very much in flux. Much of it was gathered by Tiff and his partner Bill Whitehead and sold to the National Archives in the 1980s. Further acquisitions have been made over the years until now it is a vast, sprawling collection, parts of which remain uncatalogued and inaccessible. Smaller parts of the Findley archive are held here in Calgary and in Guelph, and still other parts – important documents like his letters and photographs – are scattered in others' archives and in private hands. Because many people who knew Tiff are still alive, I am trying to find them before I continue to tackle the Findley/Whitehead Fonds in Ottawa. I am counting on fire alarms, sprinkler systems, and strict regulations to safeguard these Fonds (a misplaced trust, perhaps, given the current budget crisis at the Archives), but nothing can safeguard peoples' garages, attics, and basements, or the people themselves. All this work takes time, so when well-meaning folks ask me when Tiff's biography will appear, I (cursing inwardly) tell them politely: not for some years. I got the same question over and over again with *Making Theatre*.

Finding *the* archive, working in/with/through it, and striving to get things right, takes a lot of time. However, this much I will share with you today in hopes of arousing enough curiosity to last for some years, and it is this: I have found one stunning letter by Tiff to his ex-wife in an archive and another remarkable one in the archives that extend so far beyond our institutions. I will use these letters, and others I hope to find, to create my story of Tiff's life because I hear him, see the man as he performed himself (and wanted others to see him) in such letters. If I have any regrets when I hold and read such precious items, it is that people don't write letters like this anymore. I doubt we'll ever see another tour de force like Lowry's letter to Cape; I wonder if sons will bother to write parents in such bitter detail and at such length, as Richler did – an email or a tweet is faster and potentially as shattering; and I *hope* a person will not need to write the kind of letter Tiff wrote, even though it tells me so much about him.

The Biographer

In this final section I want to reflect on some of the tasks faced by the biographer, on the role of such a writer, and on the decisions, actions, influences, successes and failures, and challenges of being a biographer. I will take myself and "Sharon Pollock" as the examples. I am fairly certain that I got most of Sharon's story right, at least up to the time when I stopped the story. But I also know that some things escaped me, and there were other things I decided not to write about. I think I was honest in *Making Theatre* about both categories – what escaped and what went untold – except that I will never really know precisely how much escaped. If there is no trace, no faint scent, no partially obscured fingerprints to alert me to the letter or anecdote or fact that got away, then it remains an absent presence haunting the archive and my narrative. As for silences, well, I have to hope I made sound, ethical decisions on those matters.

Then there are the materials not yet deposited with the Pollock Fonds, or the materials held in private hands that I could not see or did not know I should ask to see! Can a biographer, could I, ever get it right without access to these things? And how do I navigate around a playwright or novelist who is also a biographer, an autobiographer, and an historian, who works – as I do – with archives? How does the *real* (the real?) biographer handle such slippery material? Diaries, journals, and notebooks are always pre-selected, maybe even carefully edited: remember that King had his transcribed and he edited parts; never forget what Mauberley told us about his version of his auto/biographical/historical narrative: "everything is true, except the lies." Already

I begin to feel like Winnie the Pooh going around and around in his own tracks under the illusion that I am hunting a "Woozle." This is where preparation and planning are crucial: biographers are like forensic auditors or like scientists. We open the books or go into our labs armed with theories, facts, dates, and hypotheses; we are on the watch for evidence, nothing is too small to ignore. And we know we must cross-check, verify, and confirm all our conclusions. The tests we perform on the letter, the photograph, the manuscript, the genealogy and the Will must be capable of being repeated with consistent results. The rest is intuition, craft, and luck. (Unless, as Derrida reminds us about Freud, the subject, in a fit of *"mal d'archive,"* has deliberately burned his own archive (63). And then we are unaware of our bad luck.)

I wonder what I would find, and if I could verify my findings, if I returned to Sharon's story tomorrow? She has not stopped living and working, and her archive has grown with her. At least, what has survived of that archive has grown. As far as I know Sharon does not – yet – suffer from archive fever.

If I were to return to her biography I would go back to the summer of 2008, at almost that moment when *Making Theatre* was published (or at least launched in Vancouver) and the terrible news reached me that Sharon's house had caught fire and that she was in it when it burst into flames. Shortly after receiving this news I learned that she was all right – she had got out in time with some of her beloved pets. The house itself was severely damaged, however, by a fire that started in the basement and was caused by faulty wiring. Like everyone else, my initial response was concern for her physical safety and emotional well-being, and when I later learned that she had insisted on performing her role in a play that evening I felt somewhat reassured: this was the feisty, indomitable woman I knew; the show would go on. However, perhaps *un*like anyone else – and I confess this here – my next response was horror and dread: FIRE; the basement; boxes; papers; files – an archive. Precious documents I had never seen, two decades of papers not yet organized and added to the Pollock Fonds, and god knows what other personal and family documents were stored in that basement!

For all I knew Grandmother Chalmers' letter to her son Everett was in one of those boxes and now it really had gone up in flames – real life imitating art! Did Sharon herself know – remember – what was stored down there? Could anything not reduced to ash be salvaged from smoke and water damage? Charred Lowryan fragments maybe? Alas. Such questions should not be uttered or even thought, but as soon as I realized that she was okay, these were my frantic questions: this too – this necrophilic obsession – is what it means to become a biographer.

When I agreed to give this talk to celebrate Sharon's seventy-fifth birthday, I did so knowing I would have to go back to that fire, that *mal d'archive* of demonic electrical wiring. I knew I would have to talk with her and ask nosey questions. Time passed, I hesitated, then we set a date to talk by phone, more than three years after that *auto-da-fé*. Between 2008 and 2012 she has more than *carried on*, so there was a lot to talk about. The house was restored and she was happily ensconced there again and still surrounded by cats and dogs. She has continued to act, to travel, to review plays for the CBC and, most importantly, to write. And she is, as she was before 2008, full of delight with all the things her children and grandchildren do. She also wanted an update on my children and grandson. This part of our conversation was woman-to-woman, not biographer-to-biographee. Another touch that reminded me of our many telephone conversations prior to 2008 and *Making Theatre* was the canine and feline interruptions. One rarely talks to Sharon without the dogs wanting in on the act, but this time there was an unusual feline act that I will share with you. At one point, in mid-sentence, I heard that old familiar "uhh, sigh/ groan" (only Sharon makes this sound), after which she explained that her new little cat was fascinated by push pins and would climb up on the desk to get at the board, pull them out, and put them in piles. Presumably the items on that board – items for an archive? – fell to the floor, were scattered hither and yon, even lost! Wretched puss!

Of course, I wanted to know what she had been up to. How was the trip to Kosovo? (Fine.) Did she approve of their production of *Blood*

Relations? (Yes.) How was it staged? (Expressionistically, symbolical-ly.) What language was it performed in? (Albanian.) Who directed it? (Jeton Neziraj.) And would she work with him again? (Yes, indeed – she has returned to Kosovo and he has come to Calgary; they are working on a script together.) When I asked how this collaboration was working out, she confessed her worry about their very different perspectives, but concluded: "I'm enamoured of it!"[8]

She has continued to work with Atlantic Ballet for the creation of a new work called "Ghosts of Violence," for which she did "a ton of research." And she has continued to act. Indeed, she performed in *Marg Szkaluba (Pissy's Wife)* for the conference, so I won't describe it here, except to note Sharon's observation that at eighty to ninety min-utes in length it is quite a challenge for a seventy-five-year-old memory. And there have been other activities: more than two years reviewing plays for CBC Calgary, a new CBC Radio proposal for a series that, if accepted, will fill the vacated "Afghganada" slot. And there's a new stage play brewing on a subject that has intrigued her since well be-fore the fire: Agnes Smedley (1892–1950), the American journalist, novelist, spy, Communist, and China advocate. Toward the end of our conversation, she cheerfully announced that she had bought a Kia mini-van and was planning to drive to Arizona via Fort Erie this sum-mer to consult the Smedley archives at the Arizona State University. Now, if you have ever been a passenger in a car driven by Sharon (as I have) your eyebrows will be up around your hairline, as mine were when I heard this. Oh yes: What did she think about this conference? WELL. I will leave that to your imagination, but I am sure you know that this lady does not like the spotlight, unless it is in a theatre and she's playing a role, not herself.

But I am circling the most crucial issue and I cannot avoid it any longer: Archives. The Biographer. And Fire. Much of our conversation involved revisiting the summer of 2008. "I have the ability," she told me, "of compartmentalizing," and this helped her deal with the trauma of the fire and the losses she faced over the following eighteen months while she lived in temporary digs. "It could have been so much worse," she stated matter-of-factly, and yes it could have. Not all the pets survived, but she did – with her cell phone. She had gone to her bedroom for a rest before the evening's performance: "I was asleep . . . with the door closed . . . and woke up to a flash of white light – like a bulb bursting." Then she heard a sound, like water rushing, and smelled an odd odour; she roused herself and opened the bedroom door, to be met by a wall of black smoke. She fled out the back door and dialled 911. When the District 12 firefighters arrived, all "geared up," "they were wonderful" and saved one of the dogs and her computer. Of these terrible few hours she vividly recalls the permeating, acrid, burning-rubber stench (from old plastics in the basement). The house would need to be washed and sprayed three times to eradicate the smell. And she had none of her own clothes, so borrowed shoes from this person, a T-shirt from that one, and slacks from someone else. What's more, she refused to go to the hospital, so when Melinda resigned herself to that stubborn fact, she drove her mother to the theatre, where, as if this real drama were not enough, Sharon was performing the role of Margaret in Judith Thompson's *Habitat*. If you know the play, you know it's about houses, a neighbourhood, an elderly female resident, and homeless people, and it ends with a house that *"goes up in flames"* (78). And you can begin to see how the biographer works to weave a story from the archive of facts.

Conversations, interviews really, like the one I had with Sharon a few months ago are crucial for a biographer. If the biographee co-operates, is generous with her time and thoughts, frank and open about events and responses, then the biographer's task, with a *living* subject, is certainly made easier. This ease, however, does not mean naive acceptance or belief. No one tells a nosey biographer everything and no one, even with the best intentions, remembers everything accurately. Forgetting is both inevitable and necessary. Revising is something we all do. Of far greater importance for a biographer is the archive, and so I had to ask Sharon: did anything stored in that basement survive the fire? Apparently more survived than one might think, but she has not yet found the time to go through the boxes to see what is still in them, what might have suffered serious water damage, and what is lost forever. She plans to do this difficult work – sometime, maybe soon, maybe later. And she shifts away from the topic to tell me about that Kia mini-van and the road trip she wants to take to consult Smedley's archives.

While Sharon is making her research-cum-road trip this summer, I will also be travelling (by plane and train—I don't do road trips). There are Findley interviews to conduct in Ontario, letters to find, old newspapers to study for clues to the past, and institutions to visit, from the Fisher Rare Books and Manuscripts Collection in the Robarts Library at the University of Toronto to the Metropolitan Reference Library, the Clarke Psychiatric Institute, and the National Archives. I will once more walk through the streets of old Rosedale, past the public school and the site of the Rosedale Library (which, so Lilah Kemp, the schizophrenic librarian in *Headhunter*, tells me, burned down – arson). These streets, this historic neighbourhood, with its elegant homes (now mostly divided into rented flats), and the Rosedale Ravine, surface frequently in his novels like a landscape of memory haunted by ghosts. I will probably never get Rosedale *right* – it has never been part of my identity. But neither was Fredericton, and I walked and walked its streets trying to sense the place, its past, its role in Sharon's life – trying to get it right.

If you ask me which resources are the most important in my search for Timothy Findley, I would say letters (his own, his Uncle Tiff's, others' letters to him) and geography: these two aspects of life were also crucial for him because he performed, self-consciously in his letters, many of which are descriptive, diary-like, funny, serious, and moving, and he always saw himself in his places, his Toronto houses and streets and, above all, the fields, barns, roads, and fellow creatures at Stone Orchard. All these aspects of life – these things, documents, places – belong in the archive that I am gathering. It will take time and I will do my best, with Webb's words echoing in my ears, because "the writer's work" *is* "the reason for all this diligent activity." And inextricable from the writer's work is her or his time and place, wisdom and warnings, and their significant contributions (I believe) to Canadian and human identity. Timothy Findley's biography, like Sharon Pollock's (or Richler's, Munro's, Franca's, Hirsch's, and all the others), helps tell our collective story.

My chief anxiety is not about what I will find but what I will not find and what may be unfindable. Fire haunts Tiff's work, just as it followed Lowry around and has now reached its ruthless fingers into Sharon's life and archive. As I reflect on this anxiety, I realize there are two elements fuelling my apprehension. One is comparatively simple: I hate the thought of losing, missing out on, never seeing with my own eyes, documents that may be useful. The other is more complex and troubling, and it is my fear about personal, collective, and nation-wide government-sanctioned archive fever, the death wish it represents and mobilizes, and the amnesia it produces. It was no accident, after all, that the Nazis burned books, records, and corpses. They sought to destroy the past, memory, traces of what had been (and what had been done). If we cannot find the evidence, if we do not survive, then we cannot bear witness, and biographers (like historians, artists, Holocaust survivors, and fictional autobiographers like Eme in *Getting It Straight* and Mauberley in *Famous Last Words*) are charged with bearing witness. I do not need Freud or Derrida to tell me that to live is to resist death, to hold off the "radical evil" (Derrida, 19) of a *mal d'archive*, not just for the sake of the past and the present, but for the future. Likewise, to write is to insist that this living matters, that it adds to the ongoing story of the characters, the *real* people, the places, the communities, and the always changing nation. Canada needs as much biography as we can produce because a national life-story is only as full and diverse as the memories and the archives that animate it. Of course, biographers will never get it all right, but we can resist getting it wrong by finding and preserving archives and using them to tell stories of being here now, then, and in the future.

NOTES

1   This essay, first given as a lecture in 1993, was published in *Nothing but Brush Strokes* in 1995, hence the reference to floppy disks, which none of us use anymore. This volume of Webb's essays is dedicated to "Tiff and Bill, faithful friends."

2   In "History to the Defeated: Notes on Some Novels by Timothy Findley," Woodcock observes, with his typical prescience, that Findley is part of – I would suggest a progenitor of – the "emergence of the historic imagination" in Canada that gives "our collective life an origin and a meaning [and] that has tended to shape Canadian writing during recent decades and to induce its formative myths." Woodcock also remarks that biographical writing is another sign of this "collective life" (17).

3   The Hirsch biography is a classic example of what I see as the relationship of one person's story to the wider national story because Hirsch's life in Canada is a direct result of the Second World War and Canada's policy toward Jewish refugees, especially children. By telling this part of his story his biographers have expanded the national story and filled in a part of the narrative that has been suppressed and forgotten and that many Canadians perhaps do not want to accept.

4   To find out more about the current crisis facing Library and Archives Canada, go to www.savelibraryarchives.ca. This situation has been developing for some time, but to the best of my knowledge it has received little public attention and less protest or advocacy on the part of Canadians. To the degree that the national archives are constrained by budget cuts, reductions in professional staff, and limitations in access, scholars and citizens are denied information on their cultural heritage, history, and the resources necessary to develop a larger, more complex and multiple, national story.

5   Foucault in *The Archeology of Knowledge* (first published in 1969) was the first contemporary theorist to identify the importance of archives and to develop a methodology – the system he calls archeology – that included a theory of the archive; see part 3 (126–31). Since this formulation of the archive, considerable attention has focused on the ideological nature and social/psychological role of archives. In "Archive Fever: A Freudian Impression," Derrida revisits the idea and develops it in fascinating, but troubling, ways. For Derrida, the term *mal d'archive* (translated as archive fever) names a death wish that operates by destroying memory, foreclosing on the life-affirming force of personal and collective remembering that can be enhanced, enabled in fact, through archives. Among Derrida's worst examples of such archive fever are the Nazis' attempt to exterminate Jewish books, identities, lives (corpses), and culture, and he warns against the "radical evil" of any state-authorized control of archival records. Individuals can, of course, choose to destroy their personal archives and they can put limits on aspects of an archive when it is deposited in a library, but it is the so-called *authorized* suppression or destruction of evidence that most worries Derrida.

6   In his study of the Canadian history of uranium mining and our contribution to the Manhattan Project, van Wyck describes the obstacles he met when attempting to gain access to records held in the National Archives (9–11). His frustrations make for chilling reading, especially since Canadians know next to nothing about this aspect of their Second World War history or the impact of the mining on the Dene of Deline at Great Bear Lake. This subject has been explored by Peter Blow in his film *Village of Widows* and by Marie Clements in her play *Burning Vision*.

7   See Adams, Egan, Hirsch, and Sontag on auto/biography and photography.

8   All quotations are from my telephone interview with Sharon Pollock on 29 January 2012.

Works Cited

Adams, Timothy Dow. *Light Writing and Life Writing: Photography in Autobiography*. Chapel Hill: U of North Carolina P, 1990. Print.

Bishop-Gwyn, Carol. *The Pursuit of Perfection: A Life of Celia Franca*. Toronto: Cormorant, 2011. Print.

Blow, Peter, Dir. *Village of Widows*. Lindum Films, 1999. Film.

Brown, Ian. "The Play's the Thing . . ." *Globe and Mail* 17 March 2012: R7. Print.

Busby, Brian. *A Gentleman of Pleasure: One Life of John Glassco – Poet, Memoirist, Translator, Pornographer*. Montreal: McGill-Queen's UP, 2011. Print.

Chamberlin, Edward. *If This Is Your Land, Where Are Your Stories? Finding Common Ground*. Toronto: Alfred Knopf, 2003. Print.

Derrida, Jacques. "Archive Fever: A Freudian Impression." *Diacritics* 25.2 (1995): 9–63. Print.

Egan, Susanna. *Mirror Talk: Genres of Crisis in Contemporary Autobiography*. Chapel Hill: U of North Carolina P, 1999. Print.

Findley, Timothy. *Can You See Me, Yet?* Toronto: Talonbooks, 1977. Print.

———. *Elizabeth Rex*. Toronto: HarperCollins, 2000. Print.

———. *Famous Last Words*. New York: Delacorte, 1981. Print.

———. *Headhunter*. Toronto: HarperCollins, 1993. Print.

———. *The Stillborn Lover*. Toronto: Harper Perennial, 1993. Print.

———. *The Telling of Lies*. Markham, ON: Viking, 1986. Print.

———. *The Wars*. Toronto: Clarke Irwin, 1977. Print.

Foran, Charles. *Mordecai: The Life & Times*. Toronto: Alfred Knopf, 2010. Print.

Foucault, Michel. *The Archeology of Knowledge*. Trans. A.M. Sheridan Smith. New York: Routledge, 1972. Print.

Grace, Sherrill. *Making Theatre: A Life of Sharon Pollock*. Vancouver: Talonbooks, 2008. Print.

———, ed. *Sursum Corda! The Collected Letter of Malcolm Lowry*. 2 vols. London and Toronto: Jonathan Cape and U of Toronto P, 1995, 1996. Print.

———. Sharon Pollock. Personal interview. 29 January 2012.

Hirsch, Marianne. *Family Frames: Photography, Narrative, and Postmemory*. Cambridge: Harvard UP, 1997. Print.

Levine, Allan. *King: William Lyon Mackenzie King. A Life Guided by the Hand of Destiny*. Vancouver: Douglas & McIntyre, 2011. Print.

Lind, Jane. *Perfect Red: The Life of Paraskeva Clark*. Toronto: Cormorant Books, 2009. Print.

Lowry, Malcolm. *Under the Volcano*. London: Jonathan Cape, 1947. Print.

Martz, Fraidie and Andrew Wilson. *A Fiery Soul: The Life and Theatrical Times of John Hirsch*. Montreal: Véhicule, 2011. Print.

Neufeld, James. *Lois Marshall: A Biography*. Toronto: Dundurn, 2010. Print.

Pollock, Sharon. *Blood Relations. Sharon Pollock: Collected Works*. Vol. 1. Toronto: Playwrights Canada P, 2005. 339–94. Print.

———. *Doc. Sharon Pollock: Collected Works*. Vol. 2. Toronto: Playwrights Canada P, 2006. 126–97. Print.

———. *Getting It Straight. Sharon Pollock: Collected Works*. Vol. 2. 228–62. Print.

———. *The Komagata Maru Incident. Sharon Pollock: Collected Works*. Vol. 1. 98–137. Print.

———. *Walsh. Sharon Pollock: Collected Works*. Vol. 1. 31–95. Print.

Simpson, Jeffrey. "So Much More Than a Big Nose on Our Currency." *Globe and Mail*. 10 December 2011: F9. Print.

Sontag, Susan. *On Photography*. New York: Farrar, Strauss, Giroux, 1990. Print.

Thacker, Robert. *Alice Munro: Writing Her Lives*. Toronto: McClelland & Stewart, 2005. 2011. Print.

Thompson, Judith. *Habitat*. Toronto: Playwrights Canada P, 2001. Print.

van Wyck, Peter. *The Highway of the Atom*. Montreal: McGill-Queen's UP, 2010. Print.

Webb, Phyllis. "Poetry and Psychobiography." *Nothing but Brush Strokes: Selected Prose*. Edmonton: NeWest, 1995. 87–104. Print.

Woodcock, George. "History to the Defeated: Notes on Some Novels by Timothy Findley." *Present Tense: A Critical Anthology*. Ed. John Moss. Toronto: NC, 1985. 15–28. Print. www.savelibraryarchives.ca. Web.

Sharon's Tongue

*Lindsay Burns, Pamela Halstead,
Grant Linneberg, and Laura Parken*

(Based on the words and works of Sharon Pollock)

THE WEST

WOMAN 1: I come from a country of mothers, daughters, and grandmothers.

WOMAN 2: This country's going to flower and bloom like a rose in the wreath of the Empire.

WOMAN 1: Canadians have this view of themselves as nice civilized people who have never participated in historical crimes and atrocities. But that view is false. Our history is dull only because it has been dishonestly expurgated.

WOMAN 2: You don't see the whole picture. There are other considerations.

WOMAN 1: I do not think of myself as a Canadian.

WOMAN 2: Well now, you've caught my interest. What is it? What the hell are you here for?

WOMAN 1: My region is people.

WOMAN 2: (*Addressing the audience*) In her mind's eye she'll paint his sky the colour of her sky and his fields, the colour of her fields, and the dry wind driving the grit into the back of your throat and right through your eyeballs she'll think of as a refreshing and different level of breeze, which she can hardly wait to experience. She'll think that right 'til the moment she steps off the train.

WOMAN 1: I am an Albertan in so far as I choose to live in this particular part of the world, because it speaks to me. The sky, the light, the land, that internal state of passion and challenge of the conventional embedded in Alberta's past, and resonating in its present, keeps me there.

WOMAN 2: You see it kind of makes her like she didn't come from here, like, she kinda chose here 'stead of endin' up here.

WOMAN 1: That sense of space that simultaneously enhances one's awareness of self as an individual, and self as a very small part of something infinitely large, keeps me there. Alberta and I are engaged in a dialogue, and if either of us were to stop speaking, I would no longer be an Albertan.

WOMAN 2: I know it doesn't totally explain it . . . but when someone comes to a place where they can turn around four times and see nothing but flat land and blue sky, it's a shock. Sort of like going to the moon I imagine . . . only without the press.

WOMAN 1: A *place* can be home, the sky the hills.

WOMAN 2: You're such a bullshitter, you know that?

WOMAN 1: I lie on my back in a field full of yellow mustard at midnight.

WOMAN 2:	You're a great one for stories.
WOMAN 1:	The Northern Lights are out, and I run with the dog, my feet pounding the ground with great shafts of light overhead. I run and I run with the dog. I'M TURNING THE EARTH WITH MY RUNNING UNDER A KALEIDOSCOPE SKY.
WOMAN 2:	We talk in this country, we don't sing! We talk! What the hell is goin' on here?

WOMAN'S PLACE

WOMAN 1:	I am not a possession, a thing.
WOMAN 2:	You should teach her some manners.
WOMAN 1:	I'll leave if I want to.
WOMAN 2:	Are you just gonna sit there? Aren't you gonna do anything?
MAN:	You see what she's like – who wouldn't give her a belt in the mouth, livin' with her would drive anyone nuts.
WOMAN 2:	She's what you call a liberated woman.
MAN:	Maybe you'd have accomplished more if you'd married a nice Jewish doctor and spent your time raising kids and funds for Hadassah.
WOMAN 1:	Times change.
WOMAN 2:	She's incapable of disciplining herself like a lady and we all know it. If a man can't manage his own daughter.
WOMAN 1:	Make him understand that we're people. Individual people, and we have to live separate lives–
WOMAN 2:	There are certain things we cannot change.
MAN:	You are going to end up a silly old woman with nothin' but a cat for company.
WOMAN 1:	I write! I'm good at it!

MAN:	And that means you can ignore your father and your brother and dump this Buchanan jerk and forget your kids and family?
WOMAN 2:	Look if you are going to tell your father you don't want to do what he wants you to do –
WOMAN 1:	There's gotta be other options.
MAN:	Do you know what you want?
WOMAN 1:	If I like what I'm doing, can it really be wrong? I caught a man, I sat at home, I was alone.
WOMAN 2:	Even as a child, her . . . nature was . . . irritable and impassioned.
WOMAN 1:	He likes tits and ass and whiskey.
MAN:	Enough!
WOMAN 2:	Perversion. Unnatural. What mad thoughts entered your mind?
WOMAN 1:	Which leaves the impairment of my intellect an open question, I think we can at least agree on that.
MAN:	This girl has a way of wrappin' you round with words and then she tightens them up 'til your eyes pop out and you're strugglin' just to draw a breath.
WOMAN 1:	Are you thinking about dropping dead?
WOMAN 2:	How can you say that?
WOMAN 1:	The lips move, the words come out.
MAN:	(*To Woman 1*) Are you listening to me? (*To Woman 2*) She is obstinately defiant of my authority.
WOMAN 1:	I want my words to count because they are mine and I count!
MAN:	Is it my fault that you need to be noticed!
WOMAN 1:	I will write! With this (*hand to heart*) And this! (*clutches stomach*) And this! (*both arms embrace herself*) And

these! (*strikes her legs and falls to her knees*) And this! And this! And this! (*holds her hands up hitting herself*) What have these seen and heard! (*her eyes and ears*) And what has come from here! (her mouth) What splintered shards of meaning turn and twist in here but are sometimes still and beautiful! Muddled Disjointed! Out of tune and out of time you tell me but it's all I have to Shape and Mould! What else can I make something from, but this Poor Thing? It's all I have, why can't I? It's mine! Why not? Why not, you tell me why not!

MAN: My recommendations for institutional recommitment or release will be acted upon.

LOVE GONE WRONG

MAN: There will be no more of her "artistic expression".

WOMAN 1: How is a politician like a church bell? One peals from the steeple – they say I danced too close and was too affectionate on the dance floor. I can be charming. I caught a man. When I see him, I feel myself bursting. Didn't I have the right to decide to sleep with him? To love him? I tore my heart out and flung it on the floor and he trod on it! It's here someplace. Tomorrow it will be swept up and tossed out with the trash! Unless of course that cat finishes it first. But on my heart, if no one could find it here, you'll see an imprint of a foot, oh he danced a fair fandango on it. (*Beat.*) We all got marks, shows yuh lived, yuh never gave up.

MAN: That's not a very nice story.

WOMAN 1: I'm sorry. I really am. It's just that you've caught me at a bad time – between getting up and going to bed. That's a joke. You can laugh.

MENTAL ILLNESS

WOMAN 1:   This isn't me you know. This isn't really me, this is someone else . . . My mother always said, don't snitch, and don't play with snitches. Didn't your mother ever tell you that? (*Beat*) What kind of a fool do you take me for? What are you then, I said. Are you all in my head? And I, despite the slowness of my wit, have noticed certain things. You always say don't worry. But, of course, I worry. It's natural to worry. What if the things you hear, the things you don't want to hear, what if those things really happen inside? I spent my whole life wonderin' and I'm still at it and it's a waste of time. I drove her crazy. They say that. They do. I drove her crazy, yet they're the ones taught her complete self-indulgence and not one iota of responsibility.

WOMAN 1 & 2: Listen to me! It can happen to any of us.

WOMAN 2:   Everything is always so . . . sad, isn't it? Yeah . . . why is that? I don't know. I feel as if I wasted something. Sometimes I want to scream. I just want to stand there and scream, to hit something, to reach out and smash things – to hit and smash and hit and smash and . . . and then . . . I would feel very tired and I could lie down and sleep. Sometimes I don't even think you listen, or else you listen but you don't hear what I'm saying, you hear the words, you don't get the meaning of the words! You listen like you hear other words! Sometimes you watch so close so you can see when my lips stop moving so you know I'm finished.

WOMAN 1 & 2: You don't know anything.

WOMAN 1:   I don't give a fig for regulation or rules, only ones I make myself. And if in the past I chose to observe that regulation, it was only because a suitable occasion to break it hadn't risen. Something was always about to happen and if it didn't, I made it! I knew that the edge was more interesting than the middle and the leap more interesting than the slide – If you're going to fall, Jump! I know when trains are coming . . . and when they're coming, I don't go that way then . . . You could say I was looking for human generalities made specific. It's a matter of interpretation. Why is nothing simple in this life? It all seems to me perfectly simple. Why do people make it complex? The simplest thing . . . complex. Why is everything so goddamn complex?

WOMAN 2: Sometimes if you just keep talking it will come to you . . . It doesn't always work. Nobody listens to me, can't you hear me? I said *don't* talk about it. I don't want to talk about it. Stop talking about it! Enough! The subject is closed. Closed! Do you hear me? Don't say that. Don't say that! I'll kill you if you say that to me! I try to keep my temper, I've been nice as I can be.

WOMAN 1 & 2: I've bit my tongue and smiled a lot, I've listened when they've talked a lot, I haven't really teased a lot. Except when they've been rude a lot – I guess that I found out a lot – And now I'm tired, really tired of it all, And I feel like doing something really dirty, Something nasty, mean and filthy, foul and wretched – like . . . like . . .

WOMAN 1: Well what're ya gonna do! Mope around the rest of your life? It's a dilemma alright. If I promised to be a good girl forever and ever, would anything change?

WOMAN 2: I have been loved. People have loved me . . . When they found me most loveable, I was pretending. It was not really me . . . They said I danced too close and was too affectionate on the dance floor, so I pinned mistletoe on my backside and kept on dancing, dancing, dancing! It may have been lies, but that still doesn't mean it weren't true. Knowledge is a terrible thing. It calls for action. And one must act or not act, and live with that. Which will lead to another mental and physical collapse, one that I in my present state am unable to tolerate financially, physically or mentally! I say have the courage to fear. Surely that rings a bell.

WOMAN 1:   I mean it does for me.

WOMAN 2:   Oh she may have said things, thought things, wrote things –

WOMAN 1:   It won't reflect reality. No one, it seemed, worried about her depression it was her fear of paper concerned them. I'm not mad I have a chemical imbalance.

WOMAN 2:   I need to do more, I need to . . . I need . . . I'm tryin' to build a little trust here.

WOMAN 1:   I would have to deny that.

WOMAN 2:   I don't see how distortion justifies locking me up. Is it psychiatry's view that past experience counts for nothing? Psychiatry's view is paranoia, exacerbated by drink! No trust, no deal. Shall we drink to it? You realize as well as I do that this is only the tip of the iceberg.

OUTSIDER 1

WOMAN 2:   Don't you feel anything?

WOMAN 1:   You wouldn't understand.

WOMAN 2:   Yes I would. I would try. I'm not here to argue with you. I'm here as a friend.

WOMAN 1:   I have very few friends.

WOMAN 2:   I bet you were the kinda kid that was always luggin' home birds with a broken wing.

WOMAN 1:   What've you been doin', talkin' to my mother?

WOMAN 2:	Bet you put 'em in a box by the bed and in the mornin' you discover your cat ate 'em, nothin left but feathers on the floor.
WOMAN 1:	What're you standin' there starin' at? Eh? You never seen anyone cry before?
WOMAN 2:	I'm sorry.
WOMAN 1:	You're sorry, what've you got to be sorry about? It's not your lousy life! Do you think we're aberrant?
WOMAN 2:	I don't even know what it means . . .
WOMAN 1:	To vary from normal, to stray . . . I just want to be me, take after no one.
WOMAN 2:	Hell I know it's hard, but we gotta fill out forms, and beat 'em at their own game.
WOMAN 1:	I'm a whore and what you do is offensive to me! What you do would gag me! I'm a whore and when I look at your job, I could vomit!
WOMAN 2:	You don't see the whole picture.
WOMAN 1:	I'm a puppet? Manipulate me right and everything is possible . . . I'm a person. I exist. I think and feel! And I will not allow you to do this to me.
WOMAN 2:	That sense of justice and fair play, that's a good thing, but it's got to be tempered with a sense of reality. You'll learn.
WOMAN 1:	You don't know who I am or what I think.
WOMAN 2:	What's past is past! . . . I'll stand by you.
WOMAN 1:	Nobody *listens* to me, can't you hear me? I said *don't* talk about it. I don't want to talk about it. Stop talking about it!

SEX

MAN: You're a very pretty girl. Has anybody told you that?

WOMAN 1: Don't even think about putting your hand on my ass.

MAN: It's a friendly gesture and it's a nice ass.

WOMAN 1: Never initiate action when you haven't the guts to carry through.

MAN: I'll tell you what I think . . . I think . . . that you're aware that there is a certain fascination in the ambiguity . . . You always paint the background but leave the rest to my imagination. There you are you silly goose.

WOMAN 1: Who be the goose and who be the gander here, eh?

MAN: You're a quick one.

WOMAN 1: It is not a good idea, technically or artistically, to sleep with the company manager when the producer signing the cheques is husband.

MAN: I know. Don't fuck around. Write that on something. Refer to it often.

WOMAN 1: Listen carefully . . . This has to stop. It can't go on.

MAN: Fuck Bert.

WOMAN 1: I did.

MAN: He was an asshole.

WOMAN 1: He was always nice to me! Polite, kind, he wasn't like most men.

MAN: Ladies and gentlemen! It walks! It talks! It reproduces! . . . Can we afford to be without it? I say "No!"

WOMAN 1: You're not like you seemed.

MAN: I've spent my life raisin' horses and I'm gonna tell you somethin' – a *woman* is just like a *horse*! You keep her on a tight rein, or she'll take the bit in her teeth and next thing you know, road, destination, and purpose is all

	behind you, and you'll be damn lucky if she don't pitch you right in a sewer ditch!
WOMAN 1:	You! – Are a bastard!
MAN:	Don't be like that. Say you're sorry.
WOMAN 1:	I'm sorry.
MAN:	Come talk to me. Not gonna talk to me?
WOMAN 1:	No.
MAN:	Come on, I'm all by myself. (*Beat*) Why do I bestride my world like colossus?
WOMAN 1:	Diet?
MAN:	You know, I can't help but feel you don't give full vent to your powers of persuasion.
WOMAN 1:	Two-bits-a-crack in a dark alley.
MAN:	We know we got nothing to say.
WOMAN 1:	So why are you here?
MAN:	I told you. I think you're pretty.
WOMAN 1:	Don't look at me like that.
MAN:	Like what?
WOMAN 1:	I don't know, don't do it.
MAN:	Hey, you know how things oughta to be and I know how things are. Now you put those things together, I think you got a pretty powerful thing happenin' . . . Don't you?
WOMAN 1:	You never listen, do you!
MAN:	Ready or not you must be caught.
WOMAN 1:	No! There's something you don't understand. You can't make me do one thing that I don't want to do.
MAN:	You go through men like boxes of Kleenex.
WOMAN 1:	I'll leave if I want to – I can.

MAN:	She's what you call a liberated woman. She is immune to the charms of the predatory male.
WOMAN 1:	When he gets out of the shower his penis looks like a snail that's lost its shell.
MAN:	It can happen to any of us.
WOMAN 1:	The great Canadian cocksman.
MAN:	Tell me how you account for her positive assessment? He screws her. A roar in the blood as it sped through the veins.
WOMAN 1:	Bullshit.
MAN:	Seduced, charmed and taken in by this woman who is adept at seducing and charming, when she wants to be. You are a dosser, a daughter of joy, you sail along on your bottom.
WOMAN 1:	You're a great one for stories.
MAN:	A little hand on ass – it's how business is done.
WOMAN 1:	Fuck off!

MEN

MAN:	I'm tellin' yuh somethin' now shut the fuck up and listen. Everything big. Nothing small. Put things in perspective. I come from a long line of brilliant people. I can be charming. What daddy wants daddy gets. You don't. You don't move. You don't speak. You don't do anything. If there's any doing to be done, I'll do it. I'll do it right now. Maybe it's me. Wanting my way in everything. Always had it that way. Pity to change. Don't you think? I made decisions when decisions had to be made, I chose a road, and I took it, and I never looked back. Some people value this aspect of my character and others think it just makes me a pain in the ass. And I'll tell you this . . . whatever we do, by

the time we're finished, they'll have flip-flopped to the other side of the fence. You follow me? We brought you up we can put you down. Some people talk, and some people listen, but by God, I act, and if . . . it weren't for people like me . . . people like you . . . would still be down in the slime. (*Beat.*) I don't suppose you got any idea how stupid you look. You're not very bright are you? If a man can't manage his own daughter, how the hell can he manage a business? However, we aren't here to assign guilt, we can do that later. Perhaps salvation or damnation is at hand here. (*Pause.*) You're a very pretty girl. Has anybody told you that? I'm tryin' to build a little trust here. I tell terrible lies. But I wouldn't take her word for things. That one, I tell you right from the start, her nose is in the air so far I wonder she don't drown when it rains. What a piece of bad luck, eh? Jesus my whole life's a piece of bad luck. I admit it! I loved her. I love the absence of any feeling of inferiority. I love the sincerity and selfishness. Utterly selfish. I loved knowing what others sought, I had. Glamour. They all said she had glamour. Not the usual kind. Not that kind. Special. Her own kind of glamour. Do you think she's glamourous? Let me tell you something – I think there is nothing wrong with her . . . that losing eighty pounds and tripling her intellect wouldn't cure. Maybe she's become svelte. And maybe pigs can fly. I feel ashamed. I don't know why. Or else I do know why. Guess I don't wanna face that. (*Beat*) It's a dilemma alright. It all seems perfectly simple to me. Why do people make it complex? The simplest thing . . . complex. I shouldn't be talkin' to yuh like this. Take, take, take and never give. Why does everything have to be a threat. Why can't it be a challenge? We need more challenges and fewer threats. That's what we need. Times change. That's just somethin' people say to get what they want. Real things, things that count, never change. Could I be getting old and cranky?

HAVE YOU TOLD YOUR MOTHER?

MAN: Have you told your mother?

WOMAN 1:   Not yet.

MAN: You just don't know your own mind.

WOMAN 1:   At least I have one . . . I didn't mean that.

MAN: Oh . . . you probably did . . . I always thought . . . we liked one another.

WOMAN 1:   We do.

MAN: I suppose you see me . . . in a very particular way.

WOMAN 1:   I, despite the slowness of my wit, have noticed certain things.

MAN: It's a dilemma alright.

WOMAN 1:   What do you listen to him for, he's an ignorant person, can't you tell that?

MAN: He cried and said he was sorry.

WOMAN 1:   Bullshit, Daddy.

MAN: Jesus Christ I hate to hear a woman talk like that.

WOMAN 1:   You're such a bullshitter, you know that?

MAN: I'll go back downstairs and I'll sit in the kitchen and I'll pretend that I don't know.

WOMAN 1:   What if the things you hear, the things you don't want to hear, the things they won't let you hear, what if those things really happen?

MAN: You're a great one for stories.

WOMAN 1:   Look, you and I can be straight with each other. I try to keep my temper, I've been nice as can be. I bit my tongue and smiled a lot. Well it's a secret that everybody knows. Soooo, nobody speaks of it. It's that kind of secret.

MAN: Do you know what you're saying?

WOMAN 1:	You sound worried.
MAN:	You think too much. Your head is full of scrambled thoughts and I must think of where my interests lie.
WOMAN 1:	Birds are comin' home to roost and there is not one thing you can do to stop that! Not a thing!
MAN:	Looks like all those birds are gonna be vultures.
WOMAN 1:	I say have the courage to fear.
MAN:	That's not a very nice story.
WOMAN 1:	He didn't tell it because it was nice, he told it because it was true.
MAN:	I know what you're saying but it wasn't like that.
WOMAN 1:	So what was it like, you tell me.
MAN:	You never listen, do you?
WOMAN 1:	For Christ's sake, speak the truth!
MAN:	What's honest, honest is nothing, nobody wants honest.
WOMAN 1:	Did . . . did you think you could just tell a story and everything would be right?
MAN:	I think you believe I'm as they describe me to say such things.
WOMAN 1:	I merely ask if the behaviour of the father was deviant, wicked or corrupt?
MAN:	A lie cannot endure. I don't wanna be committin' myself to a lie.
WOMAN 1:	Lying is perhaps the least of sins you contemplate in the night.
MAN:	You really want to know?
WOMAN 1:	Yeah.
MAN:	He screws her.
WOMAN 1:	Name her. Name her!
MAN:	Enough! The subject is closed. Closed! Do you hear me?

THE MENAGERIE KEEPS GROWING – SONG

MAN: (*spoken*) Listen! The animals. The animals play a big role. (*Singing*) *Birds with a broken wing.*

Cat ate 'em – feathers on the floor.

The eagle turns on its mate.

The Great Dane is poisoned.

You've stirred up a hornet's nest, haven't you?

You're a lamb looking for a slaughter.

He crawls for crumbs like a mouse – There's gotta be other options.

The mule stops in her tracks – I shoot him for meat for the huskies.

Birds are comin' home – Looks like those birds are gonna be vultures.

(*Spoken*) In Ohio a bunch of guards rounded up these pet cats the prisoners had befriended, including six, four-day-old kittens. Dashed their brains out against a wall. The incident was leaked, and letters poured in by the dozens all from irate cat lovers. Not one expressed concern for the poor buggers locked up in an institution where those guards wield power without restraint, and virtually no review. Cat lovers.

ALL: (*singing*) *I think pigs are alright . . . I've known some not bad pigs*

I think pigs are alright...It's the pigsty that turn them nasty.

MAN: (*spoken*) Did you know that if a pig falls in a trough, the other pigs will eat him. Pursue them like a wolf that tears at the soft underbelly of a fleeing doe.

ALL: (*singing*) *I think pigs are alright . . . I've known some not bad pigs*

I think pigs are alright . . . And maybe pigs can fly.

MAN:	(*spoken*) Really. The animals play a BIG role.
	(*Singing*) *A thin mangy old cat that's gone wild, chipmunks, a skunk and a squirrel,*
	Nikki a desert grey fox – I go for a walk with a husky
	Sweetie, the mule who's kept by the creek, the sled dogs, the Great Danes and Laddie a lion can lie down with a lamb
ALL:	(*singing*) *This is only the tip of the iceberg*
MAN:	(*singing*) *A big, black, silver-tipped dog. I hear the wings of insects*
	The wolves, the foxes, you silly goose – The menagerie keeps growing!
	The raccoon and the skunk; the two wildcats, Coalie my mare and Bert's gelding. The eagles, the coyotes, the deer and the elk –
ALL:	(*singing*) *And mom served them up for dinner!*

MOTHERS

ALL:	What's your mother like?
MAN:	Always there . . . cooking and cleaning and agreeing.
ALL:	What's your mother like?
WOMAN 1:	She's warm when you hug her, her eyes are blue and she wears glasses.
ALL:	What's your mother like?
WOMAN 2:	She's a thin mangy old cat that's gone wild. Nothin' left to nourish herself or her own.
ALL:	What's wrong with Mama?
WOMAN 1:	She had her heart set on a specialist.
ALL:	What's wrong with Mama?

WOMAN 2:   She had to do awful things. The milk a human kindness
           is curdled.

ALL: What's wrong with Mama?

MAN: I don't like to go anywhere with Mummy when she's like
           that.

ALL: How did Mama manage?

WOMAN 2:   Lie around, weep, cry, incapable of the simplest action!

ALL: How did Mama manage?

MAN: Making cookies for something, she holds her arms out
           to me, she cries, she says welcome home.

ALL: How did Mama manage?

WOMAN 1:   She's been like this for years, that's just Mama.

LOUSY MOTHER

WOMAN 1:   Everything's fiction. Isn't that what you say?

WOMAN 2:   Maybe I did. Maybe I didn't. What does it matter?

WOMAN 1:   I had to rely on myself cause there was fuckin' little else
           to rely on!

WOMAN 2:   Life with you necessitates drink.

WOMAN 1:   We never had a home.

WOMAN 2:   Not true.

WOMAN 1:   Is too.

WOMAN 2:   I am your mother. That's *what* I am. But it's not *who* I
           am.

WOMAN 1:   Perverse meaning deviant, wicked, corrupt.

WOMAN 2:   I feel ashamed. Wanting my way in everything. Always
           had it that way.

WOMAN 1:	You don't even see me. You don't see anybody but those stupid stupid people who think you're God. You're not God!
WOMAN 2:	Why do we always end up yelling and screaming, why do we do that? I care about you! I tell you I love you and you never listen!
WOMAN 1:	It's all make-believe, isn't it?
WOMAN 2:	I have a chemical imbalance.
WOMAN 1:	And that means you can ignore your kids and family?
WOMAN 2:	I am not prepared for the guilt.
WOMAN 1:	Perhaps it is easier to take a bullet to the body than a blow to one's prior conceptions.
WOMAN 2:	It's not my fault!
WOMAN 1:	Is it my fault that you need to be noticed? And to do what you need to do to be noticed, you need to be drunk? That is not *my* fault!
WOMAN 2:	I have caused disharmony in our family. I admit it!
WOMAN 1:	You think you can manipulate me right and everything is possible . . . I'm a person. I exist. I think and feel!
WOMAN 2:	Do you love me? (*Beat*) It is a simple question.
WOMAN 1:	Nothing's changed!
WOMAN 2:	Everything I done makes up me – the good things, the bad things.
WOMAN 1:	You've always done it! As long as I can remember! You don't know who I am or what I think.
WOMAN 2:	Course I do.
WOMAN 1:	You think you do but you don't.
WOMAN 2:	What kind of crazy talk is that?
WOMAN 1:	I don't feel anything towards you.
WOMAN 2:	Really?

WOMAN 1:   You accept no responsibility.

WOMAN 2:   God you make me mad.

WOMAN 1:   You're a lousy mother, make something of that.

ALCOHOL

WOMAN 2:   I'm present because of an invitation to an evening of entertainment amongst my dearest friends, and this is what greets me?

Are you just gonna sit there? Aren't you gonna do anything? I said come on! Get up! Do something! Do you want to spend the rest of your life in Nowhere? Where's the music – you gotta have music for a party! (*Beat*)

Come talk to me. I'm not here to argue with you. Don't be like that. Say you're sorry. I'm sorry. Hell I was drunk, I didn't mean nothing, you know that, when did I ever hit you when I was sober? (*Pause*)

You got a big mouth, that's always your problem.

Why do we always end up yelling and screaming, why do we do that? Actually I don't care. At this moment I really don't care.

You tell me, was I wrong to do that?

How many times have we had this conversation? How many times must we have this conversation? I say . . . we've had enough arguing and fighting today . . . I'm tired . . . really tired. (*Beat*)

Let me tell you something – You gotta understand everything I done makes me up – the good things, the bad things – I done things you wouldn't believe. I was successful you see. I made something of myself. I chose a road, and I took it, and I never looked back. God knows, you have to keep your wits about you. I have caused disharmony. Guess I don't wanna face that.

Is anything wrong? Only just about everything in the whole world.

I could use a drink. Life with you necessitates drink. It's a means of survival. You don't even see me. You look at me and there's nobody there.

Are we to have a drink? You stand there like a stuffed Hussar. For God's sake, pour, or move and let one act who's able.

A thing worth doing is worth doing well...May take more time, but that's not the point, is it?

Disgrace! You're a disgrace!

Get to work, your mother says.

You disappoint us.

I apologize for my stupid daughter.

You should teach her some manners.

She keeps on like this, what will she do when she's old? You see what she's like – who wouldn't give her a belt in the mouth, livin' with her would drive anyone nuts. Shall we drink to it? If you yell you can get it yourself.

Dedicated to drink.

You wanna know something funny? He said he thought getting a little cut was like pokin a hole in a plastic bag of cornmeal and everything would just drain out. Just oozed outta me over the years like jelly juice through a cheesecloth bag and all I got left inside is dry old pulp.

They say one's strongest instinct is self-preservation. I would have to deny that.

The great drunk! Not a nice drunk! A nasty obnoxious and obstreperous drunk!

How people act is a lot more truthful than what anybody can say. He cried and said he was sorry . . . he whispered . . . he said it wouldn't happen again. He said it was the pain. It was because of the pain.

We know "accidents," don't we.

I should have done something. He was an asshole. I don't know how I missed that.

I know the question. I don't know the answer! How the hell would I know? Which leaves the impairment of my intellect an open question, I think we can at least agree on that.

I said a drink would be nice. You're a good girl. I would not want you to find out anything that would make you hate me. Because I love you. And I am a judge of character. The 'bility to judge is not somethin' you cultivate, it's something you're born with. I could discern your potential to love, and to be loved, to be honest, to be loyal, to trust, to be worthy of trust.

Sounded more like a litany for a dog than a daughter.

I'm sorry.

I think you're pretty. Once I was pretty. When I was . . . 15, when I was 16. Before I got married, now I'm old. Don't look at me like that. I'm not thin and pretty. I got hair like wire.

You only love me when I do what you want!

What kind of a fool do you take me for? Because I knew, even if you did know, you wouldn't come – and my heart would've burst from that pain.

It reduces me to rely on the likes of you. I abhor you, you are beneath contempt, had I the strength I'd tilt your head and slit your throat. Well I just might do it anyway. Because it is a very strong thought in my mind.

Someday you'll be dead and I'll be happy! You all say she's sick, she isn't sick. She's drunk. What're you starin' at?

Don't like to see your mother like this? If you've got something to say, you say it. You might not . . . like seeing me like this, but once I'm outta here, I won't have to be what I have to be here.

I'll be gone, I've tried so hard to get away, and now, I'll get away, I'll be gone, leaving behind all of this.

I think of the peace of the coffin.

Write this down. One can only hope, after struggling through the vale of tears, one can only hope that the necessity of the journey, the meaning of the journey, will be made clear at the end, whether one rides a golden cloud into eternity or plummets like a stone. And you rip it out and crumple it up and throw it away.

I shouldn't be talkin' to yuh like this. I fear I'm not good company tonight. I intend to go to dinner. And you – you can go to hell.

MURDEREE

WOMAN 2: I was cast as the murderee.

Caught and crushed, close to death

Something was wrong between you and me

Strugglin' just to draw my last breath

Beaten within an inch of my life

It was my fault they are going to say

When at last my body is found

As a woman to vary from normal, to stray

This is what happens when you fuck around.

Beaten within an inch of my life soon to be found underground.

MURDER/DEATH

WOMAN 2: I was married for some years to a violent man. I spent a great deal of time planning, quite literally, murderous schemes to rid me of him. I implemented none of them for none struck me as suitably foolproof. I crept with my children into the night when it was forcibly brought home to me that in all likelihood I was cast as the murderee, not the murderer in my little dreams.

WOMAN 1: So, out we come . . . yelling bloody murder.

WOMAN 2: For me, you know it came at a moment at which I felt I either was going to kill myself, if not literally then metaphorically, or else I was going to allow myself to be born and live.

WOMAN 1: Are you death come for me now?

WOMAN 2: What makes you say that?

WOMAN 1: I didn't hear you come in. (*Pause*) This place is killing me. You are killing me.

WOMAN 2: It can happen to any of us.

WOMAN 1: Don't say that.

WOMAN 2: You have been judged and found guilty and sentenced to death.

WOMAN 1: I thought we were all sentenced to death. Will killin' me ease the ache in your heart?

WOMAN 2: I'm gonna kill you one day, see if I don't.

OUTSIDER 2

MAN: You're not nervous are you?

WOMAN 2: No. Well maybe a little.

MAN: Don't be. There's nothing to be nervous about.

WOMAN 2: You wanted to speak to me?

MAN:	Are you familiar with "he who pays the piper calls the tune?"
WOMAN 2:	Who always pays when them that can, don't? The innocent pay.
MAN:	One begins to wonder whose side you're on.
WOMAN 2:	If you have any values higher than the possession of land, money and prestige, I ask you to be outraged that your government values property more than human beings!
MAN:	Out here, you don't see the whole picture. There're other considerations . . . You play chess . . . Sometimes a pawn is sacrificed on one side of the board to gain an advantage on the other.
WOMAN 2:	They had taken the government at its word – being savages, they weren't too familiar with governments and all, so it was an understandable mistake . . . All that's needed to assure their success is a clearly defined conception of moral necessity.
MAN:	You can put it this way – we don't mind them dying for us, we just don't want them living with us.
WOMAN 2:	Who's second rate when you run out of brown people?
MAN:	I'll tell you this . . . whatever we do, by the time we're finished, they'll have flip-flopped to the other side of the fence. You follow me?
WOMAN 2:	Doesn't this tell us how little we know of their culture? Of their mindset? Of how they perceive and interpret the actions of the white man when they come into contact with him? What is shared, what is not shared? What offends, what does not offend? What do we strangers, we foreigners, know? We're ass over teakettle when it comes to knowing.

MAN:	You realize as well as I do that is only the tip of the iceberg.
WOMAN 2:	They will hate us with a perfect hatred.
MAN:	You've stirred up a hornet's nest, haven't you? You've opened up Pandora's Box. You've created a maelstrom.
WOMAN 2:	I would have to deny that.
MAN:	We brought you up we can put you down.
WOMAN 2:	I demand to know what advantage is to be gained.
MAN:	What's a critic? Why that's a legless man who teaches running.
WOMAN 2:	I'm thought of most often as a dose of salts; not palatable, but essential for the health of the body. You always say don't worry. But, of course, I worry. It's natural to worry.
MAN:	They say one's strongest instinct is self-preservation.
WOMAN 2:	Well now, you've caught my interest. What is it? What the hell are you here for?
MAN:	You disappoint us.
WOMAN 2:	I should have done something.
MAN:	Never initiate action when you haven't the guts to carry through.
WOMAN 2:	Sometimes it's the struggle that counts. I fear for my country and I fear for my people...
MAN:	You cannot stop this happening.
WOMAN 2:	What kind of a fool do you take me for?
MAN:	The two of us could quarrel about a number of things. I'm tired of quarrelling.
WOMAN 2:	Why is nothing simple in this life? I wanted to do what was right...

MAN:	We don't need rules to play, there are no rules for us. I am a gentle person, but gentle people must act when injustice engulfs them. In an operation like this there is no room for error. The smell of bubblin' tar makes a man eloquent.
WOMAN 2:	You have a heart. What does your heart say? (*Pause*) Well…it's a good day to die.

WAR

WOMAN 1:	Don't talk.
WOMAN 2:	We gotta talk sometime.
WOMAN 1:	You do the talking.
WOMAN 2:	What's your name, soldier?
MAN:	No names, sir.
WOMAN 2:	Right. No names . . . How long have you been here?
MAN:	Ever since I got here, sir.
WOMAN 2:	I see. You're not afraid?
MAN:	No sir.
WOMAN 2:	Good. Although it leads one to suspect your intellect. We will never speak of what transpires here this night, it will die with you. It will die with all of us. Would you . . . help someone die?
MAN:	Why do you ask that?
WOMAN 2:	Some people are better off dead. I might be better off dead.
MAN:	Then I'd say you're in deep shit and acting with grievous disregard for professional ethics.
WOMAN 2:	It's necessary the Government act quickly to assert its sovereignty and jurisdiction. We're in the process of determining and extending our borders geographically.

	An integral aspect of this is the extension of our boundaries morally.
MAN:	All that's needed to assure success is a clearly defined conception of moral necessity. Do you agree sir?
WOMAN 2:	A moral man don't need to think. Measures must be taken. Respect and listen. Obey. (*to woman 1*) Well are you going to sit there like patience?
WOMAN 1:	What do you want me to do?
WOMAN 2:	Your job.
WOMAN 1:	My job? I don't approve of any of this. You went over my head so I'm here. To – mediate. To witness – whatever, I'm not sure what. I won't be party to the forcing of things.
WOMAN 2:	Won't you? And isn't it a terrible job?
WOMAN 1:	What are the advantages to be gained from this . . . this sacrifice? I demand to know what advantage is to be gained.
WOMAN 2:	Hell, prime ministers, politicians and presidents kill more men than the inmates of this place ever did. Sometimes it's the struggle that counts, to struggle to keep on struggling.
WOMAN 1:	For what?
WOMAN 2:	A just cause!
WOMAN 1:	Determined by who?
WOMAN 2:	Yourself!
WOMAN 1:	Oh we'd have a great kinda order then, wouldn't we?
WOMAN 2:	What kinda order have we got now?
WOMAN 1:	You can't believe there's people willing to fight for things they're not gonna win!
WOMAN 2:	I just gotta win – and you just gotta win. I want you to look at yourself! You're not stupid, you're not insensitive

to things but . . . it's like all your choices have been made for you and . . . sometimes you rant about this or that, but you keep right on going! You never ask why am I doing this, do I really want to do this? You ask how to do it, when to do it, and where to do it, you never ask why. You just don't know your own mind.

WOMAN 1: At least I got one. There's gotta be other options.

WOMAN 2: It's a sense of responsibility, that's what it is. I take the risks, and I find my reward in the fulfillment of my task. I begin with loyalty, move on to money, end up with threats . . . I remember standing very still, scrawny and pasty, very still, afraid to move . . . in the middle of silence, listening, like a mouse on a pan, listening for the beat of the wings of the owl . . . very still . . . I'm the one who has something to lose!

WOMAN 1: Don't you feel anything for them?

WOMAN 2: You wouldn't understand.

WOMAN 1: Yes I would. I would try.

WOMAN 2: One has to make decisions. Commitments. To one side or another.

WOMAN 1: What side are you on?

WOMAN 2: The winning side. When I say move, you bloody well move, when I say jump, you say how high. In this stinking world there's two kinds, there's the rule and the ruled – and when I see the likes of you, I know where I stand.

WOMAN 1: I can save none of the others and I cannot save myself.

WOMAN 2: I don't need saving. My position assures my safety. (*Pause*) Our relationship is not an adversarial one.

WOMAN 1: Then why do I feel that it is?

WOMAN 2: I've no idea.

WOMAN 1:   Not reassuring.

MAN: I'd like to write a last letter home to me mum . . . if we
           . . . if we were on the verge of war, or anything like that.

WOMAN 2:   You aren't the first one who thought he knew. Nor will
           you be the last.

MAN: And, of course, all hell broke loose there, what with
           the kids screamin', women runnin' and men lookin'
           for somethin' to hit back with and the whole works
           naked as the day they was born, it bein' the middle of
           the night as far as they were concerned. Pursued them
           like a wolf that tears at the soft underbelly of a fleeing
           doe. She cries, oh murder! Nobody comes, she is flayed
           and gutted, nobody comes. I wanted to do what was
           right . . . and excitin' and . . . and make me mum proud.
           People ask me why did I go? People ask me what was it
           like? People ask me what do I think now that I went?
           Was it worth it?

WOMAN 2:   Suppose you could deter your neighbour from runnin'
           into you on the road by seizin' his children and tyin'
           them to the front bumper of your car. Suppose everyone
           were to do likewise. It's clearly evident accidents would
           decrease indeed the chances of a single child dyin'
           on a car bumper would be slight. Perhaps by miracle
           no child would die. In any event we can predict with
           absolute certainty that on balance more lives would be
           saved than lost and that's what nuclear deterrence is all
           about, folks. So when you hear balance of power holds
           innocents hostage I want you to think road safety and
           children!

MAN: For a long time I prayed to God. I prayed and prayed.
           I thought it was a mistake. I thought maybe he didn't
           know. I don't know what I thought. I prayed and prayed
           . . . Now, I don't believe in God. And if there is a God,
           then I don't like him.

WOMAN 2:	We all be guilty and we all be innocent. We were followin' orders and responsibility and murder don't come into it.
MAN:	How can it be so sunny, so beautiful, when such ugly things are happening. It's strange.
WOMAN 2:	What's that?
MAN:	To try so hard not to die, and now so close to death, to feel no fear, no fear.
WOMAN 2:	The whole thing has been most educational.
WOMAN 1:	Was it? I'm asking you a question! Was it worth it?
WOMAN 2:	Worth it. What is "it", what is it?
WOMAN 1:	You wouldn't know? Or you don't know?
WOMAN 2:	I just . . . don't ask myself that question.

TRUTH/LIES

WOMAN 2:	Look, you and I can be straight with each other. We know we got nothing to say.
WOMAN 1:	So why are you here?
WOMAN 2:	Same question for you.
WOMAN 1:	I told you. I thought I could help. Once I have opened his briefcase he cannot plead innocence. You know . . . you do this thing . . . you stare at me . . . You look directly at my eyes. I think . . . you think . . . that if I'm lying . . . it will come up, like lemons on a slot machine.
WOMAN 2:	I'll tell you what I think . . . I think . . . that you're aware that there is a certain fascination in the ambiguity . . . You always paint the background but leave the rest to imagination.
WOMAN 1:	What's honest, honest is nothing, nobody wants honest.
WOMAN 2:	I was thinkin' I thought hearin' the truth would help you.

WOMAN 1:	Liar.
WOMAN 2:	I'm was thinkin' I was wrong. She don't care about the truth 'cause she's built her whole life on lies, on what she wants to believe to keep that pot boilin'. That's when she feels most alive. You sit around sippin' your wine, playin' your reggae records, bobbin' your head and your ass, and singing "everybody is cryin' out for peace – none of them is cryin' for justice" – Well, someone took you at your word, this is it, people are gonna die, this is real! So fuck off!
WOMAN 1:	I wasn't even there that day.
WOMAN 2:	Do you want to drive me mad?
WOMAN 1:	Oh, yes.
WOMAN 2:	Did . . . did you think you could just tell a story and everything would be right?
WOMAN 1:	It may all have been lies, but that still doesn't mean it weren't true.
WOMAN 2:	Do you see no contradiction?
WOMAN 1:	Tween what?
WOMAN 2:	Where does the truth lie?
WOMAN 1:	Truth lie. Oh yes.
WOMAN 2:	And the truth, as you perceive it?
WOMAN 1:	Truth. Lies. Contradiction. All of em.
WOMAN 2:	Are you lying?
WOMAN 1:	About the storyline – or the timeline?
WOMAN 2:	Either.
WOMAN 1:	Everything's fiction. Isn't that what you say?
WOMAN 2:	When you say that –
WOMAN 1:	Say what?

BURNS, HALSTEAD, LINNEBERG AND PARKEN

WOMAN 2:	When you think you can do anything. You are a danger. That's something I know.
MAN:	A danger to who?
WOMAN 2:	To yourself. And to others.
MAN:	Why's that?
WOMAN 2:	She's either a fool or a liar.
WOMAN 1:	So which am I? Tell me.
WOMAN 2:	A liar. Oh she may have said things, thought things, wrote things – It won't reflect reality.
WOMAN 1:	Wrote letters home and never told them a thing that was true!
WOMAN 2:	Because you . . . you . . . are a third-rate writer, with nothing to say . . . and I, I am a writer of some talent and genius, As *assessed by others*, not myself. I speak the truth.
WOMAN 1:	Why don't I believe you?
WOMAN 2:	Because you never accept what anybody says is how anything is.
WOMAN 1:	That's not true.
WOMAN 2:	Let me tell you something –
WOMAN 1:	Bullshit.
WOMAN 2:	I wouldn't take her word for things.
WOMAN 1:	Bullshit, bullshit!
WOMAN 2:	Do you think good writing guarantees publication? Or bad writing blocks it? Quality has nothing to do with it.
WOMAN 1:	For Christ's sake, speak the truth!
WOMAN 2:	Let us forget "strictly speaking" for a moment. How about trying "laxly speaking", "loosely speaking", "informally speaking" – could you find it in your heart

to lay a charge "loosely speaking"? I could go to the press. Tell everyone what's happened here today.

WOMAN 1:   Oh they'd never believe you. It would throw so many things into question. If they believed you, they'd have to act. No one really wants to do that. It's a matter of interpretation.

WOMAN 2:   You're writing, aren't you? Inside your head, you're writing. After everything you're still writing! You're not listening! You're writing!

WOMAN 1:   I'm making something up. Maybe everything I've said in interviews, speeches, bars, lecture halls, kitchens, hotel and living rooms, on stage and off, in answer to some variation of why me and theatre is a lie. Maybe I make theatre because I make theatre. Maybe I'll stop when I die. Maybe all this is a lie.

WOMAN 2:   I need to find out which of these stories is true.

WAS IT WORTH IT?

WOMAN 2:   Was it worth it? Sentenced to the whole naked works. This . . . sacrifice? Honour, truth, and the vitality of historical crimes and atrocities. Did I think this sacrifice . . . this going to the edge of the cliff would lead to meager financial returns and a precious unique indomitable spirit? No.

WOMAN 1:   I come from a long line of brilliant savages. Unsanitary by habit, I took something nasty, mean and filthy and made something of myself. By challenging political and cultural assumptions I had the courage to fear. I avoided a life in medicine by dumping jerks. Never seeking salvation or damnation from the great imagination. And you ask was it worth it?

MAN: Artistic endeavours with lots of friends, plays for children and action figures. A roaring success makes people nervous and more often than not ends up in histrionics, windows barred, dishonesty expurgated by a blow to one's prior misconceptions. However we aren't here to assign guilt. A very strong thought in my mind is that one man's persuasion is another man's torture.

WOMAN 2: Somewhere there is an imperial directive stating rented theatres and roses for the star, are acts of self-indulgence. I gave my life to them and they inflict injury and pain. Talent and genius, the internal state of passion to make theatre has been most educational and what's past is past. I take risks with destructive acts and I chose 'her', theatre, because of my great capacity for judging lies and fascists. I know Looney Tunes when I see 'em. And you want to know if it was worth it?

WOMAN 1: I have caused disharmony with this vale of tears. Perhaps you thought I would ride a golden cloud into eternity but I have always embraced plummeting like a stone. I have learned to expect splintered shards from the indulgent and established elite. Besides, I am always up for drinking scotch. But you question if it was worth it?

MAN: This splendid spectacle 'informally speaking' was a clearly defined conception of a moral necessity. A maelstrom to some it was self-preservation to me. And you ask was it worth it? I was following orders to discern your potential to love and be loved. Using luminous aura and road apples I mastered the art of stirring up a hornet's nest for the health of the body. Does this set of circumstances – suggest that it wasn't worth it?

WOMAN 1: Circumstances force a decision, I captured it all in an orange Campfire notebook with a soft lead pencil. There's no magic formula or prizes for good behaviour for a daughter of joy. Life is savage and short and so it should be. Perhaps I will fall in dishonour in the dust.

But until then I will not surrender the huge multi-faceted crystal of truth, the passion as natural as a flower turning its face to the sun. We are all sentenced to death. It's your choice, you could escape the graveside ritual come home and choose to take my work and rip it out and crumple it up and throw it away. You'll pretend everything's alright but soon you'll see I have murdered your peace of mind with my conscience. Then you can ask yourself if it was worth it.

Pollock on Plays

WEDNESDAY, SEPTEMBER 20, 2006

Urinetown The Musical

The Calgary Theatre season is up and running. It kicks off with Ground Zero's co-production of Urinetown the Musical at The Grand Theatre, and introduces artistic director Ryan Luhning's co-producer, Joel Cochrane and his Hit and Myth Productions.

The musical hits town legitimized by 6 nominations and 3 NY Tony awards in 2001, rave reviews and numerous productions. It's even hit the college circuit in the States. Given the way Calgary's artistic directors search NY and West End stages for season offerings, the question is why was Urinetown, so long getting to our town?

Some say the title scared producers off. Some say Calgary audiences are stuck on Guys and Dolls and West Side Story. If so, this production is going to prove them wrong.

Urinetown is to musicals what Leslie Nielsen's Airplane or Mel Brook's Blazing Saddles is to movies, but its satire is smarter and more subversive.

It's a mellerdrama that shamelessly exploits the conventions of musical theatre, and the roars of laughter and standing ovation on opening night indicate all involved in this production have every right to feel flush with success.

The plot: a 20 year drought has resulted in draconian measures to conserve water. Private toilets are outlawed; public facilities are the only way to go, and if you gotta go, you gotta pay to go.

If you don't have the pennies to pay to pee, well, you're in a tight spot. Get caught relieving yourself, and officer Lockstock and his sidekick Barrel march you off to Urinetown, a mysterious and no doubt damp place from which no one ever returns.

In Urinetown it's "a privilege to pee" – words right out of the mouth of Penelope Pennywise, manager of one of those public amenities owned and controlled by the entrepreneurial and villainous villain Caldwell B Cladwell. And we're witness to his bribing a slimy senator to ensure government approval of an increase in the price of a pee.

For "the hopeless, down and out" that increase is disastrous news. Enter our hero Bobby Strong who inspires the penniless poor to revolution, and, no meller-drama being complete without romance, enter our villain's daughter, the naïve and innocent Hope.

It's all a little predictable but it's leavened by the sheer silliness of it all, as well as by throwing a few unpredictable curves when least expected.

Nothing is sacred in Urinetown. Songs and dance numbers morph into send-ups of iconic choreography, styles and stylists, movie and stage musicals. From Brecht through Les Miz to West Side Story, all is fodder for exaggeration, mimicry and mockery. Hilarity reigned on opening night and I wondered if there'd be a dry seat left in the house.

We've heard a lot about Calgary talent meeting the demands of this production but our talent pool is broad and deep. We don't need this show to prove it.

Tim Koetting as the corrupt and corrupting Cladwell, exudes a sinister charm. Every gesture and phrase holds an undercurrent of possible actions within his power, and none of them pleasant. "Don't Be a Bunny" he cautions daughter Hope, and as he dances and sings his way through the fate of bunnies in this dog eat dog, or, in this case, I suppose, dog eat bunny world, I couldn't help but think that if Fred Astaire had an evil twin it surely was Cladwell as played by Koetting.

Esther Purvis Smith as Little Sally, clutches a once plush bunny in which she conceals her not quite enough pennies for a pee as she begs for more. Purvis Smith's Little Sally shines with integrity. She finds an authentic emotional core to the character while creating within the stylistic demands of the spoof and parody of Urinetown.

Carson Natrass' Bobby Strong's stirring gospel rendition of "Run Freedom Run" came close to bringing the audience on stage to join his reluctant revolutionaries, and that was only one of a number of show stoppers.

Victoria Lamond playing Hope made a nice transition from vapid beauty to fearless leader and Elinor Holt was a spirited and hard-hearted Ms Pennywise fearlessly wielding a toilet brush in defense of exploitation and profit. Although ... although her heart will soften in time ... but that's a secret.

Lampoonery is seductive for actors, directors and for audiences, but I felt the performances of both Purvis Smith and Carson Natrass had at their centre a truthfulness that provided an emotional connect to the production, and that's needed as one tends to forget there's a serious issue buried beneath all the fun and fooffahrah.

It's a cast of 16, and the collective energy and focus of the ensemble supported and enriched the work of the principal characters, thanks to the crisp and detailed co-direction of Kevin McKendrick and Mark Bellamy, the latter also handling choreography. Deneen McArthur's costumes were appropriately grungy for the poor and dressy for the rich, while co-set and lighting designers Terry Gunvordahl and Cimmeron Meyer created a multiple level playing space which served the production well as did their illumination of the whole proceedings. And I mustn't forget the contribution of music director Randy Mueller and his five piece band that kept everyone on their toes and in fine voice.

Occasionally, not too often, I found it a bit unrelenting in volume and energy, a bit of a one note, which for me exposed a kind of vacuum beneath the busyness of it all, and there were a few sound problems rendering some lyrics unintelligible and the Act One Finale, loud but less than musical. I'm certain that's been solved even as we speak.

I must confess I find it a bit disconcerting to sit with an adult audience upon which one can absolutely rely to greet every "pay to pee" "pee for free" "privilege to pee" bit of dialogue with howls of laughter. Only recently I'd been telling a 4 year old we don't yell out, in a public place, references to peeing as it isn't really funny. It turns out I was mistaken.

And then there's a "Hail Malthus" at the unpredictable, in a good way, ending of Urinetown. I'm not sure who in the audience reads the orange insert explaining the Malthus reference. I suggest you do. And if you don't want to read all of it, just read the last paragraph.

Then you might recall a headline on the Sunday's Herald's front page "Calgary must limit water use. The province is committed to protecting watersheds while sustaining the economy."

I wondered if the authors of Urinetown had written a prologue to their musical, whether this might be it. In "Hail Malthus" we have the authors' epilogue. Scary, if it's prophecy. I hope, with all the laughter, glee and mirth, Urinetown The Musical's serious underpinnings aren't lost on an audience.

At any rate Ground Zero and Hit and Myth Productions have a hit on their hands, and Calgary has a grand opening to the 2006–2007 theatre season.

SUNDAY, OCTOBER 1, 2006

Of Mice And Men

Theatre Calgary has a new artistic director. Last Friday night Dennis Garnhum introduced himself and his first season of plays with the classic "Of Mice and Men" by John Steinbeck.

A brief summary of the plot for those who need a reminder – two migrant farm workers in California during the Great Depression share an impossible dream and goal, to own their own small farm and stop their wandering. Lennie is a giant of a man with the mind of a child. His love of stroking soft things has led to never-ending trouble including a charge of rape from which the men are fleeing. George's compassionate nature has burdened him with the care and protection of Lennie and just when their impossible dream of owning a farm seems possible, tragedy intervenes and George must make a dreadful decision.

As an introduction to the new artistic director the production gives a somewhat ambiguous hint of things to come. We have new boy, old play. 70 years old. Which shouldn't be held against it. It won the NY Drama Circle Award in 1937. Perhaps it seemed a safe bet for director Dennis Garnhum to open his season. He's directed 2 other productions of this play. He obviously loves it well as he tells us in his notes. Maybe too well. They say familiarity breeds contempt, but it also can breed adoration, and when the revered object is a play you run the risk of sucking the life right out of it. It becomes a beautiful thing in performance, but a beautiful inert thing.

There are no safe bets in theatre. With every production you undertake risk. Hedging your bets in theatre brings its own risk. I'll mix metaphors here and say you have to play in theatre without a safety net. Many Calgarians were hoping for a braver production choice to serve as our introduction to the new artistic director.

As for the production – the stage is framed by a rough wood border. The title of the play is projected on a scrim prior to the play's beginning which opens with a brief sequence of men working the fields. That scrim closes the play with a projected quote from Robbie Burns telling us what the play has illustrated. I got it without the quote.

Allan Stitchbury and John Jenkins' set design of multiple interiors and exteriors are gorgeous to look upon and ingeniously manipulated and transformed from one location to another by a cadre of farm workers. These transitions are scenes in themselves and are all quite graceful but they impede the forward action of the play.

The soaring classical music which accompanies the scenes of scene changes lends an air of romanticism which seems at odds with the gritty depression era of these indentured migrant workers.

I don't know whether it was that wooden framing of the stage or the scrim or the moving set scenes within the scenes proper of the play but the production had a cinematic feel and look to it. Much of the action, or perhaps I should say dialogue, took place centre stage with a panorama view of what could be seen around and behind with the odd character coming on in the background, sitting or standing a while and moving off. It made a wonderful picture but when I try to understand why there was such a static or tepid feel to character interaction centre stage I wonder if it diluted focus. The unfolding of the play's story often seemed like a series of still photos which failed to carry and build dramatic tension.

Steinbeck's "Of Mice and Men" is beloved by all who know it and on the curriculum of schools without number. I have no doubt it will sell well. But that is not the only criterion for theatrical success. Theatre Calgary is our flagship regional theatre. It has more human, technical and financial resources than other Calgary theatre companies along with a host of talent at its contractual fingertips. All involved with this production have resumes documenting their many roles, raves and experience. When you have much, more is expected of you. And when a classic is produced I want it to be as alive as the day it was written. I don't want to feel I'm viewing a skeleton, beautifully rendered, but still a skeleton.

Down With Up With People

The Calgary theatre scene is bubbling with activity. It's curtains up on One Yellow Rabbit's season opener "Down With Up With People: The Untold Story of Anthony Curtola" at The Big Secret Theatre, starring Andy Curtis.

Anthony Curtola is a wannabe celebrity, best known, if known, for his hosting of the Big Rock Eddy Awards. He's a mid-Atlantic David Niven in a white dinner jacket who oozes ersatz charm reminiscent of a waiter at the Keg. Anthony Curtola is a great pretender, just a boy from Alberta with pretensions, and even his Medicine Hat origins change with his telling of them. The character is the alter ego of One Yellow Rabbit's comedic master Andy Curtis and when Curtis slips into Curtola's skin it's a seamless fit. Every twitch of the thin penciled on moustache, or lift of the similarly applied eyebrow, a bite of the thumb, a touch to the nose, elicits laughter. He takes the stage with confidence knowing he holds the audience in his hand and they'll go where he takes them. In fact when house lights go out and the stage is still black, audience members burst into laughter so wide spread I can only assume it was in anticipation of what was to come.

Curtola' "untold story" is a series of monologues, I could call them rambling, or a stream of consciousness, made up, as Curtola tells us, of digressions, anec-dotes, some amusing, some iffy, revelations, epiphanies and sidebars. They're interspaced with musical song and dance by Curtola and his back-up 3 member chorus of The Oh Lay girls. Krysten Blair, Onalea Gilbertson and Denise Clarke. Denise Clarke is a pleasure to watch. Back-up, background or not, every fiber of her being and body is committed to the moment. I found my eye drawn to her, not that she was drawing focus in any way, or that Curtis' performance was lagging, but primarily because I found the material itself slight, and not up to the usual One Yellow Rabbit standard.

One can't fault Andy's performance, and the Oh Lay girls are a treat. The lyrics and choreography are ersatz renditions themselves drawn from musical sources from Bobby Sherman to Loverboy; I found them the cleverest and best aspect of the show. Shades of Urinetown, we even have Curtola's major epiphany, brought on by either a bad olive or a nasty pudding, accompanied by the evacuation of body wastes. I won't be more specific. Blake Brooker's script just seemed thin, a quickie kind of thing, an anorexic Rabbit that didn't hop despite the sparkly Oh Lay Girls and the considerable talents of Andy Curtis.

Overall the show doesn't have the sizzle we've come to expect from One Yellow Rabbit but is worth taking in for Rabbit fans.

Wait Until Dark

It's Vertigo Theatre's 30th anniversary and they're celebrating 3 decades of mystery theatre with the 60's thriller "Wait Until Dark" made famous by its incarnation in film with Audrey Hepburn. The plot relies on a suspension of disbelief so great that it strains one's imaginative powers and reveals how the unfolding of story on stage and our expectations of what constitutes thrilling and terror has changed over the last 40 years.

As for the plot, criminal mastermind Harry Roat enlists a couple of ex-cons to attain a drug-packed doll Roat believes is hidden somewhere in the apartment of Susie who's blind and her husband who's unwittingly brought the doll into the country and apparently mislaid it. The baddies concoct an elaborate plan with more twists than a corkscrew to gain Susie's confidence and assistance in finding the doll during her husband's absence. Her blindness seems to make her an easy mark but appearances are deceiving. With the help of a neighborhood kid the tables are ultimately turned, the lights go out and the disadvantage is in the criminal's court for Susie has been in the dark all along.

I thought Adrienne's Snook's Susie hit one note – that of high anxiety. It was as if her blindness was her character. There're more notes to be played in that character than I got from the performance. Christian Goutis as Mike the ex-con masquerading as an old Marine acquaintance of Susie's husband moved from manipulating Susie to, despite his best, or worst intentions, finding himself having a degree of sympathy for her which he knew he must suppress. I found his characterization and that of Sydney Nicole Herauf as the smart and sassy Gloria, the most fully formed of the evening. Trevor Leigh's Roat was sinister if not terribly believable but perhaps I wasn't working hard enough with that suspension of disbelief so essential to the play itself. And I just felt really sorry for Chad Norbert as Mike's partner in crime for having to wear that awful wig. I tried to convince myself it was part of his character, but failed. It ended up having more presence than he did which was not his fault.

Scott Reid's set was utilitarian as needed and Glenda Stirling's direction kept things moving. I didn't get shivers and tingles along the spine and you'll have to wait until the dark of the final confrontation between Susie and Road before thrilling and terror sets in.

THURSDAY, OCTOBER 5, 2006

10 Days On Earth

Alberta Theatre Projects has launched its current season with Ronnie Burkett's latest puppet creation "10 Days On Earth" which premiered earlier this year in Toronto and concluded a successful three month run.

The Village Voice describes Ronnie Burkett as "one of the world's geniuses" and adds "seeing his troupe every few years has become a necessity of civilized theatre-going." He's a grand master of puppetry, with an international reputation and is truly a Canadian national treasure. To top it all off, he's one of our own, a real Alberta boy born and bred in Medicine Hat.

Calgary theatre-goers have a long, warm and heart-felt association with Burkett's Theatre of Marionettes from 1986's "Fool's Edge" to "Provenance" in 2003. So electricity was in the air, and the theatre crackled with audience excitement and anticipation as lights went up on Burkett's latest creation. That's the way it should be particularly when the work is by one of the world's significant theatre artists. And for those who may not be sufficiently aware of Ronnie's work, it's puppetry for the legitimate stage and an adult audience. He deals in serious themes with outrageous wit that cuts to the core.

Burkett has spoken in interviews of a catalytic and haunting experience that inspired "10 Days On Earth." In an English shopping mall he saw an elderly woman with a developmentally disabled adult, her son or so he thought. Burkett was touched by the woman's loving care and attention to the needs of this child in a man's body and the man-child's affectionate response to his mother. The question of what would become of him when his mother died solidified in Burkett's mind as "if you were alone and didn't know it, would you feel lonely?" And so "10 days On Earth" came into being.

In the play Burkett presents us with Darrell a mentally challenged middle-aged adult who lives with his elderly single mum who was abandoned by Darrell's father when she found herself pregnant. One day she retreats into her room, closes the door, and dies. Darrell returns home from his shoe shining job, knows he mustn't intrude when the door is closed, and continues on for 10 days, talking to her through the door, mourning the loss of the rituals and routines that have governed his life, and gradually realizing that something is not right.

He finds solace in recalling his favourite book in which a terrier, Honeydog, nattily attired in a cranberry waistcoat and bow tie, and a tutu-clad duckling, Little Burp, search for a home. They meet a variety of animals from a raunchy rat in pink to a seductive sheep, Blanche Dubaa. The story of Darrell's 10 days, his simple conversations with street acquaintances from Lloyd, a foul-mouthed preacher who just may or may not be God, to Irene, a Salvation Army worker, and the story of Honeydog and Little Burp's quest for a home are interwoven and, for me, subtly reflect each other.

"10 Days On Earth" is a deceptively simple story told with wit, insight, sensitivity and affection. But the plot is merely the surface of "10 Days on Earth." Burkett's Theatre of Marionettes is hypnotic and multi-dimensional which deepens and enriches our engagement with the characters and the story. And that has something to do with the art of puppetry itself.

First we have Ronnie Burkett's marvelously and beautifully crafted puppets with their faces permanently etched into an expression, a smile, a frown, a grimace. I see those expressions change and I know that cannot be. Yet it is. A theatrical miracle. Then there's Ronnie's manipulation of his cast, each broad or subtle manipulation true to the character of the individual puppet and the emotion or action of the moment. But economical as well, conveying the essence of that movement and moment. And the characters' voices, all given voice by Ronnie ring authentic for each.

The puppets are real, as real as you or I am. In fact they're more real than we are, and more real than any actor could be for Burkett's puppets are people stripped to their essence. Our awareness that the source of this magical multi-dimensional world is given life and unfolds before us through one multi-talented individual amplifies our engagement and entertainment. Viewing that world is like looking through a microscope at our own world. It magnifies, penetrates and illuminates.

Some have an unfortunate tendency to define and circumscribe, an individual's work. "Ah, that's the kind of thing he or she writes or directs or paints or role he or she plays." The work and the artist are labeled and his or her new work compared to old work. If the label no longer quite fits, there is a sense of unease, an unwillingness to reassess the trajectory of the artist' creations. I think Burkett is exploring a slightly different path than in his previous work. With the Honeydog and Little Burp story Burkett reveals himself as the Narrator. He's lit and speaks directly to the audience. The Creator is acknowledging himself, inserting himself in the work, in a way I find significant. And I find it exciting.

I wonder if it is an indicator of where Burkett will go next. I know he'll go where his vision takes him. It won't be determined by the expectation of those who prefer an artist to run in the same spot.

As for his central question "if you were alone and didn't know it, would you feel lonely?" One answer is you can never be lonely so long as you have access to stories. Unlike Darryl most of us are seldom alone, yet we're told feelings of loneliness are pandemic. Perhaps Honeydog and Little Burp's story is an offering by Ronnie to us, as well as comfort for Darrell.

Popular as Burkett is, there are often good seats left in the run so try not to miss this latest work by a master of his art form.

TUESDAY, OCTOBER 10, 2006

Insomnia

Theatre Junction has joined forces with the Toronto theatre company Necessary Angel to open its 2006–2007 season. The two have co-produced "Insomnia" authored by award-winning theatre artists Daniel Brooks and Guillermo Verdecchia.

Necessary Angel and Brooks have almost iconic stature in Canadian theatre with a lengthy list of awards and recognition of the contribution of both to the national theatre scene. Calgarians may remember a 2003 Theatre Junction production "The Good Life" which introduced them to Brooks and laid the groundwork for this co-operative venture.

In "Insomnia" we have a central character John F. and his whiny wife Gwen. John is riddled with anxiety over almost everything. His deteriorating marriage, his unfinished "opus", his finances or lack thereof, the responsibilities of fatherhood, the state of the world, and his insomnia. And that insomnia gives rise to the structure of the play. The plot, if plot it is, unfolds in a series of short concise scenes. Landmarks that move things along and often seem to emerge from that dream-like state brought on by extreme lack of sleep. Things pick up with the arrival of John's brother William, a successful Disney executive, and his narcoleptic wife, Kate.

John yearns for Kate but they're ill-matched, given his insomnia and her narcolepsy. And William is apparently boffing Gwen. Or maybe not, given the central character's altered state of consciousness due to insomnia. There are laughs, but it's not a comedy. Unless I'm sadly mistaken. To be honest, I didn't find the text of the play compelling.

The production of the text, however, was stunning, a visual treat.

Set designer Julie Fox creates a stark stage curtained in black. A dark void with a forced perspective leading the eye to a red exit sign. Above it a small window through which we can see a bedroom lamp and a few metal bars of a crib's headboard. Downstage an easy chair, and a floor lamp in a cool pool of light.

All minimalist. There's a sense of restraint. But restraint suggests an explosion of emotion or a physical act that requires restraint. So there's a tension in the set's classic simplicity. There's a red floor. So when lit we have red corridors delineated and piercing through areas of charcoal and black. Characters move through the light and shadow. Come and go randomly but with strong intentions. They enter and exit through passageways in the black void that envelops the space.

Lighting by Andrea Lundy is ever so precise. She paints the stage and characters with a palette of light and dark that surprises us on occasion. A bar of lights for example will suddenly expose the audience reminding us that we are participating in this imagined series of events in performance. We might ask who and how real are we. And enriching all this is designer Richard Feren's soundscape. It adds an aural dimension heightening, pointing and counterpointing key moments.

Every production choice enhances a theatrical expression of John's insomniac state of mind.

There's no deficit of talent in the cast. Daniel Brooks' John is understated and naturalistic. He can turn on a dime, effortlessly and credibly transforming into an emotionally charged violent individual. A stylized physicality that sets us back in our seats. Randy Hughson is William, irritatingly successful, liberal with his advice, certain and secure. Fiona Highet as Gwen and Columbe Demers as Kate ably inhabit their characters. Well, what there is of character. The text doesn't really give them much to work with.

Direction is clean and clear. Christopher Abraham maximizes the effect on the audience of the highly theatrical elements of set, light and sound. He creates images that imprint on the eye. Stage pictures that we carry with us as we leave the theatre.

With this wealth of talent in performance, design and direction I should be over the moon. But I'm not. I'm high in the sky but not over the moon.

Maybe it's because I'm a woman, or maybe because I'm a playwright. The script strikes me as 90 minutes of male angst. But male angst with the pretensions. We're supposed to find a deeper universal meaning resonating within what is essentially just a domestic drama. It has vapid female characters and a central male character whinging on about his wife, his work, his child, his sex life, politics and the state of the world. At one point he engages in a long political rant. I had to fight the urge to mutter "yeah yeah yeah. I know that. Stop yelling at me". I don't know. Maybe that was the desired effect. Then there's a dinner scene near the end with a surprising meat entrée. It's reminiscent of the playwright who finds the only way to end a play is to shoot someone and go to black. Something I confess I did myself in an early work.

With "Insomnia" the rich theatrical spectacle floods our senses. So we don't pay much attention to What is being presented and a lot of attention to How it's being presented. The lushness of the production blinds us, in a manner of speaking, to the thinness of the material being produced.

It's a polished production. My reservations around the written text are fairly apparent. But the sheer theatricality of the production, its visual impact, the command of the art and craft of the theatre artists involved make "Insomnia" a production worth seeing.

THURSDAY, OCTOBER 12, 2006

Trainspotting

Calgary's Sage Theatre is attracting audiences with its present production of "Trainspotting", a stage version of the 1996 hit movie and novel by Irvine Welsh.

It's darker in tone and content than the movie. And it has nothing to do with spotting trains. But it's still definitely not for the faint of heart or stomach. The play rubs our face in the grim underbelly of Edinburgh Scotland. And it does this through a series of monologues and short sketch-like scenes. These reflect and reveal the junkie high jinks and heroin hell of addiction.

The play's principal character, a kind of narrator, is Mark. Monologues and scenes shadow disconnected events in Mark's life. He opens and closes the play as he wakes covered in his own vomit and excrement.

Mark's caught in a circle of addiction and death. "Caught" may not be the right word for he apparently chooses this over a life of bourgeois boredom, tedium, or employment in any job for which he might be qualified. Although it's difficult to imagine what that job could possibly be. He's surrounded by a variety of characters played by three actors. They ride a heroin roller coaster of highs and lows, their lives driven and defined by their need of the drug. It's not a pretty picture.

Between the start and stop of the play this crew of desperate deadbeats cook up smack, pop up veins, and shoot up. All is most realistic. A pregnant girlfriend is sadistically beaten. Mark fishes for opium suppositories in a filthy blocked toilet and reinserts them in his rectum. He has sex with his dead brother's wife at the funeral. All mourn briefly an addict's overlooked and dead baby discovered between cooking up hits. A waitress dips a used tampax into a rude customer's soup; this and more fueled by a cynical humour and rage. "Trainspotting" is what's known as "in yer face" theatre. It's a bleak and shocking comedy laced with dark despair.

The actors handle the text with a great deal of energy and emotional intensity. Geoffrey Ewert plays Mark. He hits all the bases of rage, anguish, despair and depression. It's mixed with a kind of contemptuous joyful exuberance at giving the finger to society's conventions. Christopher Austman is triple cast. His most significant role is Tommy, a lamb looking for a slaughter. Mark introduces him to heroin and it's not long before this gentle soul staggers naked on stage, and slumps to the floor. With his veins collapsed, he injects his penis for a final and fatal hit.

David Trimble is Franco Begbie, raw, violent, sadistic and abusive. He roars dialogue in a staccato stream punctuated by a torrent of profanity rarely if ever heard on Calgary stages. And Jennie Esdale capably takes on the roles of June and Alison and delivers a couple of monologues recounting small victories in an otherwise dreary existence. I couldn't really keep each female character straight, but it didn't seem to matter. One character is a bit more spirited than the other; I think that's June. My clue is her costume.

In any other play this might constitute a major flaw but not so in this one.

I think it's because there's a certain sameness to all the characters. Their brutal and squalid existence. The onslaught of horrific images and actions that most of us don't ordinarily see. The bombardment of profanity. The audience experiences shock and awe mixed with laughter and that tends to disguise the lack of any real depth or dimension to the characters. It seems not to matter. We're swept along in the play's sheer audacity, anecdotal story-telling and great dialogue. Although I had a small difficulty there.

Remember the play takes place in Edinburgh Scotland. The Scottish accent is most evident. Accent work's a challenge. The line between a seeming authenticity, and the audience's comprehension of what's being said is a fine one. The actor needn't duplicate exactly the thick Scottish brogue for it to ring true for the setting. I felt some actors walked, or talked, that fine line better than others. Quick calculation – I couldn't understand probably 20 to 25% of what was said.

Maybe it's my ears. Maybe the director feels that's acceptable. It's certainly true I didn't find that percentage of dialogue loss an insurmountable barrier to the play. One just goes with the play's flow of energy and action.

The portrayals of the characters, as far as they go, feel honest and true. But it's not a play that's delving into how these people individually got to be where we find them. If a finger is pointed, it's pointed at society in general, class and economic distinctions, consumerism, and I suppose I could say etc.

And I could say it suggests subliminally the characters' drug-addled lives reflect a slice of life in our own city's underbelly for the same reasons. I should mention the play has a caution – stimulated sex and drug-taking, violence, nudity and profanity – plus a ray of hope the program said, although I missed that. It must have been a very very small ray.

"Trainspotting" plays in the Joyce Doolittle Theatre at the Pumphouse. It's a small intimate space. Very intimate and sometimes a challenge. This play suits the space well. Set and lighting designer Ian Martens places a couple of seedy bits of furniture against a the theatre's worn brick wall, It's spare and bleak, and the lighting projects a gloom matching the characters' lives. Small changes, a table here, a chair or a coffin there are slipped in or out by the actors when needed. The violence is carefully choreographed and realistic.

Director Kelly Reay uses the space well although I found the end of Act One unfocused and unclear. And there was that one note quality to the characterizations which I'm not sure lies at the feet of the director or the actors. It may be inherent in the play. All in all, "Trainspotting" is a good production as well as an example of theatre of the "in yer face" genre. If the warnings don't scare you off, it's worth seeing.

TUESDAY, OCTOBER 17, 2006

The Goat

Alberta Theatre Projects is causing a stir with its present production of Edward Albee's acclaimed and controversial "The Goat or Who is Sylvia". Why the controversy? In two words, interspecies sex. Thus the Goat, named Sylvia.

Here's the plot. An opening scene of marital bliss. Martin, a successful architect at the top of his game. Stevie, his liberal and loving wife of 22 years. Billy, their

17 year old gay and much adored son. Martin seems a trifle distracted. But no, it's not Alzheimers, as we learn when he confides in best friend Ross – Martin's having an extra-marital affair. With a goat. Named Sylvia. Ross gives the game away in a letter to wife Stevie, and as you might imagine this shatters Martin and Stevie's idyllic union. That's mirrored in Stevie's smashing of all breakable objects and overturning of furniture. Understandably she's upset. But determined to learn every detail of her husband's bestial relationship. Well, maybe not every detail, but enough. After releasing a torrent of disbelief, anger and pain, she storms off, warning Martin she'll bring him down. I can tell you this does not bode well for the goat

The playwright has laced all this with a mega dosing of wit and humor. The audience laughed a lot on opening night, and were suitably hushed when a comforting hug between father and son turned into a passionate embrace and more passionate kiss. Gotta tell you I didn't buy that for a minute. I feel an immensely talented playwright has done a con job on us. He's baiting the audience with a shocking situation, and what makes it controversial is that a lot of people rise to the bait.

Somewhere I've read that Albee's plays "command our attention not because of their depth but because of the extraordinary vitality of their surface." Tolerance, which we're told the play is about, is not actually addressed but we do get sparkling clever dialogue, fireworks on stage, witty digs at political correctness as well as descriptions of the epiphany of gazing into a goat's eyes.

Set designer David Fraser gives us a tastefully decorated living room as befits an architect. The walls are slatted, subtly echoing for me, sophisticated barnyard fencing. Jennifer Morehouse provided the fireworks as Stevie. She teeters on the edge of overplaying an overwrought Stevie confronting the destruction of her happy family unit. David McNally is Martin, at first serene, if a bit distracted, in his love for both Stevie and Sylvia. Complacent, believing he can explain his happiness and the rightness of it all. And into depression with his realization of the destruction unleashed. In Martin's view it is not his own actions but the meddling and judgmental best friend Ross played briskly and competently by Paul Cowling that's led to his family's break-down. The cast is rounded out by Christopher Duthrie's Billy and directed by Kate Newby.

Much as I wanted to be engaged emotionally, intellectually or morally, I was unmoved by the production (with the exception of feeling badly for the goat). Don't know if the failure is mine, the production or the play's.

WEDNESDAY, OCTOBER 18, 2006

Glorious!

Theatre Calgary's founding artistic director has returned to Calgary to direct "Glorious" which we're told is the true story of Florence Foster Jenkins. The first question for me was – who is Florence Foster Jenkins?

Florence is, or was, the worst singer in the world, usually referred to as "the soprano of the sliding scale". She was wealthy, came from Pennyslavia, and financed her own career. "Glorious" by Peter Quilter is a hilarious and charming comedy tracing Florence's career, from her performances at recitals for NY society ladies to her last performance, a sell-out at Carnegie Hall in 1944.

Canadians have a national treasure in Nicola Cavendish who plays Madame Jenkins. She simply takes command of the stage, embodying this Pennyslavanian "artiste" with every gesture, tilt of the head, and vocal cadence. She sings operatic arias, and she sings them atrociously. She's a dreamer but a pragmatic dreamer who will let nothing, not even a lack of talent, stand in her way.

Supporting Florence's dream is a covey of friends. Her pianist, Cosme McMoon, as played by Jonathan Monroe is sensitive, shy, gay. He's a sweet man, at first appalled by Jenkin's vocal abilities (or lack thereof) and later moved by genuine affection for her. Dixie Seatle is Dorothy, a stalwart friend and would-be theatrical designer. Seatle is captivating with a lightness of touch that plays perfectly with and against Cavendish's straight-ahead drive to achieve her dream. Maria Vacratsis as the insubordinate Mexican maid has us in the aisles without our ever understanding a word she says. Gesture and expression tell all we need to know. Florence's "significant other" St Clair Byfield is played by Calgary's Christopher Hunt. He's a bluff fellow with a hearty guffaw, a failed actor with a British accent that comes and goes.

Theatre Calgary's founder and Shaw Festival's former artistic director Christopher Newton directs the production with a sure hand. He's drawn out the humanity of a glorious cast of characters never allowing the production to slip into caricature and cartoon. Every aspect of the production comes together to create a jewel of a show.

A lush set by David Boechler leads us through a doorway to Florence's NY apartment, and on to a recording studio, a ballroom, a cemetery and finally Carnegie Hall. And then there's elegant and fantastic costume design by Phillip Clarkson. As for lighting design – I urge you to see this production if only for the lighting design by Adam Brodie. It's beautiful and evocative, illuminating external settings and heightening internal moments. "Glorious" is a polished and delightful production. The night I attended we all laughed ourselves silly.

If you're looking for frothy, funny, well played and produced, don't miss "Glorious".

In Fine Form

A couple of wild and crazy guys have taken over One Yellow Rabbit's Big Secret Theatre to present "In Fine Form". They appear in pajamas, and invite you to wear your pj's when you attend. I declined the invitation but did take in the show on opening night with a host of others, some in pajamas.

Mark Chavez and Shendoah Allen, are a madcap duo who offer up a "faster than the speed of light" series of sketches and characters. They blend physical, mimed and stand-up comedy, spice it with improv, add strands of mini-plots and recurring characters, and turn up the heat with amazing performance skills and high energy. The two reveal an astounding on stage ability to read each other's minds and creative intentions. They seamlessly morph from one character to another to another, even exchanging characters within a sketch. "In Fine Form" manages to keep two balls in the air. It's hilariously chaotic, and at the same time it gives us fragments of multiple stories and plot lines we can follow.

"Chaotic" and "stories we can follow" may seem a contradiction but the style of "In Fine Form" is the bond between the two: lighting speed of presentation plus instantaneous physical and vocal transformation from one character to another. Once Chavez and Allen step on stage we're caught in a riptide of hilarity. There's no stopping. We're propelled from one bit to another bit to another bit. That's what gives the sense of chaos but it's also what weaves the recurring characters and stories into a unified theatre piece.

The show's a wonderful example of the saying "less is more" in the theatre. Particularly when you have performers possessing the degree of art and craft Chevez and Allen display. The production begins with a completely bare stage. Two conservative looking guys in their conservative pj's enter with two folding chairs. They stand there, awkward and embarrassed, have nothing to say, don't know what they're doing there – it's the actor's nightmare. The pj guys slink off stage. They reappear – and from then on, the audience is on the comedic ride of their life. The stage is suddenly populated with a world of characters. There's

Leopold and his talking horse Fredrick, Mr X and Lower Case t, two old fogies, a father and his adenoidal daughter Jennifer, a haunted hotel, its eerie night clerk, a couple of old ladies. Each mini scene reveals a changing relationship, a conflict, an event. Jennifer and her dad, for example, seeking accommodation at a hotel where every opened door reveals freaky inhabitants, some of whom we've previously met in their own mini scenes. Then Chavez and Allen flip the audience back and forth between the various comic tales. They weave them together in surprising ways.

The Pajama Men defy easy description. "In Fine Form" is certainly more than a comedy revue, at the same time less than play. It's in a class of its own, an excellent performance piece and the genre really is irrelevant.

There're some good shows playing in Calgary at present. I hope folks can find the time to take them in. There're always one or two "pay what you can" performances as well as cheaper matinees. Check that out if ticket price is an issue.

And don't forget – wear your pajamas to a performance and you'll receive the admiration of Chavez and Allen.

TUESDAY, OCTOBER 31, 2006

Show No. 1: Archeology

If you're thinking of "archeology" as commonly thought of, that ain't what you're gonna get. In fact you're not gonna get much of anything. "Show No. 1: Archeology" is a grab bag of disconnected and incoherent bits and pieces. Some of the bits are self-indulgent and personal, others are a party piece to show off the performer's particular talent or lack thereof. A monologue here, a banal platitude there, some video clips, an exceedingly physical movement piece, some songs, less said about them the better, a rap with the rapper writhing about on the floor – we even got some male frontal nudity at which I wanted to scream "Is that all there is?"

In addition the production attempts to ingratiate itself with the audience by having performers greet friends as we enter, serve a beverage mid show, join us to watch parts of the performance, and then hang out in the lobby as we exit the theatre. The whole thing is pointless and directionless. I was torn between weeping with despair and chewing my tongue off in a rage.

The production has failed badly. The net result of this introduction to Mark Lawes' new direction for Theatre Junction and its ensemble creation work was a

SHARON POLLOCK | DONNA COATES

collective shudder throughout the audience. Disappointment and disbelief was palatable on opening night.

Any performance piece requires a spine. It can be any one of a number of things, including such things as a story, or a thesis, or a style of presentation. That spine is an organizational principal. It determines what you keep and what you discard in creation. This piece has no spine. It can no more stand upright than you or I could minus a spine. That's one problem.

Next is Lawes' idea of ensemble creation as evident on the stage. Talk is cheap and we've heard a lot of it about Theatre Junction's ensemble. Ensemble creation in theatre means more than a long-term contract. It's not a mutual admiration society, nor is it a company hopping up and down more or less in unison on the stage. There is not an iota of ensemble creation, in the true meaning of the word, evident in "Show No. 1: Archeology." The phrase seems to be used to deflect and deny any critical assessment of the work.

Theatre Junction has a prestigious production history in the city. With "Show No. 1: Archeology" some money and a great deal of trust and good will has been lost. One can only hope that someone in the company has the brains, the guts, the artistic integrity or the financial responsibility to ask some hard questions.

If they're still selling tickets the theatre police should be arresting someone for fraud. Lovers of theatre are threatened with "Show No. 2: Atlantis" in March 2007.

MONDAY, NOVEMBER 13, 2006

Something True and Wonderful

"Something True and Wonderful" is a light lunch. Steve, an inveterate liar, and Evelyn who's seeking a truthful mate, meet up at one of those self-improvement retreats. There's an attraction between the two. But Evelyn demands truthfulness only in so far as it meets her needs, and Steve can't seem to break out of his habitual lying. The play's mildly amusing. And the amusement is heightened slightly by the video documentation of their attempts at establishing a relationship. Both the characters and the audience are aware of the camera and the video is played on a screen centre stage simultaneous with the story unfolding. Evelyn turns the tables on Steve and what may be true love triumphs.

There's solid performances from Curt Mckinstry as Steve and Shari Watling as Evelyn. Mckinstry's Steve is a kind of "ah Shucks" likeable liar, a bit bumbling and easy to forgive, even as he tries to negotiate his way into Evelyn's bed, while Watling gives Evelyn a nice underplayed desperate edge to her search for a truthful partner. There's an ironic twist in that it's ultimately a lie that brings them together.

The script by playwright Doug Curtis is slight and skips across the surface of the characters. A little tonic is added by the video camera. It becomes a kind of character with Steve and Evelyn acknowledging it and playing to it and with it. It's a fun device that both Mckinstry and Watling use to their advantage.

Margaret and Bartley Bard, the founders of Lunchbox Theatre, returned from a busy schedule in L.A. to direct "Something True and Wonderful". They've made the most of the material with the assistance of a strong cast. Nevertheless I find the script minor fare and a strange choice to showcase the Bard's comedic directorial talents. Their brief return to Calgary is a welcome one.

MONDAY, JANUARY 14, 2008

Sylvia Plath Must Not Die

Every year the appetizer on One Yellow Rabbit's menu for the Rodeo is their sponsorship of Ground Zero's 10 Minute Play Festival, a one night stand of 6 sketches by "Calgary's rising theatre stars" created in the 24 hours proceeding the presentation. It's a hit and miss affair with a most forgiving audience and I was only able to take in the first half. It was "miss" but the folks around me ate it up and for all I know the "hits" could have strutted their stuff in the second half, which a prior engagement prevented my taking in.

All of that is merely prelude to what is billed as the Rodeo's highlight: One Yellow Rabbit's celebratory 25th anniversary creation "Sylvia Plath Must Not Die" – Sylvia Plath being the young American Poet, born in 1932, first poem published at the age of 8; first book at 28, married to and essentially abandoned by English poet Ted Hughes, mother of 2 children, suicidal from an early age and prone to severe bouts of depression, killing herself at age 30. In 1982 Plath, already an iconic figure, became the first poet to be posthumously awarded a Pulitzer Prize,

I wouldn't say "Sylvia Plath Must Not Die" offers any real exploration, theatrical or otherwise, of the poet's life and relationships. What the One Yellow Rabbit ensemble has done is pair the poetry of Sylvia Plath with that of Anne Sexton. The two met at a poetry workshop in Boston, and though living on different continents, apparently remained friends. They are generally described as belonging to the school of "confessional poets".

Sexton, born in 1928, suffered from bipolar disorder, with manic episodes that fueled her poetry writing – writing which originally began as therapy suggested by her psychiatrist. The raw emotion and confessional aspects of her work drew immediate attention and success. She married, had 2 children, was divorced, had many affairs as well as an incestuous sexual relationship with her young daughter that was revealed after her death. She received the Pulitzer Prize in 1967, and committed suicide in 1974.

A mother lode of rich material here, as well as questions without number about literary genius, madness, love, lust, family, friendship, and the female, as manifested in the lives and deaths of Plath and Sexton. But One Yellow Rabbit really doesn't dig into any of that in the sense of a conventional play or drama, except in so far as the women reveal themselves in the poetry they created.

So what we have is Onalea Gilbertson as Plath (looking very much like her) and Denise Clarke as Anne Sexton delivering as the characters 23 of the poets' works. The poems are separated by transitional scripted mini-scenes primarily between Sexton's husband Kayo played by Andy Curtis and Plath's Ted Hughes played by Michael Green.

The two men share biographical information about their wives in an informal and sometimes amusing fashion. For the most part they seem structural devices for exposition and to illustrate the women's marital relationships, as well as to provide some physical movement to the piece. There's a funny little sparring scene between the two men with Green describing most poetically what poetry is, while Curtis counters with what poetry is not – as in "poetry is not your drunken wife falling face down in the mashed potatoes." We hear a large number of the women's poems and learn something factual of their lives. It's a kind of Wikipedia approach but with the added attraction of One Yellow Rabbit's considerable performance skills and the opportunity to hear some wonderful poetry.

The production takes place on the open expanse of the full Vertigo stage surrounded by blacks with two cape cod chairs isolated in pools of light. The chairs are sometimes moved and the lighting design takes our eye where the director wants it to go. Plath's poetry is dense and detailed. Because of this I felt the additional time one has to digest it when reading it on the page allows greater access and engagement with the words and images than when they're spoken. But I thought Gilbertson captured an internal repression, like a spring wound too tight in an effort to prevent its flying apart, and yet leading to that very thing. Her last two poems "Daddy" and "Lady Lazarus" were most powerful. I loved her red shoes, reminiscent of the fairy tale of the girl with the red shoes that danced her spirit to death. Although we don't hear it Sexton has a poem "The Red Shoes", and husband Kayo's refrain of "You're a good girl" is essentially saying to both women don't try to escape the snare of being a good girl, continue the dance of domestic isolation, child-rearing and society's norms though it leads to depression, madness, and death of the self.

Everything we know of Anne Sexton tells us her mental illness was on public view and she reveled in it. Denise Clarke portrays this with physical contortions and a fairly broad comic delivery. This Sexton might be nothing more than a maudlin drunk with a dark wit and a way with words. What I found missing was the bitterness, bite, deep pain and anguish that was the stimulant, catalyst, and foundation for the poetry. And perhaps because of the resonance of Gilbertson's red shoes my mind occasionally wandered to why Clarke's unattractive black and white dress? I kept thinking this costume must mean something, perhaps Sexton was drunk or maniac when she bought it – or it means black, white, polarizing? She's bi-polar and the dress illustrates this? I had to pinch my arm and get back to listening to the poetry.

Curtis as Kayo doesn't say much but exudes a kind of droll long-suffering husband wedded to a mad woman and at one point driven beyond endurance to violence. Green gives a moving rendition of Hughes poem "Lovesong" with an accent that is ... or isn't . . .whatever, I'm not quite sure. However the two contrasted each other nicely.

The evening was more of an introduction to the lives and poetry of two important figures in the literary world. For those who were aware of them and their work it was probably wonderful to hear their words spoken on stage, a kind of beefed up poetry reading. For those who were unaware, it may lead them to a Google search and a bookstore to learn more.

Essentially, I think the Rabbits achieved their objective: A celebration of the poetry and a showcase for two talented women in the ensemble. As an intro to the High Performance Rodeo it's no high risk ride.

SHARON POLLOCK | DONNA COATES

Security

Calgary is home to the world's longest running professional lunchtime theatre. It enters its 33rd year with the present production, a premiere of "Security" by Calgarian Neil Fleming.

In recent years the company in its search for scripts that meet its mandate has taken to annually commissioning and work-shopping 6 plays via their Petro Canada Stage One program. At the end of the season the plays are read before an audience, feedback solicited, and the favoured few, or many in some cases, continue on to production in the following season. You could say the scripts are tailored to meet the particular demands of their theatre. Audiences are juggling coffee in one hand, sandwich in the other, and a number are coming from and returning to work in the city centre. So the plays are under an hour in length, the form is comedy, with cast numbers and staging requirements that match the intimate venue and the company's budget.

While some see this as the restrictions of lunchtime theatre, I don't. I do see challenges to the playwright's imagination, to the actors and designers' interpretative art, and a test of the artistic director's vision of what theatre can be as it tickles our funny bone and revives our spirits. Lunchtime theatre is like knocking back a shot glass of energy as we take a mid-day break.

The present production, "Security" by Calgarian Neil Fleming, was commissioned and developed through the Stage One program, and deemed ready for production. It's billed as "a feel-good farce" so we know off the bat we're into broad comedy and amusing improbable situations, a hallmark of Fleming's other plays "John Doe/Jack Rabbit" and "Gnomes".

The plot: Miles McInnes (Curt McKinstry) and Andy Bastichuk (Trevor Rueger) are two security guards, hence the title. They work in a high end apartment complex that caters to celebrities and on this occasion they receive word that movie star Anna Monk (Nicole Zylstra) and her friend/agent/fellow star Patricia McGovern (Jane MacFarlane) are arriving. Andy is a little guy, shy, nervous, and Anna Monk's biggest fan. He just happens to have written a film script for Anna who also is shy, nervous, and not the brightest bulb in the box.

Miles is as large and imposing as Andy is small and timid. Miles is a fan of Patricia who is as brash and sexually aggressive as Anna is self-conscious and retiring. Andy's no salesman so at Andy's request Miles will pretend to be Andy and pitch Andy's script to Anna. But Anna, trying to avoid a stalker, has exchanged identities with Patricia.

So we have the stallion Miles passing himself off as Andy connecting with the cougar Patricia passing herself off as Anna. (Apparently this works as Anna always wears a mask in her serial movie role. I'm unsure why Miles doesn't recognize Patricia.)

The stalker (who never appears) is also a star with a household name and fortuitously for the farce a cat bearing the same name is loose in the complex and must be caught. Of course Anna thinks it's the stalker, but, as you may guess, the real Anna and the real Andy meet around this, discover they're kindred souls and go for coffee and perogies at the French Maid strip bar while Patricia and Miles, foregoing the script pitching, are having it off in an off stage bedroom. Everyone discovers who everyone really is and Anna and Andy end up producing their film starring Miles and Patricia. I think. That bit, though elaborately costumed, was a trifle unclear. Or possibly I wasn't paying attention.

I mentioned the playwright's imagination in meeting the perceived needs of a particular theatre when writing on commission. There may be certain patterns to any dramatic form, like farce, but imagination and invention make character and situations fresh and new. They render the formula invisible. With this script I'm too aware of a farce template, a visible contrivance to the characters and events. The playwright gives us two couples, the individual personalities of each of the couples are as opposite as possible, as if one had sought antonyms in a thesaurus to characterize them. Then you have exchanged identities Andy / Miles, Anna / Patricia and mistaken identity, the cat and the stalker. The events, the "this happens which makes that happen which leads to this" is thinly plotted and highly predictable. "Security" seems rushed and insufficiently thought-through writing.

Perhaps a different performance style would have diminished the overt formula feel to the script. Instead, for me, it highlighted it. Performances were broad, cartoonish and one dimensional. Too shallow for stereotypes. There was a forced element to the vocal delivery of lines. Everyone was pushing the volume button and striking poses on the stage. A lot of the dialogue was delivered full front to the audience, directorial choices that did nothing to silence my inner voice whispering "if you really think this is so funny why are you working so hard and making it so artificial?"

On the other hand – Terry Gunvordahl's marvelous set and lighting, with multiple inverted city skylines as background provided numerous locales with minimal means. Two benches in front of two large glass panels that by turns were

SHARON POLLOCK | DONNA COATES

revolving doors, an airport lounge, an elevator, living room, lobby, you name it. Set and lighting served in both utilitarian and elegant ways the needs of the play. I couldn't find a costume credit in the program but I thought they were appropriate and visual indicators of the characters. Word of mouth gives the credit to Amy Dettling.

Farce is easy to imitate but difficult to create. What makes it so funny is the tension between the credible and the ridiculously improbable. The further you can stretch that line of tension without snapping it, the funnier the farce. I'm afraid "Security" is no high wire act nor is it well served by the production.

SUNDAY, FEBRUARY 3, 2008

Our Town

In 1938 American playwright Thornton Wilder grew weary of sumptuous set elements, chronological time and realism in the theatre of his day. He did something about it by breaking with convention and writing a Pulitizer Prize winning play which virtually eliminated any set and props, and jumped through time with a narrator who filled the audience in on past, present and future events. The author created, on basically an empty stage, and with a large cast, a simple portrayal of life in small town Grover's Corners, New Hampshire. Universal, timeless truths were revealed, at least in theory, in the commonplace events and ordinary lives of the town's citizens on an average day in 1901, in 1904, and in 1913.

Wilder's "Our Town" is said to be the most produced American play of all time with a production running somewhere on each and every day of the year. While I don't vouch for the veracity of that claim, "Our Town" is indeed the production chosen by Theatre Calgary to celebrate its 40th birthday.

The play unfolds in 3 acts each dedicated to a day: "Daily Life" followed by "Love" followed by "Death". It focuses in an understated way on two families and their oldest offspring, the son of one and the daughter of the other. I suppose you could say the town itself, Grover's Corners, is really the central character and the play is that central character's monologue delivered in the multiple voices of the townspeople.

The portrait of Grover's Corners begins with the Stage Manager (aka. Narrator) setting two tables and chairs plus two ladders on the empty stage. The top of the ladders will represent the sill of two upper story windows. A couple of arches are pushed out for "those who need scenery" as the S.M. puts it. He's a chorus-like figure who speaks directly to us in describing the layout of this imaginary town, providing background to the characters, the town and the day, sprinkling his monologues with tidbits of homespun observations and a kind of Farmers' Almanac philosophy with a gentle "ah, shucks, we're just plain folks" humour.

An imaginary street separates the home of Dr. Gibbs and his family from that of the local newspaper editor and his family, the Webbs. Each residence is defined by the table and chairs on opposite sides of the stage. Folks eat breakfast, kids go to school, the milkman and paperboy deliver, wives garden & gossip & go to church choir, the town drunk staggers by, the policeman walks his beat - you get the picture.

Teenagers George Gibb and Emily Webb, neighbours since birth, converse through their respective bedroom windows, visually represented by each perching on the top rung of their respective ladders. They will sip drugstore sodas at the local pharmacy, graduate high school, and marry. Their relationship is a primary thread in the tapestry of ordinary life around them as a father-in-law gives advice, the bride and groom have prenuptial doubts, and the guests cry at their wedding.

In the final act, the Dead of Grover's Corners, some of whom we've met previously, sit peacefully in their graves "waitin' for somethin' they feel is comin'. Somethin' important and great," "somethin' eternal". It's the day of a funeral, and the Dead welcome Emily who has died in childbirth shortly after marriage. The Stage Manager allows her to relive one day, her 12th birthday, but her stay is brief. She quickly returns to the dead sobbing with the realization that life rushes by too quickly to apprehend and appreciate it.

"We don't have time to look at each other . . . do human beings ever realize life while they live it?" she asks. The Stage Manager's answer is "No". And Emily, weaned from Earth, settles in with the Dead, as the day ends in Grover's Corners, and the play ends for us.

If one thinks of drama as a series of exciting or emotional events (as some do) nothing happens in "Our Town", although a lot goes on. The days on view are full of small, routine and predictable details of life that, even when first produced in 1938, is a nostalgic and romanticized look at life in the first decade of the 1900's. I'm afraid I question its dramatic viability in the first decade of the 21st century. The playwright was breaking with the theatre conventions of his time and place with his minimalist, next to non-existent set, actors miming props and actions as they played out the minutiae of life in placid small town New Hampshire. In 1938 that approach was fresh and new. That's not true anymore.

Sumptuous sets and technological spectacle have recently been the earmark of Theatre Calgary productions, thus it may be innovative for the company to mount a minimalist production on a relatively bare stage. But theatre audiences generally have become more familiar with the power of such minimalist settings, mimed action, non-linear time, and the diverse ways of creating drama in performance of what appears to be non-dramatic. So my attention is caught and maintained, not by the uneventful minutiae, but by the stage direction and the performances.

I'm looking for visual moments that imprint on my mind and my eye, images that I carry away with me as I leave the theatre. I'm looking for a style of production in which the stripping away of set and props is matched by a clarity and preciseness in the physical realization of the script. Actors playing surface as opposed to depth in characters and relationship is a sure path to tedium for an audience. Every action and movement is significant because these characters in all their normality nevertheless stand for more than themselves. It is in finding the essence of a moment between characters and within characters that the images I speak of are created.

I didn't find a strong directorial concept regarding this production's style or staging, thus those resonating images that stand for more than themselves were few and far between. And though we may be looking at a broad overview of life in Grover's Corners it does not dictate what I found to be a general flatness to the lighting design. It all added to a prevailing lack of focus.

I'm not sure if there was a fear that dialogue would drift off into the wings or up into the fly gallery but actors on opening night, with the exception of Dave Kelly as the Stage Manager and Tyrell Crews as George, too often delivered dialogue in a declamatory tone, I suppose to assure that audience in the back row could hear. Then there was the New England accent everyone assumed, and that lent an air of artificiality to the proceedings rather than authenticity. Plus it kept giving rise to the question, why is an American play set in a Northeastern state at the turn of the 20th century seen as an appropriate production with which to celebrate TC's 40th birthday season? We were informed in that now ubiquitous pre-show chat that all "Our Town" are played by Calgarians, but that hardly answers the question.

What about "Farther West" by John Murrell, or any play by W.O. Mitchell, both playwrights whose identity and work were founded and formed by the Canadian West and both having a past connection to Theatre Calgary?

Back to "Our Town" which certainly holds a rightful place in the American historical canon of classics. But how well does it translates to a contemporary audience? I can't help suspecting the S.M.'s assertion that "This is the way we were in our growin' up, our marryin', our livin' and our dyin'" in Grover's Corners, N.H. is not the full truth. All the characters are white, protestant with anglo-saxon names, and Emily, the smartest of the lot, is destined for an early marriage and death, despite her brains and suggested ambition. We're told there's a factory in town plus a Polish area just off stage but no one from there figures in the growin', livin' marryin' or dyin'; these kinds of things rattle around in the back of my head as I watch "Our Town". The only way to avoid them is to experience a stunning production of a deceptively simple but really difficult play.

This isn't it.

FRIDAY, FEBRUARY 8, 2008

The Premature Burial

It seems as if Calgary births a new company every day. It speaks to the wealth· of emerging young theatre artists in the city, as well as to the interest of many in collaborative creation. Perhaps that's in reaction to larger companies' more hierarchical rehearsal and production structures, and the lack of opportunity within most established companies for young, emerging, or even old established artists, to explore and stretch the boundaries of live performance, often by mixing and melding artistic disciplines and mediums.

Motel is an intimate theatre space opposite One Yellow Rabbit in the Epcor Centre. It's the birthing place for many artist-generated projects – and kudos to the Rabbits for making the space available.

Raven Theatre, at Motel, is the new kid on the block. Its mandate is the creation of experimental projects and performance pieces employing diverse artistic mediums. Their introductory production is the company's Artistic Director Simone Saunders's adaptation, or performance extrapolation, of Edgar Allan Poe's "The Premature Burial."

In Poe's story a narrator gives various examples of people being buried alive and relates it to his and our fear of death that until confronted, symbolically through premature burial, prevents life being lived to the fullest. Raven's acting ensemble of Simone Saunders, Leda Davies, Lorianna Lombardo with Director Charles Netto gives us three Raven shape-shifters who narrate Poe's story in a multi-textured way by breaking the prose into individual voices, and by expressing an action, character or emotion by gesture or stylized movement.

Visually there are arresting moments – a long stretch of rich bright red material drawn slowly from a coffin entraps wrists and arms signifying a woman' struggle with illness; then represents her death when wrapped round and encasing her head and eventually becomes the shroud that strangles her and from which she hangs when prematurely entombed. There's a most effective scene with masks (created/constructed by Douglas Witt) and their power of mask work seems ideally suited to the play's content and style.

Designer Anton de Groot, composer Brian Bergum and the Raven Theatre ensemble have done well with minimal means but boy oh boy, do I ever wish they had access to all the bells, whistles and time with which to continue the R & D on this text and process. That's not a comment on the quality of the production. It is a comment on my unhappiness (and sometimes rage) that the full realization of Simone Saunders' vision, the achievement of its theatrical potential, and that of other creative artists drawn to this kind of process and performance, is so dependent on resources that may not be within their reach.

I always say creativity can replace money but sometimes you just need more lighting instruments, a venue in which a true velvet blackout with pin spots of light is possible, a state of the art sound system, plus other elements and tools that contribute, support, and reveal performance – and time, precious time to play, to try out, to discard and to choose. The first public presentation of "The Premature Burial" is really the first step. I hope Raven will find the resources to continue refining this performance piece.

SUNDAY, FEBRUARY 10, 2008

Snake in the Grass

At Motel in Epcor Centre is Raven Theatre's A. D. Simone Saunders' performance adaptation of Edgar Alan Poe's "The Premature Burial." It's only a block and a half walk from Motel to Vertigo, but it's a world away in terms of theatre.

At Vertigo the mandate is Mystery Theatre and "Snake in the Grass" by Alan Ayckbourn fills that bill. Author of over 70 plays, Ayckbourn's generally acknowledged as a Master Wordsmith. With an Ayckbourn play on the boards one's pretty well guaranteed a leisurely night out with engaging characters, entertaining dialogue, in this case with a light comedic touch, and a plot that will keep your interest.

The playwright refers to "Snake in the Grass" as a ghost play. Though no ghosts appear, the spirit of a deceased abusive father inhabits the minds and memories of his two offspring. Annabel Chester escaped in her teens leaving behind her younger sister Miriam. Miriam has cared for her father over the years, sacrificing any life of her own and enduring his verbal and physical assaults. None of this bodes well for her mental health and one would not be surprised were she driven to desperate measures that did not bode well for papa.

The play begins with Annabel's return, in ill health herself, to claim her inheritance such as it is. There is much to be resolved between the two sisters but the most immediate problem is a former employee, Alice Moody, who'd assisted Miriam in caring for the old man before his death. An untimely death, claims Moody, and threatens blackmail. We know Miriam, under stress, is prone to impulsive actions and as things go from bad to worse for Annabel, as well as for Moody, the very air vibrates with malevolent intention.

Laura Parken is, at first, a confident Annabel. But as events and memories overcome her, her strength in fleeing a past abusive marriage, and her careful planning for the sisters' future, are gradually eroded. In Val Planche we see a Miriam, abandoned, isolated and victimized, who has survived by erasing who she once was or might have been. She's rendered the real Miriam invisible and thus invulnerable, creating a public persona somewhere between an eccentric bag lady and a stubborn impulsive child. The subtle conflict between the two as to who is the pawn, and who is moving the pieces, is nicely played by Parken and Planche.

An important figure is Alice Moody, the blackmailing nurse. Kathryn Kerbes as Moody captures the smugness and self-satisfaction of the employee, finally in a position of power over her supposed betters and intent on taking full advantage of it.

Terry Gunvordahl's set deserves star billing. It's truly stunning in its realistic exterior of an English cottage, the garden, summerhouse, and portion of a tennis court. It's lovely to look at and yet has an ambient mustiness and hint of decay just beneath the surface. Vanessa Porteous' direction is detailed and seamless, the production delivering what Vertigo promises to its loyal patrons.

http://www.sharonpollock.com/pages/Reviews/Archive.html

Contributors

LINDSAY BURNS is an actress and playwright living in Calgary. She was fortunate enough to attend *Blood Relations* in 1980 at Theatre Calgary. A professional actress since 1988, Lindsay had her first one-woman show, *Naming Names*, produced in 1995. In 2000 she co-wrote the popular one-act *I Eat* for Lunchbox Theatre, followed by *Risking Rapture* in 2002. In 2005 she wrote and performed *Dough: the Politics of Martha Stewart*. In 2007 Lindsay debuted *The Vajayjay Monologues* at Urban Curvz. It has travelled to the Winnipeg, Edmonton, and New York Fringe Festivals. *Sharon's Tongue* was designed as a deep dive into the work of Ms. Pollock served with delicious food and sparkling company.

KATHY K.Y. CHUNG received her Ph.D. from the Centre for Drama, Theatre and Performance Studies, University of Toronto, where she completed a dissertation on the drama of Sharon Pollock. She has published on Pollock's plays, on Vancouver arts history, and on the experience of co-editing Margaret Atwood's juvenilia.

DONNA COATES has published dozens of articles and book chapters on Australian, Canadian, and New Zealand women's responses in fiction and drama to the First and Second World Wars and to the Vietnam War. With Sherrill Grace, she has co-edited and selected plays for *Canada and the Theatre of War, Volumes One and Two* (2008, 2010). With George Melnyk, she has edited *Wild Words: Essays on Alberta Literature* (2009). She is currently completing a full-length manuscript on Australian women's fictional responses to twentieth-century wars and coordinating and editing a series of volumes on Women and War for Routledge's History of Feminism Series.

CARMEN DERKSON works as an assistant professor (Limited Term) at the University of Lethbridge where she teaches Modernism and Children's Lit in twentieth-century, nineteenth-century, and contemporary literatures. Currently a PhD candidate at the University of Calgary, she is writing her critical dissertation on a brief history of the fragment across Modernisms using tactics of mimesis, aural awareness, and recognition with immersive place-practice, or *Coeurographies/ Chorographies*, to examine embodied movement and sensory dissent as modes for situational decoding of un/disciplined bodies on various scriptural economies and sites. She has recent critical and creative publications forthcoming and published from *Theatre Research in Canada, Canadian Literature: A Quarterly of Criticism and Review, Event, Substance: A Review of Theory and Literary Criticism* and various other venues. Her recent creative project, a poetry manuscript, *Pine*, is written from the perspective of a pine tree and engages the biopolitics of pine trees, various goblin markets, and figures of nostalgia.

SHERRILL GRACE is an Officer of the Order of Canada, a Fellow of the Royal Society of Canada, and a University Killam Professor at the University of British Columbia, where she has taught Canadian literature and culture for many years. She has published extensively on twentieth-century Canadian literature and lectured across Canada and Europe and in Australia, China, Japan, and the United States. Among her books are *Canada and the Idea of the North*, *The Collected Letters of Malcolm Lowry*, *On the Art of Being Canadian*, *Landscapes of War and Memory*, and studies of theatre and autobiography, Margaret Atwood, and Tom Thompson. She is the author *of Making Theatre: A Life of Sharon Pollock*, and is currently writing the biography of Timothy Findley.

PAMELA HALSTEAD is a freelance director, dramaturg, actor, teacher, and arts consultant. She is the former Artistic Director of Lunchbox Theatre (Calgary) and Ship's Company Theatre (Parrsboro, Nova Scotia). In her ten years between these two companies she directed and/ or produced over sixty productions, the majority of them premieres of new works. Pamela is co-founder and Artistic Producer of DMV Theatre (Halifax, Nova Scotia), Artistic Adviser to Valley Summer Theatre (Wolfville, Nova Scotia), and the PERFORM! Coordinator for Theatre Nova Scotia. In 2013, Pamela was awarded the inaugural Evans Award at the Calgary Critics' Awards for her contribution to the vibrancy of the Calgary theatre community.

GRANT LINNEBERG has performed in theatres across Canada, from Stratford to Vancouver and most points in between. Favourite roles include Bob in *Nisei Blue* (Alberta Theatre Projects), Squash in *Victor/Victoria* (Stage West), Lenny in *Of Mice and Men* (Vancouver Playhouse), Big Jule in *Guys and Dolls* (Stratford and Stage West), Falstaff in *The Merry Wives of Windsor* (Shakespeare in the Park), Gordon in *Some Assembly Required* (ATP), Roy in *Middle Age White Guys* (Lunchbox Theatre), Joe Gage in *The Ginkgo Tree* (The Arts Club, Vancouver), and John Chisum in *The Collected Works of Billy the Kid* (ATP). He is a Betty Mitchell Award Nominee and a Jessie Richardson Award Nominee. He lives in Calgary with his wife, actress and writer Lindsay Burns, and their son, Jasper.

MARTIN MORROW is an arts journalist and critic who has been covering the Canadian theatre scene since the 1980s. Originally based in Calgary, he served as the *Calgary Herald*'s chief theatre critic from 1988 until 2000, and as the Arts & Lifestyle Editor for *Fast Forward*, the city's alternative weekly (2003–2006). In between, he published *Wild Theatre: The History of One Yellow Rabbit* (Banff Centre Press, 2003), a popular chronicle of one of Canada's leading avant-garde theatre companies, which was nominated for an Alberta Book Award. Since 2007, Morrow has been based in Toronto, where he has continued a long relationship with *The Globe and Mail* as the paper's second theatre critic. He has also served as an arts producer for CBC.ca, the Canadian Broadcasting Corporation's website (2007–2011), and as a film and theatre columnist for *The Grid* (2011–2014). A two-time winner of the Nathan Cohen Award for Excellence in Critical Writing, he is president of the Canadian Theatre Critics Association and a jury member of the Toronto Theatre Critics Awards.

JETON NEZIRAJ is a former professor of dramaturgy at the Faculty of Arts of the University of Pristina (2007–2008) and former artistic director of the National Theatre of Kosovo. He is the founder and director of Qendra Multimedia, a cultural production company based in Pristina. He has written over fifteen plays, some of which have been translated from the Albanian and published and performed in both Kosovo and abroad.

LAURA PARKEN, a native Calgarian, has been performing locally and nationally for over thirty years. Laura has worked with virtually every professional theatre company in Calgary, but her favourite and most rewarding achievements have been in the independent realm, creating and collaborating with other artists in productions including *Sharon's Tongue*, as well as her solo show *Might As Well Live*, a fictional, emotional autobiography of Dorothy Parker, created with Ken Cameron, and *Adventures of the Trick-Riders* with Sheri-D Wilson for the One

Yellow Rabbit High Performance Rodeo. Laura has also collaborated and performed in acclaimed productions with Michael Green, Doug Curtis, Gail Hanrahan, Andy Curtis, Sharon Stevens, and Sandi Somers, among others. Laura is the recipient of two Betty Mitchell Awards for Acting.

Wes D. Pearce is professor of theatre and currently an associate dean (Undergraduate) in the Faculty of Fine Arts at the University of Regina. He co-edited *OutSpoken: Perspectives on Queer Identity* (2013), which was nominated for a Saskatchewan Book Award and has been published in a number of anthologies exploring a variety of topics and interests. He is also an accomplished scenographer and has over the past twenty years designed elements for nearly a hundred productions across western Canada (including Alberta Theatre Projects, Prairie Theatre Exchange, Stage West Calgary, Western Canada Theatre, Globe Theatre) and is a frequent collaborator with Saskatoon's Persephone Theatre. His work has been honoured with two Betty Mitchel and three Saskatoon and Area Theatre Awards nominations for Outstanding Costume Design. He is currently editing an anthology commemorating the fiftieth anniversary of the production of George Ryga's landmark play *The Ecstasy of Rita Joe*.

Tanya Schaap received her Ph.D. from the English Department at the University of Calgary in 2015. Her areas of research include trauma theory, women and war, and 9/11 fiction. Her most recent work, an essay examining the war diary of Canadian artist Molly Lamb Bobak, is forthcoming in *Working Memory: Women and War, 1939–1945*, eds. Jeanne Perreault and Marlene Kadar (2015). Tanya has presented at numerous conferences and won a number of awards and prizes, including the Izaak Killam Memorial Scholarship (2011 and 2012) as well as the Joseph Bombardier 3-year Graduate Scholarship (CGS) from SSHRC (2011).

SHELLEY SCOTT is a professor in the Department of Theatre and Dramatic Arts at the University of Lethbridge and the associate dean for the Faculty of Fine Arts. She is the past president of the Canadian Association for Theatre Research. She has published two books: *The Violent Woman as the New Theatrical Character Type: Cases from Canadian Drama* (2007) and *Nightwood Theatre: A Woman's Work is Always Done* (2010). She has published articles in *alt.theatre: Cultural Diversity and the Stage*, *Canadian Theatre Review*, *Modern Drama*, *Theatre Research in Canada*, *Resources for Feminist Research*, and the *British Journal of Canadian Studies*, and contributed to several essay collections. Most recently she co-edited, with Reid Gilbert, issue 150 of the *Canadian Theatre Review* on the topic of burlesque.

JERRY WASSERMAN is a professor of English and Theatre at the University of British Columbia in Vancouver with specializations in Canadian and American drama and performance, theatre history, blues literature and popular entertainment. Recipient of a Killam Teaching Prize, the Dorothy Somerset Award and the Sam Payne Award, he is editor of the two-volume anthology *Modern Canadian Plays* (now in its 5th edition), *Spectacle of Empire: Marc Lescarbot's Theatre of Neptune in New France*, and *Theatre and AutoBiography: Writing and Performing Lives in Theory and Practice* (with Sherrill Grace). As a stage, film and TV actor he has more than 200 professional credits. He is also a longtime theatre critic for Canadian newspapers and radio. More than 500 of his reviews are archived on his website, www.vancouverplays.com.

JASON WIENS is an instructor in the Department of English at the University of Calgary, where he teaches Canadian literature. He has published articles on prairie poetry, Dionne Brand, Margaret Avison, the Kootenay School of Writing, and George Bowering, and regularly reviews contemporary poetry for *Quill and Quire* and *Alberta Views*. He recently received a grant to develop a new undergraduate course that will ask students to digitize selected papers in the Canadian literature collection of the University of Calgary's Archives and Special Collections. In recent years he has delivered conference papers on Frederick Philip Grove, John Glassco, and Roderick Haig Brown, as part of a developing interest in modernist non-fiction. This is his first published article on Sharon Pollock's work, although he has taught her plays – including *Blood Relations*, *Walsh*, *Whiskey Six Cadenza*, and *Generations* – numerous times.

CYNTHIA ZIMMERMAN has been a commentator on Canadian playwriting and on the voice of women on the Canadian stage throughout her career at Glendon College, York University. Now professor emerita, she continues to publish and teach in her research specialty areas, Canadian theatre and contemporary women playwrights. Previously book review editor of *Modern Drama*, an omnibus reviewer of drama for "Letters in Canada," the *University of Toronto Quarterly* annual survey of publications, she has authored or co-authored a number of books and produced numerous articles, chapters, and public papers. Her most recent works are as editor of the three-volume *Sharon Pollock: Collected Works*, *The Betty Lambert Reader*, and *Reading Carol Bolt*, all published by Playwrights Canada Press. *Reading Carol Bolt* is both an anthology and a collection that commemorates and celebrates Bolt's important pioneering contributions to Canadian theatre.

Index

SHARON POLLOCK | DONNA COATES

mysteries. See also *Blood Relations*;
  Constance; *Death in the Family*; *End
  Dream*; *Saucy Jack*
  audience enjoyment, 43–44
  contradictory evidence convention, 42
  detectives in, 30–31, 32, 36
  gender issues, 44
  as genre, 30–31, 43–44
  investigator's role, 31, 41
  justice issues, 34, 36, 43–44
  missing-clothing convention, 36
  motivation for crimes, 34
  SP's plays as, 7, 29–34, 43–44
  SP's views on, 29–30
  truth and ambiguity, 33, 39
  unsolved real-life murders, 29

N

Nail Biter (Thompson), 192n1
Nation Maker (Gwyn), 219–20
National Arts Centre, 2, 102n6
National Energy Policy, 8, 52–53
National Theatre of Kosovo, 208–9. *See also*
  Kosovo theatre
Natives. *See* Aboriginal people
Natrass, Carson, 275
naturalism, dramatic, 56, 58–59, 60, 90–92
naturalism, prairie, 54–56
NDWT Theatre, 85, 102n3, 102n5
Necessary Angel Theatre, 282–84
Netto, Charles, 300–301
New Brunswick. *See also* Theatre New
  Brunswick
  Atlantic Ballet Theatre, 4, 228
  setting for *Doc*, 80–81
  setting for *Fair Liberty's Call*, 111–13,
    115–17, 132
  SP's early life in, 66
Newby, Kate, 287
Newman, Peter C., 18
Newton, Christopher, 288
Neziraj, Jeton, 3, 10–11, 207–11, 211n1,
  228, 306. *See also* Kosovo theatre
9/11 terrorist attacks. *See* September 11
  terrorist attacks

Norbert, Chad, 279
Nothof, Anne F.
  collected essays on SP, 6
  on *End Dream*, 40
  on *Generations*, 92, 93
  on impossibility of knowing, 32–33
  interviews with SP, 85
  on mysteries, 39
  on *Saucy Jack*, 37
  on scenography, 93
  on staging of *Doc*, 98
Nunn, Robert, 98

O

Of Mice and Men (Steinbeck), 200, 201, 203,
  276–77
Oh Lay Girls, 278
oil and gas industry, 3, 8, 52–53, 54
Omar Khadr, Oh Canada (Williamson, ed.),
  192n1
One Flew Over the Cuckoo's Nest
  (Wasserman), 4, 203
One Night Stand (Bolt), 43
One Tiger to a Hill (Pollock), 24–25, 44n1,
  148
One Yellow Rabbit
  10 Minute Play Festival, 292
  Down With Up With People, 278
  In Fine Form, 289–90
  historical background, 200, 306
  Sylvia Plath Must Not Die, 292–94
O'Neill, Eugene, 65
Our Town (Wilder), 297–300
Ouzounian, Richard, 66

P

Page, Malcolm, 25n2, 97–98
Palace of the End (Thompson). *See also* Abu
  Ghraib prison; torture
  Lynndie England's life, 10, 169, 173–78,
    185, 190–91
  female torturers, 171–74
  "Harrowdown Hill," 169
  historical background, 170–71

Second World War
  citizen internments, 154–55, 170, 183,
    193n5
  Jewish refugee policy, 232n3
  uranium mining, 221, 232n6
Security (Fleming), 295–97
Sedgwick, Eve Kosofsky, 45n4, 109–10
Senier, Siobhan, 109
September 11 terrorist attacks. See also
    Man Out of Joint
  predictions of, 148, 151, 170, 186–87
  pretext for Iraq War, 189
Sexton, Anne and Alfred (Kayo), 292–94
sexualized torture, 152, 170–74, 184, 192n3.
    See also torture
Shanker, Thom, 192n4
Sharon Pollock: Collected Works
    (Zimmerman, ed.), 3
*Sharon Pollock: Critical Perspectives on
    Canadian Theatre in English* (Grace
    and La Flamme, eds.), 6
Sharon Pollock: Essays on Her Works
    (Nothof, ed.), 6
"Sharon's Tongue" (Burns, Parken,
    Linneberg, and Halstead), 11,
    237–72
Sheppard, Allan, 53
Show No. 1: Archeology, 290–91
Simon, Jack, 101
Simpson, Jeffrey, 219–20
Sitting Bull, Chief, 13–20, 22–25, 25n2
Smedley, Agnes, 4, 228, 230
Smith, Janet, 39–41, 44
Smith, Russell, 66
Snake in the Grass (Ayckbourn), 301–2
Snook, Adrienne, 279
social class and female soldiers, 174, 175–76,
    192
social justice
  collective responsibility, 9–10, 157–58
  fatally compromised males, 24–25
  historical murder mysteries, 34, 36
  moral conflict and, 86
  at national beginnings, 141–42
  as theme, 5, 34

Something True and Wonderful (Curtis),
    291–92
song. *See* music and dance
Sontag, Susan, 171, 174, 182–87
Soulpepper Theatre, 66–67, 76–81, **78–80**
sound and listening. See also *Fair Liberty's
    Call*
  auditory *vs.* visual recognition, 114–15,
    123
  Bakhtin's ideological consciousness,
    117–18
  listening as reparative practice, 108–11,
    113–14, 118–19, 121–23
  listening *vs.* hearing, 114
  recognition *vs.* acknowledgement, 109
Spidell, Jane, 79
Spirits of the Trail (Mitchell), 25
Sprung, Guy, 65, 76, **77**, 79
Stage One program, 295
Standard Operating Procedure (film), 177
Stein, Alexander, 110, 114
Steinbeck, John, *Of Mice and Men*,
    200–201, 203, 276–77
Steward, Dan, 150
The Stillborn Lover (Findley), 216
Stirling, Glenda, 279
Stitchbury, Allan, 277
Stone, Martin, 53
Stratford Festival
  Fair Liberty's Call, 201, 202
  SP as associate director, 2
  Walsh, 25n1, 99, **99**
Stuck in a Snowbank Theatre, 2
Sturken, Marita, 162
Summerscale, Kate, 36
Sursum Corda! (Grace, ed.), 222
The Suspicions of Mr. Whicher
    (Summerscale), 36
Sussex, Lucy, 30–31
Sylvia Plath Must Not Die, 292–94

T

Tarragon Theatre, 53, 62n1, 102n3, 220
TC. *See* Theatre Calgary
The Telling of Lies (Findley), 216

as memory play, 93, 95
multiple viewpoints, 94, 96
productions of, 93, 102n8
prologue, 94
reception of, 93
SP's views on, 93
White, Hayden, 16–17
Whitehead, Bill, 224
Whittaker, Herbert, 25n1
Wiens, Jason, 7–8, 47–63, 308–9
Wild Theatre (Morrow), 306
Wilder, Thornton, 297–300
Williams, Kayla, 191–92
Williamson, Janice, 192n1
Wilson, Andrew, 219, 232n3
Witt, Douglas, 301
women. *See* gender
Wong Foon Sing, 39–43
Wood, John, 99
Woodcock, George, 218–20, 232n2
Woods, Grahame, 19
World Trade Centre attacks. *See* September
        11 terrorist attacks
World War II. *See* Second World War
writer-in-residence, SP as, 2–3. *See also*
        Pollock, Sharon, life in the theatre

Y

Young-Bruehl, Elisabeth, 72, 74, 76, 81n9
Yugoslavia, theatre. *See* Kosovo theatre

Z

Zimmerman, Cynthia, 309
    on collection of SP's plays, 3
    on *Doc*, 65–82
    on *Fair Liberty's Call*, 127, 143n8, 143n11
    on *Generations*, 62
    on loss and mourning, 127, 143n11
    on multiple vantage points, 30
    on murder mysteries, 29–30, 34
    on scenography, 91, 92
    on social justice issues, 34
Zylstra, Nicole, 295–96